Minnesota's Own

MINNESOTA'S OWN

PRESERVING OUR GRAND HOMES

LARRY MILLETT

Photography by Matt Schmitt

MINNESOTA HISTORICAL SOCIETY PRESS

www.mnhspress.org

The Minnesota Historical Society Press is a member of the Association of American University Presses.

Manufactured in Canada

10 9 8 7 6 5 4 3 2 1

♾ The paper used in this publication meets the minimum requirements of the American National Standard for Information Sciences—Permanence for Printed Library Materials, ANSI Z39.48–1984.

International Standard Book Number
ISBN: 978-0-87351-929-8

Library of Congress Cataloging-in-Publication Data
Millett, Larry, 1947– author.
Minnesota's own : preserving our grand homes / Larry Millett ; photography by Matt Schmitt.
     pages   cm
Includes bibliographical references and index.
ISBN 978-0-87351-929-8 (hardback)
1. Architect-designed houses—Minnesota. 2. Architect-designed houses—Conservation and restoration—Minnesota. 3. Minnesota—Biography. I. Schmitt, Matt, photographer. II. Title.
NA7235.M6M55 2014
728'.3709776—dc23
                                                    2014027769

Minnesota's Own was designed and set in type by Chris Long at Mighty Media, Minneapolis. The typefaces are Verdigris and Sweet Sans, designed by Mark van Bronkhorst; and Garamond Premier Pro, designed by Robert Slimbach.

Elevation and floor plan illustrations by Todd Grover, Katie Kangas, Stuart MacDonald, and Angela Wolf Scott of MacDonald and Mack Architects.

Color and retouching by Tim Meegan.

Map of homes by Matt Millett.

The Jeffris Family Foundation
Dedicated to Midwestern Historic Preservation

JFF

THIS BOOK IS GENEROUSLY FUNDED by the Jeffris Family Foundation of Janesville, Wisconsin, which is committed to funding projects that preserve cultural history in the Midwest through the preservation of regionally and nationally important buildings and decorative arts projects. ❧

As a historian and archaeologist, I do not usually encounter a donor or private individual who so obviously respects and encourages academic scholarship as a means to accurately identify and restore the past. It is a pleasure to be working on a project where establishing and maintaining historical integrity is a requirement and not an afterthought.

Leah Rosenow, Collections Manager,
Mid-continent Railway Historical Society and Museum

Dedicated to Royce Yeater

Few people have Royce Yeater's knowledge of and enthusiasm for their profession. Preservation is fortunate to have him as an advocate.

Thomas M. Jeffris, President, the Jeffris Family Foundation

Contents

❧ Preface

Minnesota's Own IS THE STORY OF TWENTY-TWO REMARKABLE HOMES and the families who built them. It does not pretend to be a best-of list, although the houses are indeed among the state's finest. They vary widely by period, style, size, and location. The oldest dates to 1865; the newest, to 1950. Architectural styles extend across almost the entire range found in Minnesota, from Gothic Revival all the way through Queen Anne and period revival to Arts and Crafts and Midcentury Modern. The largest house—James J. Hill's commanding sandstone fortress on Summit Avenue in St. Paul—encompasses 36,000 square feet. The smallest—Frank Lloyd Wright's intimate Willey House in Minneapolis—is a much more modest 1,300 square feet. And although many of the houses are located in and around the Twin Cities, others are in communities scattered across the four corners of the state, from Duluth and Bemidji to Worthington and Winona.

It will come as no surprise that choosing the houses to include in this book was a daunting task. I began by creating a list of more than a thousand homes statewide, culled from a wide range of sources gathered over my many years of writing about architecture in Minnesota. Among them were quite a few homes I had been fortunate enough to visit at one time or another, but there were many more I knew only from photographs or written descriptions. Once I had compiled a satisfactory list, I began to winnow. This was the devil's work, the stuff of second thoughts and dreaded decisions, but it had to be done. The process took several months, and I eventually settled on a list of about seventy-five houses I thought would make good candidates for the book.

The next stage was to hit the road in an effort to see as many of the houses as possible. These scouting expeditions consisted of several tours of homes in greater Minnesota as well as trips across the Twin Cities area. The traveling team included my wife, Jodie Ahern, an artist with a fine eye for form and color who made many contributions to this book, and Matt Schmitt, who shot the hundreds of superb photographs that bring *Minnesota's Own* to life. Almost without exception, the homeowners we contacted were gracious and welcoming, and the road trips became not only once-in-a-lifetime opportunities to experience some of Minnesota's most beautiful houses but also chances to meet many wonderful people.

After visiting the houses, we began the second stage of the winnowing process, using Matt's scouting photographs as our guide. We first pared down the list to about thirty-five houses and then, after much thought and discussion, reached the final tally of twenty-two homes. Royce Yeater of the Jeffris Family Foundation, whose generous funding made this book possible, participated in the final selection of houses, as did Pamela McClanahan, director of the Minnesota Historical Society Press, and her team. All of us lost a favored house or two as the list of candidates shrank, but in the end we felt confident that we had managed to gather a representative sampling of Minnesota's best homes.

Despite their many differences, the houses that make up *Minnesota's Own* are linked by at least two common threads. Architectural quality is one of them. While styles and tastes inevitably change, good design is a constant, and all of the houses exemplify the best architectural thinking of their time. They also represent the work of such outstanding Minnesota architects as Cass Gilbert, Clarence Johnston, Edwin Lundie, and the firm of Purcell and Elmslie. Other houses highlight the skills of exceptional craftspeople, such as decorator John Bradstreet, wood-carver Johannes Kirchmayer, stone sculptor Herman Schlink, and ironmaster Samuel Yellin. To see the houses in *Minnesota's Own* is to appreciate just how much the state has been blessed over the years by the work of brilliant designers.

Another common element is that all of the houses speak to the value and importance of historic preservation. In some cases, public or nonprofit institutions led the preservation effort; in others, individuals with a deep love of history stepped forward to bring old houses back from the brink. There was a time when preservation had few advocates or practitioners, but today the idea of protecting and maintaining the best of our built history is a positive force in many communities. The work of preservation is never ending, but the houses in this book demonstrate that its rewards are profound and lasting.

Houses, of course, are much more than just wood and brick and doors and windows. They also function as deep reservoirs of memory that collect and store the life stories of their occupants. The stories in this book highlight the lives of many significant figures from Minnesota's past, from territorial and state governor Alexander Ramsey to lawyer and iron ore investor Chester Congdon to Harry Blackmun, author of one of the most controversial rulings in the history of the U.S. Supreme Court. There are also stories of lesser-known lives. One recounts the career of a millionaire lumberman who met a tragic end in a St. Paul hotel room. Another tells of an unlikely genius who revolutionized the American breakfast table. Yet another recounts the memorable day when the Duke and Duchess of Windsor enjoyed dinner at a home in the St. Paul suburbs.

The men and women who built the splendid houses that grace *Minnesota's Own* are long gone now. But the power of architecture is such that their memories live on in the places they called home, even as a new generation of owners adds stories of its own to the saga of history. ❧

Larry Millett

Minnesota's Own

URBAN MANSIONS

Lawrence S. Donaldson House
Minneapolis, 1907–1908

Lawrence S. Donaldson, circa 1920. He founded the family department store in 1883 with his older brother, William.

Opposite: The Donaldson House, built for the owner of a large department store, is among the outstanding mansions in Minneapolis's exclusive Lowry Hill neighborhood.

THE MANSIONS THAT CROWN THE STEEP NORTHERN FACE OF LOWRY Hill in Minneapolis were built mainly by transplanted Yankees who came west at just the right time to make their fortunes in flour, timber, and manufacturing. One of the hill's greatest mansions, however, has a different provenance. Its original owner, Lawrence S. Donaldson, was a native of Scotland, and he had little interest in grist mills or pineries. He was instead a draper (retail merchant) by trade, and within a decade of his arrival in Minneapolis, his name—emblazoned on the huge department store that he helped found—was among the most famous in the city.

Donaldson's mansion at 1712 Mount Curve Avenue is not the largest or most ostentatious property on Lowry Hill, where many of the city's wealthiest businessmen built sumptuous homes in the 1890s and early 1900s, but it is among the very best, conveying a sense of quiet refinement inside and out. The mansion's history, which includes a dramatic tale of loss and renewal, is more tumultuous. Some of its finest interior features were stripped away in the late 1970s, only to be reacquired two decades later by a loving new owner, Mark Perrin. Today, the impeccably restored mansion offers a window into Minnesota's golden age of architecture in the early 1900s, when the best homes featured a quality of materials and a level of craftsmanship that has not been equaled since.

The man behind the house was a classic American success story. Just twenty-two years old when he immigrated to the United States in 1878, Donaldson arrived with little money but with the advantage of considerable training in the retail business. By 1880 Donaldson had found his way to St. Paul, where he took a job with one of that city's largest dry goods wholesalers. Two years later, he relocated across the river to Minneapolis to join his older brother, William, who worked at Colton's Department Store. The store—a small, one-story affair at Sixth Street and Nicollet Avenue—hardly qualified as a retail colossus. Nor does it seem to have been very well managed. Despite a thriving local economy, Colton's failed in 1883, and the Donaldsons quickly raised enough money to take it over.

Donaldson's Glass Block Department Store, circa 1920. The store was expanded several times as business grew.

An iron-and-steel canopy supported by hexagonal columns shelters the front door, which is set between art-glass sidelights.

Their timing was auspicious. Minneapolis in the 1880s was a prime playground of American capitalism, its economy fueled by a decade of explosive growth that saw the city's population more than triple from just under 47,000 to nearly 165,000. In this superheated environment, riches awaited entrepreneurs with vision and know-how, and the Donaldsons did not let the main chance escape them. As business boomed, the brothers in 1888 built the first recognizably modern department store in the Twin Cities. It was called Donaldson's Glass Block, and it offered a glamorous world of shopping unlike anything ever seen before in Minneapolis.

The five-story glass-and-iron store, with its gleaming white facade and sixty-foot-high Parisian-style corner dome illuminated by thousands of lights, was an instant success. William was the company's president, while Lawrence (who often went by his initials, L. S.) served as general manager. In 1899 William died, and Lawrence assumed complete control of the store. Not until George Draper Dayton opened his department store a block away on Nicollet Avenue in 1902 did Donaldson's have any serious competition. Even so, the store continued to grow and prosper under Lawrence Donaldson's leadership. He oversaw the construction of several additions to the original 1888 building, and by 1920 the store occupied an entire downtown block.

A rather jaunty-looking man who sported a brushy mustache and often wore bow ties, Donaldson cut something of an unusual figure among the city's merchant elite. He was a prominent Catholic in what was then the overwhelmingly Protestant business world of Minneapolis. Active in Catholic affairs, Donaldson in 1905 gave perhaps his greatest gift to the church, donating the land in downtown Minneapolis on which the Basilica of St. Mary was later built. Donaldson could be generous with his employees as well (he once sent an ailing elderly employee on a two-week vacation, covering all the costs himself), but like other businessmen of the time, he wasn't above hiring private detectives to investigate suspicious employee behavior.

Donaldson was also a bit unusual among his fellow business magnates in that he remained a bachelor for many years. As such, he preferred apartment-style living, and as late as the 1890s he maintained his residence in a suite at the West Hotel in downtown Minneapolis. He was finally married in 1901, at age forty-four, to twenty-eight-year-old Isabel McDonald, and the couple soon had their only child, a son also named Lawrence.

A few years after their wedding, the Donaldsons began planning a new house on Lowry Hill. Named after entrepreneur Thomas Lowry, who'd built the first mansion there in the early 1870s, the hill offered high ground in a mostly level city and was conveniently situated only a mile or so from the heart of downtown Minneapolis. Despite its natural advantages, the hill didn't begin to fill out with costly homes until the 1890s. Among those

Donaldson's Glass Block

When the L. S. Donaldson Company began to build its Glass Block department store in Minneapolis in 1883, the idea was to create not only a dry goods store but also a total shopping experience. Inspired by the Parisian retail phenomenon of Bon Marche, Donaldson's displayed its wares—from clothing and furniture to cosmetics and fine jewelry—in glass cases and street-level window showrooms, tantalizing in their abundance and quality. Donaldson's was unique in Minnesota in that the store also included six cafés and tearooms, created by the great interior designer John S. Bradstreet.

For Donaldson's, Bradstreet designed the Gentleman's Café, a Gothic smoking den; the Art Nouveau–style Dutch Room; the decorative Japanese Room; the Ivory Room; and the elegant Arts and Crafts–style Silver Grey Room. Customers enjoyed their time at Donaldson's, taking shopping breaks in the tearooms. Refreshed, they continued to purchase even more merchandise. The rival Dayton's Department Store, just across the street, seized this profitable idea and in 1912 enlisted Prairie school architects William Purcell and George Elmslie to draw plans for its own tearooms. These rooms were never built, but Dayton's later established its popular Oak Grill (famous for its popovers) and Sky Room.

The two rivals went out of their way to one-up each other in their quest for customers, eventually hosting bargain basement events, bridal discount sales, and holiday displays complete with a parade of Santas. But only Donaldson's undertook a children's train ride, suspended from its ceiling, allowing kids to peer down at their parents from above.

Donaldson's was also well known for its shoe department ("America's Finest Shoe Store," according to a 1908 store catalog) and its own greenhouse plants, drug store, optical department, spa/salon, and furniture repair service. All of these amenities were ingenious inventions for dry goods retailers at the time.

Donaldson's stately Glass Block flagship enjoyed a long life but lost much of its original appearance over the years. Its dome was sold for scrap during World War II, and its glassy facade was covered over in the late 1940s. The remodeled store figures prominently in the opening credits of the *Mary Tyler Moore Show*, the backdrop for Mary's famous tam toss.

The building was abandoned in 1982 when the store moved into the new City Center, a pinkish-tan skyscraper and shopping complex derisively labeled "The Giant Salmon Loaf." The final blow to the empty Glass Block building occurred on Thanksgiving Day 1982, when it and the adjacent Northwestern National Bank were destroyed in an enormous fire set by two juvenile arsonists.

By the time of the fire, Donaldson's maintained stores all around the Twin Cities area, including one in the nation's first enclosed shopping mall—Southdale—which opened in Edina in 1956. But Donaldson's was not destined to last. In 1987 all of the company's stores were acquired by Carson Pirie Scott and Company of Chicago and later went under a variety of names.

A John Bradstreet–designed tearoom at Donaldson's Department Store, circa 1910. The tearoom was a comfortable place for customers, mostly women, to take a respite from shopping.

John Scott Bradstreet and His Crafthouse

An extraordinary tastemaker, John S. Bradstreet came to epitomize an eclectic and global design style in Minnesota that would eventually influence the entire country. He was at the heart of a design theory he called "a harmony of good things," drawing influences from Moorish, Japanese, Art Nouveau, Arts and Crafts, and Prairie styles to create a uniquely American aesthetic. His vision touched many of the best homes in Minnesota at the end of the nineteenth century, including rooms at the Lawrence S. Donaldson House and at Chester Congdon's Glensheen estate in Duluth.

Raised in New England, Bradstreet began his career at Gorham Manufacturing Company, a Rhode Island producer of fine silver wares. He left New England in 1873 for the drier climate of Minnesota after a bout with tuberculosis. Ten years later, he convinced the owners of Gorham to move west and join him in the furniture trade. By then, Bradstreet had established himself as a purveyor of fine home furnishings and an inveterate world traveler in search of grace and beauty. He maintained Minneapolis businesses that showcased and sold both original furniture and examples of the exotica he collected during his travels. Bradstreet acknowledged public fascination with all things Japanese, traveling often to Japan to observe and collect its arts firsthand. He eventually adapted his own version of the Japanese technique of *jin-di-sugi*, a process by which cypress wood was smoked and wire brushed to bring the hard grain fibers into prominence. The patterns of the grain then influenced the shape, decoration, or carving of a piece of furniture, celebrating the harmony between nature and craftsmanship.

Bradstreet affiliated with the design elite of his time. He had a special fondness for Louis Comfort Tiffany's glasswork and used it throughout the Donaldson House. On display at the Minneapolis Institute of Arts (MIA) is an entire Bradstreet-designed living room reassembled from the Duluth home of William and Mina Prindle, complete with Tiffany glass and Bradstreet's signature Lotus Table. The MIA itself owes a debt to Bradstreet, who helped inspire the formation of the Minneapolis Society of Fine Arts, which evolved into the renowned art institution it is today.

Bradstreet's crowning achievement in Minnesota was the establishment of his Minneapolis crafthouse, opened in 1904 in a renovated Italianate mansion at Seventh Street and Fourth Avenue South. It included showrooms of fine arts and crafts from around the world, along with museum-quality antiques and furniture and decorative arts made on site. The crafthouse became not just a retailer but also a destination, where people gathered for exhibitions, concerts, lectures, and cultural events that propelled the arts in Minnesota far beyond their humble prairie roots.

In 1914 Bradstreet, an early and enthusiastic supporter of the automobile, died in a car accident and was the recipient of lengthy eulogies in the city's newspapers.

John Bradstreet's crafthouse, circa 1918. Bradstreet remodeled an old mansion to create his Japanese-themed workshop and display room, which opened in 1904.

The richly appointed living room includes a beamed ceiling with intricately carved corbels and a Renaissance Revival–style fireplace made of pink Minnesota travertine.

The canopy columns display stylized thistles, the national flower of Scotland, where Donaldson was born.

drawn to the neighborhood as it began to develop into a mansion district was William Donaldson. In 1893 he moved into a massive new stone mansion (torn down in 1933) on the southern flank of the hill at 21 Groveland Terrace.

When Lawrence Donaldson was finally ready to build a home of his own, he chose a site at the crest of the hill on Mount Curve Avenue, almost directly above his brother's old house. He began assembling land in 1905, when he purchased two lots, at 1700 and 1712 Mount Curve. A house on the lot at 1700, just east of where Donaldson would soon build his mansion, was demolished. Another home, directly to the west, was later torn down to make way for Donaldson's carriage house. Eventually, Donaldson acquired six lots (about an acre in all), including two along Kenwood Parkway at the base of the hill, to provide ample grounds for his mansion.

Donaldson's selection of the Minneapolis firm of Kees and Colburn to design his home was hardly a surprise, since he had enjoyed a long working relationship with architect Frederick Kees. The Donaldson brothers' groundbreaking department store of 1888 had been the work of Kees and his then partner, Franklin Long. The firm of Long and Kees, best known today for its mighty Municipal Building (now Minneapolis City Hall), broke up in 1898. Kees then joined forces with Serenus Colburn in about 1900 to create another highly successful architectural partnership that lasted well into the 1920s.

The mansion in its original form was completed in 1907, but it appears the Donaldsons weren't satisfied with the result. In 1908 they undertook

This elevation drawing illustrates the balance and scale of Kees and Colburn's Renaissance Revival design for Donaldson's home.

This floor plan shows how the home's 1908 addition expanded the house to the rear, including an enlarged dining room and a new sunroom.

a significant addition, extending the north (rear) side of the house by several feet to accommodate a larger dining room, a spectacular new sunroom, and an extra bedroom upstairs. The mansion, which in its revised form approached ten thousand square feet in size, must have pleased the Donaldsons, both of whom remained in the home until their deaths.

At first glance, the mansion—with its buff Roman brick walls, careful symmetry, double bay windows, elaborate marquee, and decorative terra-cotta trim—seems to be a fairly standard essay in the Renaissance Revival style that was popular for high-end houses in the early 1900s. A closer inspection reveals that the home is in fact quite eclectic, as were many mansions of the time. Some details, most notably the railings that guard the front terrace, evoke the intricate, swirling ornament of the Chicago architect Louis Sullivan. Other features, such as the broad front dormer and the art-glass windows surrounding the entry, call to mind the Arts and Crafts style and even hint at the work of Frank Lloyd Wright and his followers (the so-called Prairie school).

There are more exotic touches, as well. Scotland's national flower—the thistle—is worked into much of the home's cast-stone, stained-glass, and carved-wood ornament. This design theme is established immediately at the front entry, where sculpted thistles burst out from the cushion capitals atop two massive octagonal columns that support the marquee. Kees and Colburn's use of a unifying decorative motif was fairly common practice at the time, with stylized flowers of one kind or another often favored for this purpose.

The stained-glass window in the living room is an exact replica of the original, which was fabricated by Louis Comfort Tiffany's studios in New York. The three circular panels depict thistle flowers.

The elegant library is one of two rooms in the home that showcase the work of celebrated Minneapolis decorator John Bradstreet.

Opposite: A domed gold-leaf ceiling hovers over the dining room, which is reached directly from the front hall. The room's original Tiffany light fixture was removed in the 1970s and later sold at auction to singer Barbra Streisand.

The house's eclecticism is even more evident inside, where the rugged simplicity of the Arts and Crafts style plays off against the lush classicism of the Renaissance Revival. The Arts and Crafts elements serve the house especially well by toning down its lavish tendencies, so the mansion, unlike some of its more aggressively opulent peers, never feels like just another naked display of wealth. As built, the mansion was also an outstanding repository of light fixtures, lamps, fireplace surrounds, and stained-glass windows designed by Louis Tiffany's famed New York studios. Minneapolis decorator John Bradstreet, a friend of Tiffany and a first-class designer in his own right, also contributed superb furnishings and ornamental features.

The mansion's many delights begin at the entrance, where an elevated front terrace, not a common feature in Minnesota houses, extends to either side of a glass-and-iron marquee. Distinctive metal railings that incorporate a pattern of repeating circles and curves guard the terrace. It is no accident that these railings evoke the work of Louis Sullivan, since his influence is readily visible in other designs by Kees and Colburn, most notably their Minneapolis Grain Exchange of 1902.

The mansion's front door, set between wide sidelights, features iron grillwork and opens into a gorgeous foyer richly decorated with Arts and Crafts–style crackle glass. Beyond the foyer is a broad oak-paneled hall that provides access to the living and dining rooms, a front reception parlor (which doubles as a study), a sunroom, and the main staircase. Next to the stairs, a side hall leads to another entry sheltered by the mansion's porte cochere. A full-length mirror conveniently placed in the side hall was undoubtedly designed to let visitors perform last-minute clothing or makeup adjustments before joining the party. Another small hall near the side entry leads to a powder room and a large, remodeled kitchen.

Each of the mansion's main rooms has a distinctive character. The thirty-by-fifteen-foot living room, finished in mahogany-stained birch woodwork, cen-

Murals painted by Russian-born artist Alfons A. Baumgart form a decorative frieze above the dining room's zebra-wood paneling.

The rear of the house overlooks a broad yard and gardens, with views of the Minneapolis skyline. The porte cochere, hidden for many years behind a garage, was restored by the current owner, Mark Perrin.

ters around a beautifully carved fireplace made of pink Minnesota travertine. Here, too, is one of the home's most fanciful touches: ceiling beams that rest on corbels, each carved with a face and other features designed to depict one of the four seasons. The room also includes a superb bronze-and-glass-bead center light fixture and a delicate stained-glass side window with three circular insets depicting the thistle plant. The original window came from Tiffany but was one of many items removed from the house by later owners and sold at auction in 1978. Perrin was unable to restore the window, so he had an exact reproduction made by Century Studios of Minneapolis.

To the rear of the living room is the mansion's most extraordinary space—a glorious sunroom designed by Bradstreet, the most popular interior decorator of his time in Minneapolis. Bradstreet had opened a Japanese-themed studio and crafthouse in downtown Minneapolis only a few years earlier, and he used his deep knowledge of Japanese art to create a truly remarkable room for the Donaldsons.

The sunroom is paneled in cypress wood fumed in the traditional Japanese manner known as *jin-di-sugi*, a technique that brings out the grain of the wood and produces subtle color effects. The room, which conveys a sense of all-encompassing serenity, showcases Bradstreet's mastery of *jin-di-sugi*. Among its outstanding features are eleven carved transom screens (reacquired by Perrin) that portray variations of the peony blossom. Stylized flowers and other motifs also appear in a series of delicate carved panels on the room's upper walls. One especially fine panel shows a pair of cranes in flight with a rising sun in the background. The largest panel of all, above the fireplace, also depicts birds and flowers. The original fireplace surround included Tiffany glass mosaic tiles, but it, too, was removed and has now been replaced with marble. A unique Bradstreet-designed light fixture with Tiffany glass completes the room's *jin-di-sugi* ensemble.

A side porch (not shown on plan) was added to the east side of the sunroom in 1912 and converted to three-season use in 2001. To the west is the dining room, which features a domed white gold-leaf ceiling, classically inspired murals attributed to Russian-born Minneapolis artist Alfons A. Baumgart, and zebra wood and mahogany paneling. Here, the luxurious spirit of the Renaissance Revival style is more apparent than anywhere else in the house.

The dining room once included a magnificent Tiffany glass light fixture that sold for $15,000 at the 1978 auction at Christie's in New York. The buyer was Barbra Streisand, an avid Tiffany collector at the time. She sold the fixture fifteen years later for $72,000. It was sold again at auction in 2010, fetching just over $110,000, which is probably more than Donaldson paid for the entire house.

The main staircase and front hall feature quartersawn oak woodwork. A broad doorway with side columns leads to the living room.

Bradstreet also designed the reception room at the front of the house. Here, the decoration and furnishing are more traditional: fine oak paneling, a pressed-copper fireplace screen depicting a medieval village scene, and built-in bookcases identical to those Bradstreet used at Chester Congdon's contemporaneous Glensheen estate in Duluth.

The main staircase, guarded by sturdy Arts and Crafts oak balusters, was once lit with a Tiffany light fixture and a Tiffany stained-glass window above the landing. Both are now gone, but Perrin has reacquired another portion of the original landing window. Fortunately, one piece of the staircase's literal historic fabric, a twenty-three-foot-long runner made of camel hair, remains in place. At the top of the stairs on the second floor, a wide hall leads to five bedrooms, most of which have been remodeled or rebuilt over the years. There is, however, a restored white-tile bathroom equipped with an exceptional piece of plumbing: a deluxe surround shower made in 1906 by the Crane Company.

The spacious attic initially included servants' quarters and a nursery decorated with playful tiles featuring Mother Goose rhymes. The mansion, unlike others on Lowry Hill, never had a formal ballroom in the attic—perhaps Donaldson wasn't much for dancing—but there is a handsome basement billiard room that includes stained-glass windows depicting pool balls and cues. A fireplace topped by another Baumgart-painted mural kept the players warm. The basement also offers access to a long concrete tunnel that connects to a carriage house constructed in 1916.

In addition to the occasional game of pool, Donaldson's interests included horticulture, and the property once featured an elaborate sunken garden located to the east of the mansion. He also seems to have been a very enthusiastic golfer, since he belonged to at least seven clubs, including one in New York and another in Chicago.

Donaldson suffered a heart attack late in 1923, and it produced lingering effects. In July of 1924, he slipped into a coma and died two days later in his man-

John Bradstreet's glorious sunroom features cypress wood paneling fumed to bring out its grain in a traditional Japanese technique known as *jin-di-sugi*. The room's eleven carved transom screens were reacquired by Perrin after previous owners had removed them.

sion at age sixty-eight. Shortly before his death, Donaldson had announced plans for a new building that would include a 445-foot tower. As it turned out, the tower (which would have been the tallest in Minneapolis) failed to materialize, but the department store was remodeled and expanded. Donaldson's remained in business until 1982, when another retailer bought the firm, ending its century-long presence in Minnesota.

Isabel Donaldson died in 1937, and the couple's son, Lawrence, became the new owner. He lived in the house until his death in 1958, after which new owners subdivided the property into three lots. A new house was built to the east (on the site of the old garden). The carriage house to the west, where Donaldson's 1923 Rolls Royce remained in storage, was also purchased by the new owners and remodeled into a residence. A fourth lot was carved out of the old estate in 1964 and became the site of a small house just to the west of the mansion.

The mansion itself stood relatively intact until 1978, when its owners began stripping away all of the Tiffany light fixtures, lamps, and stained-glass panels, which were sold at Christie's. The owners removed many other original decorative features, such as the screens in the sunroom and the carved corbels in the living room, before selling the mansion in 1979.

When Perrin, a biotechnology executive, bought the house in 2000, he and his then partner, landscape architect Ron Beining, faced a daunting challenge. Although Perrin had grown up in an 1820s-vintage home in Upstate New York filled with antiques collected by his parents, the Donaldson House was his first restoration project, and he quickly discovered it would not be easy. The mansion was missing many of its original ornamental details; its mechanical and electrical systems were in desperate need of attention; the stately porte cochere had been defaced by a garage placed directly in front of it; and the grounds themselves were less than stellar. Nor was the decorating much to write home about. "The living room walls were painted a Pepto-Bismol pink," Perrin recalls.

Over the next decade, Perrin brought the mansion back to its original grandeur, aided in part by a bit of serendipity. A chance encounter revealed that the family who had sold off the Tiffany furnishings still had at least thirty items from the house in their possession. Perrin bought them all back and returned them to the house. He also restored or refurbished every major room, added new amenities such as a basement entertainment center, modernized the mechanical and electrical systems, purchased the carriage house and restored it as part of the property, and undertook new landscaping for the grounds. Perrin also wrote and published a history of the house, which has once again become one of the jewels of Lowry Hill. ☙

A carved relief panel above the sunroom's fireplace portrays two birds amid flowers and stems.

Henry Myers House
Duluth, 1910

A sculpted head (one of two found on the house) adorns an upper gable. The heads and all of the home's exterior trim appear to be carved from granite but are actually made of concrete blocks faced with terra-cotta.

Opposite: Random chunks of charcoal-gray basaltic rock form the rugged walls of the Henry Myers House in Duluth. Myers obtained the blast rock from a nearby street excavation.

DULUTH HAS ALWAYS SEEMED A WORLD APART AMONG MIDWESTERN cities, a kind of San Francisco on ice, home to steep hills, fog banks, great ships, and dazzling vistas of land and water. Its history is just as extraordinary as its natural setting on the shores of Lake Superior. Founded in the 1850s amid rumors of nearby gold and copper deposits, the city at first grew slowly and in 1880 was home to fewer than 3,500 people. But with the discovery of vast iron ore deposits on the Mesabi Iron Range in the late 1880s, Duluth—where shipping, lumbering, and railroading also flourished—became a fevered boomtown, its population soaring to 53,000 by 1900.

The boom, which was both quick and powerful, produced enormous wealth for the city's business elite, so much so that by the early 1900s Duluth boosters began to claim their city was home to more millionaires per capita than any other place in America. Even if this claim wasn't true, it must have seemed as if the city were awash in riches, as block after block of new mansions, most built between 1900 and 1910, sprang up on the city's East End (far away from the industrialized West End, where most of the money was made).

The largest and most lavish Duluth mansion of all was Chester Congdon's incomparable Glensheen, but many other big houses appeared nearby, particularly along East Superior, First, and Second Streets. The houses here, by virtue of their often unusual designs, form one of Minnesota's most distinctive architectural colonies—a mansion district quite different from any in the Twin Cities, for example. Among the most peculiar and delightful of these homes is a dark, rugged mansion built at 2505 East First Street for Henry Myers, one of the many businessmen who had profited from Duluth's wave of prosperity. Restored in 2013 by new owners Johan and Nicole Bakken, the muscular home is at once roughhewn and sophisticated, and it could have been built nowhere except Duluth.

A financier and real estate broker, Myers was born in Mansfield, Ohio, in 1857. Little is known about his early life, but by 1884 he had moved to

The Seventh Avenue West Incline Railway, 1915. Henry Myers was likely among the Duluth businessmen who invested in the railway, which operated from 1890 to 1939.

Duluth in search of opportunity. His two brothers, Jacob and Benjamin, arrived in Duluth at about the same time. Jacob, perhaps feeling the chill, later moved to Texas, but Henry and Benjamin stayed on.

Myers soon had a hand in many enterprises in Duluth, including the construction in 1889 of one of the city's early marvels—an incline railway that ascended six hundred feet up the bluffs on the West End. Known as the Duluth Beltline Railway, it was intended to serve a new hilltop residential development and prospered for a time before shutting down in 1916. It's likely Myers also invested in Duluth's second—and better-known—incline railway, which was built along Seventh Avenue West in 1890 and remained in operation until 1939. Duluth's incline railways were the only two of their kind ever built in Minnesota.

Myers also invested in real estate, and in 1890 he and his brothers built Park Terrace (razed, 1936), one of Duluth's great Victorian-era landmarks. Park Terrace was a row house that stepped up steep hills on two sides to create a stunning, one-of-a-kind architectural profile. Myers and his wife, Lucy, lived in one of the units. His two brothers were also residents, creating a small family compound. Henry and Lucy moved out in 1895, and their only child, Cecil, was born three years later.

In 1907 Henry and Benjamin Myers formed a company that according to one newspaper account was "authorized to do practically every kind of business, real estate, warehouses, halls and buildings, exploration work and mining, lumber and merchandise." Despite its all-purpose corporate credentials, the Myers Brothers Company specialized in real estate, investing in iron ore lands north of Duluth as well as on the Cuyuna Range in Crow Wing County. The brothers also had substantial real estate interests in Duluth itself.

By 1909, with his business flourishing, Henry Myers hired the Duluth architectural firm of Bray and Nystrom to design a new home in the heart of the city's mansion district. William T. Bray, the firm's chief designer, was a New Yorker who had been practicing in Duluth since 1891. He formed a partnership with the Swedish-born Carl Nystrom in 1906. The firm's work, like that of many Duluth architects of the period, was wildly eclectic. At the same time they were working on Myers's picturesque fantasy, they were also designing a home just blocks away in the sleek Prairie style of Frank Lloyd Wright. The Myers House demonstrates Bray and Nystrom's ability to scramble a mélange of stylistic ingredients into a distinctive concoction. The home's round corner tower, massive rock walls, and broad overall proportions evoke the Romanesque Revival style. Why the architects and their client chose this style is a mystery, since it was well out of fashion by 1910. The house, in fact, is possibly the last example of Romanesque Revival built in Minnesota.

Even so, the house is far from an exercise in pure Romanesque nostalgia. The battlements atop the porte cochere, for example, point to a Gothic influence (also dated at the time). Two of the house's four gables are rounded rather than peaked, a stylistic quirk that seems to have been borrowed from Tudor or even Spanish Colonial Revival sources. Inside, however, the home's generally simple detailing is mostly in the Arts and Crafts manner, which was very popular in 1910, although the dining room inhabits yet another stylistic world—Classical Revival. All told, the house is a very eccentric mix, unusual even by Duluth's freewheeling standards.

Much of the home's character derives from its craggy walls, which are laid up in thick, random chunks of the charcoal-gray basaltic rock that crops up all around Duluth. Myers didn't have to go far to find the basalt, which

Park Terrace Apartments, circa 1891. Myers and his brothers built these visually astonishing apartments, which were torn down in 1936.

The Myers House offers a spirited mélange of styles ranging from Romanesque and Gothic Revival to Tudor and Arts and Crafts. Other Duluth mansions of the period embrace a similarly eclectic approach to design.

Duluth's Greatest Victorian

Almost all of Duluth's historic mansions are located in the city's East End, well removed from the grittier environs to the west of downtown. But Duluth's working-class West End once had a fabulous mansion of its own, a Queen Anne–style extravaganza that had few, if any, equals in all of

Minnesota. Built for industrialist DeWitt Clinton Prescott in 1890, the house stood for just over a half century before age caught up with it.

Prescott, who was named after New York governor and Erie Canal promoter DeWitt Clinton (1769–1828), built the home the same year he moved his company, which manufactured sawmill machinery, from northern Wisconsin to Duluth. Unlike the mostly brick and stone East End mansions of the early 1900s, Prescott's house, at 4831 West Fifth Street, was a festival celebrating the wonders of wood. It was also a delightfully over-the-top example of Queen Anne at its most exuberant.

The style's name—after England's Queen Anne, who ruled from 1702 to 1714—is a curious misnomer. The classically inspired English architecture of her era was quite staid, whereas the Queen Anne style as it evolved in the United States, beginning in the 1870s, was a kind of free-for-all characterized by complex forms, an eclectic array of materials, and a sense of boisterous energy. Prescott's three-story mansion—a visual riot of towers (three), gables, dormers, chimneys, balconies, porches, bargeboards, finials, cresting, and gingerbread ornament—perfectly expressed the anything-goes spirit of American Queen Anne. It's not known who designed the house, but pattern books were readily available at the time as inspirations.

Inside, the house was well stuffed with Victorian goodies, including inlaid floors, hand-carved woodwork, stained-glass windows, and plumbing imported from England. A third-floor ballroom provided a place for entertainment. Guests could even avail themselves of a gold-plated washbasin in the reception room before heading upstairs for a round of dancing.

Like many another outsized mansion of its time, Prescott's improbable house did not function as a family home for very long. Prescott and his wife, Sarah, moved to Chicago in 1896. Another owner occupied the house into the early 1900s, but keeping it up—or, for that matter, simply keeping it painted—must have been a struggle. Around 1914 the house was offered to the Duluth Catholic Diocese as a children's hospital, but it may never actually have been used for that purpose. The house was vacant for many years thereafter and eventually fell into tax forfeiture.

In 1944, a new owner bought the sagging old pile for $1,500 and began dismantling it piece by piece. Some of the better interior elements, including three fireplaces, were later installed in a new home built by the owner. Dimensional lumber was also salvaged and used to construct several tourist cabins along Highway 61 in Duluth. By 1948, Duluth's greatest Victorian was only a memory, and today modern-era homes occupy the mansion's lot.

The Clint D. Prescott House is one of Duluth's—and Minnesota's—greatest lost Victorians. Built in 1890 for an industrialist, the Queen Anne–style house was dismantled in the 1940s.

A series of receding Tudor arches surrounds the front door, which is sheltered by an open porch. The porch's curved wood braces are also Tudor in character.

was blast rock from the construction of Twenty-Fourth Avenue East only a block away. It's possible Myers got the idea for using it from his experience with the incline railway projects, which had also required dynamiting large amounts of rock. Myers probably acquired the rock for not much more than the cost of hauling it to his property.

The home's rock walls are trimmed with what looks to be pink granite but is actually a type of concrete block faced in terra-cotta. This rather unusual material, made by the long-gone Winkle Terra Cotta Company of St. Louis, shows up in other Duluth buildings but is not commonly seen elsewhere in Minnesota. The home's terra-cotta array includes an elaborate series of receding arches around the front door, scrolled gable ends, a

The richly finished front entry hall features a magnificent staircase that begins its ascent with a giant scroll rather than the usual newel post. All of the woodwork is Circassian walnut.

swirling rail above the side porch, and two sculpted heads that were possibly standard items from the Winkle Company catalog.

Structurally, the house is as solid as it looks. The stone exterior walls support an interior structural system that includes brick walls and a concrete-tile ceiling system. This sort of "fireproof" construction was used for many mansions in Minnesota and elsewhere at the turn of the twentieth century.

In addition to the main house, which encompasses well over six thousand square feet, the property includes a two-story carriage house to the rear, also built of basalt. The house itself cost $35,000, according to the building permit, although the actual price tag, including land and furnishings, would have been much higher. Construction required about eighteen months. It's not known who actually built the house, but the stonework certainly required the skills of a master mason. The house occupies an exceptionally large corner lot that provides space for an ample side yard. An aerial photograph of the house from the 1920s shows much of the yard being used as a garden.

The experience of the house begins with its massive front porch, which rises from low, battered walls to a series of heavy piers with thick curved-wood braces. The front door is set within a layered series of terra-cotta arches. In a faithful version of Romanesque Revival, these arches would be rounded, but here they are flattened in the manner of English Tudor architecture—another example of the home's unapologetic eclecticism.

A small, tiled vestibule leads from the front door into a spacious entry hall paneled in golden-brown Circassian walnut. Often used for fine furniture, the intricately grained walnut was an unusual choice by the architects, since oak was the favored interior wood for most houses of the period. The main staircase, which features the same walnut along with subtle inlays, is a few steps in from the front door. Positioned beneath a high skylight, the staircase forms the literal center of the house. Its outstanding feature is an Arts and Crafts–style railing that seems brawny enough for a warehouse. But instead of ascending from a sturdy, square newel post, as would be the usual case, the railing begins its upward march with a voluptuous scroll. Surprises of this kind abound throughout the house, which more often than not defies architectural convention.

To the left of the hall, through a broad opening flanked by pocket doors, is the living room, which includes a rounded front parlor in the base of the tower. The living room's centerpiece is a fireplace set within an outsized surround of white Italian marble accented with bands of mosaic tile. A mahogany overmantel provides contrast, as do similarly dark ceiling beams. With its foursquare woodwork and generally simple detailing, the living room has a strong Arts and Crafts feel, albeit of a very luxurious kind. As with other rooms in the house, the baseboard and top moldings here are exceptionally tall, creating well-defined wall borders.

The circling parlor in the tower is one of the home's most charming spaces. Lit by three double-hung windows, it adds welcome curvature to what is otherwise a resolutely foursquare house. The parlor's fabric walls

Much of the home's character derives from its craggy walls, which are laid up in thick, random chunks of the charcoal-gray basaltic rock that crops up all around Duluth.

While renovating the Myers House, the current owners discovered these elegant sconces, long hidden under previous remodelings.

I. Vernon Hill

Duluth's unique architectural heritage, so evident in the Henry Myers House, includes a series of unusual homes designed by an architect whose career was at once unlikely, brilliant, and tragically short. His name was Isaac Vernon Hill, and though he is little known today outside Duluth, it's possible he might have made a national name for himself had he lived longer.

Born in England in 1872, Hill (who always went by I. Vernon Hill) immigrated with his family to Duluth when he was sixteen years old. In 1891 he found work as a bookkeeper with a Duluth home builder. He was apparently a natural-born designer, and within three years he abandoned his accounting ledgers to become a draftsman for the company. In 1896, at age twenty-four, he formed his first architectural partnership. He would go on to have two other partners during his brief career, including William Bray (later one of the architects of the Myers House).

Architecture is a field in which mastery usually comes late, but Hill was a meteor. Afflicted with tuberculosis, he perhaps sensed that his time was short, and he moved quickly to establish himself in his chosen profession. By 1900 he was designing homes like no others in Minnesota, in a variety of styles. One of the most spectacular, high above Duluth at 501 West Skyline Parkway, was built for a druggist named Arthur Cook. Rising above a series of stairways, walls, terraces, and rock gardens made from stone quarried on the site, the house became an instant landmark featured on postcards, and it remains one of the city's most photographed architectural monuments.

Most of Hill's other houses are in Duluth's East End mansion district. Two of his most exciting designs—the F. A. Patrick House (1901) and Hill's own house (1902)—are dynamic reworkings of the then-popular Tudor Revival style. The Patrick House, at 2306 East Superior Street, is notable for its double front gable. The house Hill designed for himself and his wife, Cora, at 2220 East Superior, is even bolder, with a steep front gable thrusting above a narrow two-story bay and then intersecting with equally large cross gables that hover over a cascading array of smaller roofs. The house's complex interplay of forms is reminiscent of some of the early work of Frank Lloyd Wright.

Hill also designed a number of foursquare homes that are much different from his Tudor-inspired residences. One of the best is a house at 2029 East Superior built in 1902 for George Crosby, a founder of the Cuyuna Iron Range. Mixing the Arts and Crafts and Art Nouveau styles in a highly creative way, the sandstone house includes carvings by local master George Thrana, whose work can be found on many other buildings in Duluth.

In 1903 Hill left Duluth for good, moving to Los Angeles with his wife and their two young children. He hoped the mild California air would improve his health, but it did not, and he died of pneumonia in February of 1904 at age thirty-one. He never had time to build a career in California, and his small but superb body of work in Duluth remains his sole architectural legacy.

The A. P. Cook House, circa 1915. Located on Skyline Drive, the house is one of many superb designs created around 1900 by short-lived Duluth architect I. Vernon Hill.

and hand-painted ceiling were restored in 2013, as were most of the home's other interior finishes.

To live in Duluth is to be a sun seeker during the long winter months, which in some years seem to flirt with eternity. A sunroom on the southwest side of the house, off the living room, provides a bright, warm spot in winter. The Bakkens upgraded the room with new floor tile as well as in-floor heat. They also cleaned and repaired the tile around the room's fireplace.

The dining room is the home's most elaborately decorated space. Its lush plaster ceiling, organized in bands around a central oval, offers a mini-encyclopedia of Classical Revival ornamental motifs. But other prominent elements—a painted frieze band, a mahogany sideboard, and an arched

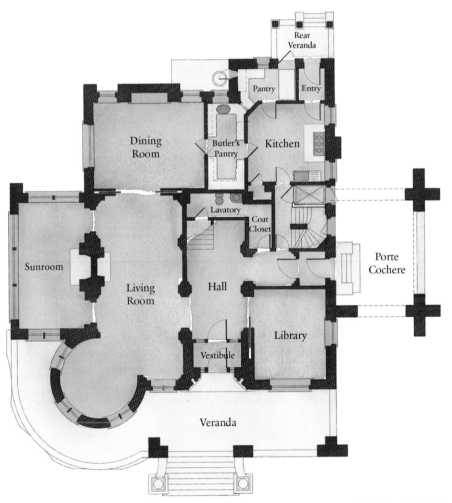

The main rooms of the Myers House are arranged around a central hall, with a side hall leading to the porte cochere.

The staircase, lit by an eight-foot-square skylight, features exceptionally hefty railings. The Circassian walnut panels beneath the stairs showcase the wood's intricate graining.

A fanciful witch's-hat roof rises above the home's massive corner tower. Johan and Nicole Bakken restored and renovated the house after purchasing it in 2012.

picture window—aren't especially classical in their inspiration, and the room as a whole, like the house itself, is an elusive amalgam of styles.

The main floor also includes a handsome library across the hall from the living room. Finished in walnut, it features built-in bookcases and drawers and a beamed ceiling. A renovated kitchen at the north-east corner of the house completes the main-floor ensemble.

Upstairs, there are four corner bedrooms, three bathrooms, and a sewing room on the second floor. The master bedroom, which extends into the tower, offers views toward Lake Superior. All of the upstairs hallways receive daylight from the multipaneled sky-light above the stairs. This eight-foot-square skylight is one of the home's crucial features, sending streams of light all the way down to the first floor.

Most of the third floor is taken up by what was originally a ballroom, which could be reached by a small elevator as well as the stairs. The ballroom (which the Bakkens use as a billiard and entertain-ment room) was carefully finished with hardwood floors, wainscoting, and stenciled walls. A scene depicting two peacocks in full plumage is among the decorative highlights.

The Myerses moved into their new home some-time in late 1910 or early 1911 and never lived any-where else. The couple seem to have led a full life. The *Duluth News-Tribune* reported frequently on their travels, which, not surprisingly, were mostly to warm places. In September 1920 the Myerses made more news because of their invitation to a dinner party in St. Paul for Senator Warren G. Harding of Ohio, who would soon be elected president. The invitation probably came about because Henry Myers was a first cousin of Harding's wife, Florence.

Henry Myers died in Duluth in 1931, and Lucy, in 1938. Over the next seventy years, as owners came and went, the house was remodeled to vary-ing degrees, although its essential features remained

Opposite: The dining room includes a decorative plaster ceiling organized around a central oval, a painted frieze band, and a beautiful mahogany sideboard.

A luxurious white-marble fireplace with a mahogany overmantel serves as the centerpiece of the living room, which, like much of the interior, reflects the influence of the Arts and Crafts style popular in the early 1900s.

The library, across the front hall from the living room, includes beamed ceilings and built-in bookcases, all finished in Circassian walnut.

intact. In 2012, the house came up for sale for the first time in more than twenty-five years, and when the Bakkens saw it, they knew immediately they had found their home.

Johan, a gastroenterologist and the son of a doctor, grew up in Oslo, Norway, but moved with his family to Duluth when he was nine years old. Nicole, a nurse practitioner, was born in California. Like her husband, she received some of her medical training at the Mayo Clinic in Rochester, Minnesota. Even before leaving Rochester, the couple made trips to Duluth to look at houses, searching for a home with character that hadn't been too deeply disturbed by modern interventions.

The Myers House turned out to be exactly what they were looking for. They closed on the house in November 2012, a month before their first child, a daughter, was born. The couple then undertook the lengthy process of restoring the home's faded beauty while also upgrading its tired wiring, plumbing, and heating systems.

Restoring the home's original interiors required the work of master craftspeople to hand paint and stencil walls and ceilings, recast damaged plaster-work, and refinish woodwork and floors. There were some serendipitous moments along the way, among them the discovery of elegant bedroom sconces long hidden under earlier remodelings. The Bakkens were also able to repurchase some of the original furnishings from the home, which had been sold by an earlier owner.

At the same time, all manner of fixing had to be done, on everything from sinks that no longer worked to leaky windows. The skylight was in particular need of repair, and the couple had to replace the entire roof as well. They also decided to completely rebuild the kitchen, which had been remodeled in the 1970s.

The Bakkens completed their work of renewal in 2013, and the house that Henry and Lucy Myers built has once again taken on its rightful place as one of Duluth's—and Minnesota's—most unusual architectural treasures. ❧

Swan J. Turnblad House
Minneapolis, 1908

An oil portrait of Swan Turnblad, commissioned after his death in 1933, suggests his aloof and imperious nature.

Opposite: Draped in fresh snow, the Swan Turnblad House in Minneapolis resembles an old-world castle plucked from the pages of a fairy tale. Turnblad, a Swedish immigrant, made his fortune publishing the nation's largest Swedish-language newspaper.

I N THE EARLY 1900S, A MILE-LONG SECTION OF PARK AVENUE IN MINneapolis formed one of the Upper Midwest's most impressive mansion districts. The families who lived there—with names such as Barber, Bell, Forman, and Phelps—largely hailed from old Yankee stock, and their big houses tended to follow the standard architectural styles of the time. There was, however, one great exception, a fantastic castle of a house, full of delirious detail, built at 2600 Park Avenue between 1904 and 1908 by Swan J. Turnblad, the son of poor Swedish immigrants. Carefully avoiding the niceties of understatement, Turnblad built his thirty-three-room mansion to show his neighbors, and all of Minneapolis, how far he had come in the world.

Yet the mansion, which has been listed on the National Register of Historic Places since 1971, was more than just an expensive exercise in architectural one-upmanship. It was also designed as a vessel for the display of Swedish art and culture, and there is evidence to suggest Turnblad always intended his flamboyant showpiece would ultimately serve a broad community purpose. This ideal was realized in 1929, when he donated the mansion to what became the American Swedish Institute, which still flourishes today.

Although the story of Turnblad and his mansion is one of great achievement against the odds, it also resonates with deep strains of Nordic melancholy. Despite its manifest splendors, the mansion never seems to have brought great happiness to its builder. Its completion, in fact, inspired a chain of lawsuits accusing Turnblad of financial skullduggery in his role as publisher of the *Svenska Amerikanska Posten*, then the nation's largest Swedish-language newspaper. How, former stockholders of the supposedly unprofitable newspaper wondered, had Turnblad been able to afford such splendor? The answer would not prove to be especially edifying.

Very slender, with a long, austere face punctuated by piercing blue eyes, Turnblad in photographs conveys a sense of imperious distance. His business dealings, and the numerous lawsuits they inspired, paint the picture of a sharp-elbowed operator who did not leave many friends in

his wake. Witnesses in court cases called him "avaricious," "deceitful," and a "prevaricator," among other choice terms. A caretaker at the mansion in the late 1920s described Turnblad as "an odd sort, a kind of dominating sort." The man also recalled that during the entire time of his employment, he never saw anyone visit the mansion, where Turnblad, his wife, and their daughter spent most of their time on the second and third floors, never using the magnificent suite of rooms downstairs. At other times, it appears the family occupied the mansion only during the day, returning at night to an apartment above Turnblad's downtown newspaper office.

The mansion's design is as unusual as its provenance. Although it falls within the general realm of the French Revival style called Chateauesque, the mansion is at heart a poor boy's fairy-tale fantasy, decked out with towers, mock battlements, sculpted gables, and carved grotesques. The interior, organized around a central hall that features the grandest fireplace in Minnesota, is equally over-the-top, teeming with intricately carved woodwork and fine furnishings, including eleven superb *kakelugnar* (tiled stoves) imported from Sweden. Turnblad spared no expense in building the home, which some estimates report might have cost as much as $1.2 to $1.5 million by the time the last interior flourishes were installed in 1910.

When he arrived in America with his parents at age eight in 1868, Turnblad hardly appeared to have the makings of great wealth. Sven Johan was the youngest of eleven children born to the Månsson family, farmers in the province of Småland in southern Sweden. Farming the province's rocky ground was a difficult proposition even in the best of times, and crop failures in the late 1860s brought widespread famine. Turnblad's parents, like thousands of their countrymen, finally sought a better life across the Atlantic. Upon their arrival in the United States, the family changed their surname to Turnblad, and the boy's first name became Swan—an Americanized version of Sven common at the time.

The mansion mixes French and northern European influences in a loose version of the style known as Chateauesque. Its architect, Victor Cordella, was born in Poland.

As conceived by architects Christopher Boehme and Victor Cordella, the Turnblad House features two towers and an elaborate roofline.

The American Swedish Institute, which has owned the mansion since 1929, built a large addition in 2012 to help accommodate its numerous programs and activities.

One of his much older half brothers had settled some years earlier in Minnesota near the town of Vasa, not far from Red Wing, and it was there the Turnblad family took up farming. Only a few miles away, Alexander Anderson—another son of Swedish immigrants who would go on to an extraordinary career—also toiled as a farm boy, but there's no indication that he and Turnblad ever crossed paths.

Little is known about Turnblad's life on the farm, except that he didn't stay long enough to make a living at it. By 1880 he was residing in Minneapolis's Cedar-Riverside neighborhood—home to many Scandinavian immigrants—and working as a compositor for the *Minnesota Stats Tidning*, one of the city's four Swedish-language newspapers. It was in Minneapolis that he met Christina Nilsson, also a Swedish immigrant. Her family farmed in southwestern Minnesota, but she had come to Minneapolis in the 1880s to find work. She and Turnblad married in 1883 and a year later had their only child, a daughter named Lillian.

Turnblad's work with the *Stats Tidning* put him in what today would be called a growth industry. With an average of 32,000 Swedes a year immigrating to the United States in the 1880s, the number of Swedish-language newspapers across the country steadily increased, to forty-one by 1890. Turnblad, better than anyone else, found a publishing formula to appeal to this large Swedish-speaking audience, and it made him a rich man.

Swan Turnblad with his wife, Christina, and their only child, Lillian, circa 1890. It was about this time that Turnblad became publisher of the *Svenska Amerikanska Posten*.

The main floor plan of Turnblad's thirty-three-room mansion seemed to provide for a lavish lifestyle, but Turnblad and his family quietly spent much of their time on the third floor.

Turnblad's newspaper maintained its own office building, now gone, at 500 Seventh Street South in downtown Minneapolis.

His rapid climb to wealth began in 1885 when he went to work for the newly formed *Svenska Amerikanska Posten*. His first job was as a typesetter, but he soon became the weekly's manager. He was also an early stockholder in the company. The circumstances behind Turnblad's rapid rise to wealth are murky, but by 1889 he had become the newspaper's largest stockholder and publisher. In 1897, in a deal that was to inspire future lawsuits, Christina Turnblad—obviously acting on her husband's behalf—purchased the supposedly profitless newspaper for one dollar while also assuming $4,000 in debt. Four years later, Turnblad bought back the *Posten* from his wife. He would remain its owner for the next two decades.

The *Posten* had begun as a rather dull four-page affair devoted to the cause of temperance. But Turnblad, a salesman and promoter at heart, gradually enlarged the newspaper to more than twenty pages. He also made it much livelier, with breezy articles, serial stories, comic strips, a women's section, photographs, and even some use of color as early as 1904. The recipe worked, and at its height in the early 1900s the *Posten*'s circulation reached 55,000, making it the nation's biggest Swedish-language newspaper.

Turnblad's fortunes rose with the newspaper's. In 1893 he built a combination town home and apartment building at 1511 Stevens Avenue South (on the present site of the Minneapolis Convention Center), but it wasn't large enough to contain his dreams. By 1899, he was ready to do something big. That year, he bought a prime piece of property along Fifteenth Street, extending into what is now Loring Park, and announced his intent to build a mansion there. The Minneapolis Park Board opposed the idea, however, and moved to condemn the property for park purposes. The board won its case after a long court fight, forcing Turnblad to look elsewhere for a suitable mansion site. In 1903 he purchased six lots at the southwest corner of Park Avenue and Twenty-Sixth Street and began planning a mansion like none other on the avenue.

Although it's not known how Turnblad went about selecting an architect, three firms, including one from Philadelphia, submitted plans. The firm Turnblad chose, Boehme and Cordella, was hardly among the most prominent in Minneapolis. Its partners, Christopher Boehme and Victor Cordella, had only recently come together and had no major buildings to their credit when Turnblad hired them. But Cordella, the firm's designer, had extensive experience as well as a sophisticated European sensibility. The son of a sculptor, he was born in Poland and educated there at the Royal Academy of Art in Kraków. He moved to the United States in 1893 and worked as a draftsman for several leading Twin Cities architects, including Cass Gilbert, before going into partnership with the German-born Boehme. Castles and other buildings Cordella knew in his native Poland undoubtedly influenced his design of Turnblad's mansion.

Situated behind a high wrought iron fence, the mansion—its walls built of smooth, light-gray Indiana limestone—does indeed seem like a castle, built perhaps for a slightly daft king. Its four distinct and asymmetrical facades offer a cheerful accumulation of towers, bays, gables, dormers, porches, balconies, and chimneys, all arranged for picturesque effect. The mansion's visual signature is its front tower—an inset cylinder of stone that shoots up three stories to a series of battlements surmounted by a steep conical roof before terminating in an ornate copper finial. Just below the battlements, a small pulpit-like balcony swells out from the tower, as fanciful as a child's dream.

An array of stone carvings, all executed by Herman Schlink, further contributes to the mansion's sense of the unreal. Born in Winona, Minnesota, and trained at the Chicago Art Institute, Schlink decorated the mansion with a bestiary that includes lions' heads, a horse's head (for the mansion's superb carriage house), and a small colony of gargoyles. Two of the fiercest gargoyles thrust out from the corner of the front entry porch, and whether they're welcoming visitors or trying to scare them off is an open question.

Inside, the mansion opens up into a glorious two-story grand hall that offers a depth and richness of ornament matched by few, if any other, homes in Minnesota. A polychromed plaster ceiling executed by Schlink hovers over the hall, which conveys a sense of baronial grandeur. The hall's focal point is an astounding piece of Baroque theater—a two-story fireplace featuring a white-onyx surround and an elaborate multi-level mantel carved from African mahogany. A work of architecture in its own right, the mantel sports columns, cornices, a clock, and five sculpted figures, among them a Viking, two maidens, and a pair of "barbarian" caryatids, as carver Albin Polasek described them.

Polasek was one of eighteen wood-carvers who labored inside the mansion. Born in what is today the Czech Republic, Polasek learned wood carving in Vienna before immigrating to the United States in 1901 at age twenty-two. He studied at the Pennsylvania Academy of the Fine Arts in Philadelphia and then traveled to Wisconsin, where he met another highly skilled carver, the Swiss-born Ulrich Steiner. Both men, and all the other carvers who worked at the mansion, were employed by the Aaron Carlson Company of Minneapolis, a firm founded in 1891 by its namesake, who, like Turnblad, was a Swedish immigrant. The company is still in business today.

The other first-floor rooms, arranged around the hall, offer a variety of architectural finishes and styles. Most sumptuous of all are the music and

Among the mansion's many playful features is a pulpit-like balcony set just beneath the mock battlements of the front tower.

Park Avenue's Mansions

By the time Swan Turnblad built his Swedish Castle, as it was often called, Park Avenue reigned as the most desirable residential territory in Minneapolis. In the early 1900s thirty or so mansions lined the avenue's "golden mile," which extended from about Eighteenth to Twenty-Eighth Streets. Lumber, grain, and flour-milling barons, representing the city's emblematic industries, all had fine homes along Park at one time, and Turnblad must have taken great pride in being among such elite company.

The avenue's rapid rise to prominence began in the early 1880s, when wealthy home builders began to exploit its convenient location on the flatlands directly south of downtown. Minneapolis's largest mansion district at that time was located in the downtown area, roughly south of Nicollet Avenue and west of Fifth Street South. But commercial growth was already threatening the mansions there, and well-to-do families sought other places to build. One area that attracted a colony of mansions in the 1880s was the Washburn–Fair Oaks neighborhood near today's Minneapolis Institute of Arts. Flour miller and politician William Washburn in 1884 built what was then the city's largest house, at Twenty-Second Street and Stevens Avenue. Other mansions quickly materialized around his ten-acre estate (now Washburn–Fair Oaks Park, created after the mansion was razed in 1924).

Park Avenue, a few blocks east of Washburn–Fair Oaks, began to acquire its collection of mansions at about the same time. Although a few big houses had appeared on Park in the 1870s, the avenue saw its first big wave of mansion building in 1885. That year alone, five Queen Anne–style mansions (all of them now gone) were completed between Twenty-Second and Twenty-Sixth Streets. The John E. Bell House, a flamboyant pile at Twenty-Fourth and Park, was perhaps the most notable of the quintet.

The late 1880s and early 1890s saw the construction of additional mansions, in styles ranging from Richardsonian Romanesque to Shingle. Meanwhile, the avenue's well-heeled residents took steps to ensure its continued cachet. They formed an improvement association in 1890 and inaugurated an early example of zoning by establishing minimum setback requirements for new houses. In 1892, the residents also provided funds to pave the avenue with asphalt. It was the first street in the city to offer this amenity.

The depression of 1893 slowed mansion building, but by 1900 contractors were again at work on new homes. One of the largest, just across Twenty-Sixth Street from the Turnblad mansion, was built in 1902 for grain magnate Charles Harrington. His Beaux-Arts house, like Turnblad's, took on a new use in 1929 when it became home for many years to the Zuhrah Shrine Temple. Park Avenue's complement of big houses was largely in place by 1910, although one mansion was built as late as 1927.

A range of factors, from shifting residential patterns to urban renewal to institutional expansion, began eating away at the avenue's stock of mansions by the 1930s. Over the next fifty years, at least fifteen mansions along the golden mile were torn down, while most of the survivors were converted to institutional uses. Today, Park Avenue might best be described as a vestigial mansion district, its old glory days still visible amid the tides of urban change.

The Frank Heffelfinger House, 2205 Park Avenue, circa 1905. The house, razed in 1983, was one of many mansions that once made the avenue Minneapolis's most prestigious residential address.

A small solarium rises over the porte cochere on the mansion's south side.

A semicircular alcove off the music room is one of the mansion's many charming nooks and crannies.

dining rooms. The music room overlooks Park Avenue and includes among its furnishings one of the mansion's original Austrian-made rugs, woven from Swedish wool. Trimmed in Honduran mahogany, the room combines a sense of monumental formality with a dose of whimsy in the form of fifty-two winged cherubs stationed with military precision along a frieze band. The cherubs, like all of the room's carved wood, are Steiner's work. His pay was forty cents an hour, considered a good wage at the time.

Steiner was also in charge of carving the wood—a mix of white oak and bleached Honduran mahogany—in the mansion's incomparable dining room, which includes a stunningly intricate sideboard. A fireplace mantel with caryatids, a beamed and coffered ceiling, and the room's ornate table (reputedly carved in place) also showcase the skills of Steiner and his assistants. It was in every sense a royal room, fit for Minneapolis's Swedish king, and the wonder is that Turnblad rarely, if ever, appears to have used it. A Rococo Revival salon with enameled wood and delicate plasterwork, a Moorish Revival–style den, a kitchen, and a breakfast room finished in the fashion of an eighteenth-century Swedish manor house round out the main floor.

The mansion's grand staircase, inaugurated by a duo of winged lions that guard the first few steps in lieu of banisters, offers yet another remarkable sight—the Visby window, a church-sized expanse of painted glass said to have cost $17,000. The window is a copy of a painting by nineteenth-century Swedish artist Carl Gustav Hellqvist that depicts a scene from 1361 when a Danish king forced the people of the town of Visby to surrender their valuables or face destruction. Made by a glass company in Stockholm, the window was shipped in sections to Minneapolis. Beneath the window a door flanked by two more stained-glass windows leads to the mansion's solarium, located above the porte cochere.

Three large bedrooms, a dressing room, a seamstresses' quarters, and a library/reading room occupy most of the second floor, where an open balcony encircles the grand hall. Some of the bedrooms are now used for exhibits. The third floor contains a skylit ballroom, now an exhibit hall, as well as servants' quarters, a studio, and several guest rooms. Original plans called for a basement swimming pool and gymnasium, but these were never built. Other rooms in the basement are now used for meetings, exhibits, ASI's library, and special events. The mansion's large carriage house, where it is believed Turnblad once had a turntable for his automobiles, has been converted to office space.

Even before he built the mansion, Turnblad's penchant for public display made him a well-known figure in Minneapolis. He claimed to own the

A two-story grand hall dominates the mansion's luxurious interior. The elaborate multistage fireplace at the center of the hall has no equal in Minnesota.

city's first private electric automobile, a Waverly purchased in 1899. He liked to deck out the car with flowers for parades and also took it on a number of highly publicized excursions. He was active in Democratic Party politics, serving as a delegate to three national conventions, and he also traveled extensively—junkets he wrote about at great length in the *Posten*. But it was publicity generated by his new mansion in 1908 that quickly earned Turnblad a less welcome form of notoriety.

In April of 1908, just as Turnblad and his family were moving into the mansion, a former *Posten* stockholder filed a lawsuit asking for $1 million in damages. The suit and others that followed all claimed Turnblad had lied for years about the newspaper's profitability in order to enrich himself at stockholders' expense. The deal by which his wife purchased the newspaper in 1897, supposedly with her own funds, came under particularly close scrutiny. It didn't take long for the lawsuits to become a public circus covered in exhaustive detail by the Minneapolis newspapers.

Turnblad won a decision in his favor after a five-month trial in 1909, but the Minnesota Supreme Court reversed the ruling in 1911 and ordered a new trial. Turnblad finally settled most of the claims against him out of court, but the trial and its attendant publicity hardly burnished his reputation. Court records as a whole suggest Turnblad was indeed dishonest in his business dealings and that he milked every cent he could out of the *Posten* to support his lavish way of life. Turnblad finally sold the newspaper in 1920, only to repurchase it eight years later after it had failed under the new ownership. But even Turnblad couldn't revive the *Posten*'s sagging fortunes, and it was one of the nation's last remaining Swedish-language newspapers when it was sold in 1940.

Despite his dubious business ethics, Turnblad throughout his often enigmatic life maintained a true devotion to his Swedish heritage, and by the mid-1920s he clearly was thinking about the possibility his mansion could be used as a place to celebrate and sustain his native culture. Turnblad would claim

Winged lions guard the sumptuous grand staircase, which ascends to a landing where a huge stained-glass window depicts a dramatic scene from Swedish history. A custom replica of the original carpet was installed in 2011.

in newspaper interviews that he had intended all along to donate the mansion for just such a purpose, but there's no way of knowing whether he was being truthful. He once said he wanted the mansion "to endure for a hundred thousand years"—presumably as a monument to himself.

What's certain is that as Turnblad grew older, the mansion became more of a burden than an asset. It was vacant except for a caretaker in 1921, when four boys, believing the place to be haunted, got through a gate and onto the grounds before being spotted. They were later fined five dollars apiece for their transgressions. As time went on, a number of possible buyers for the mansion emerged, but Turnblad declined to sell. He also suggested at one point that he might give the mansion to the City of Minneapolis, which probably wouldn't have wanted it.

After consulting with the Swedish consul to Minnesota and later receiving a letter of support from Sweden's Crown Prince Gustaf Adolf, Turnblad in 1929 agreed to donate the mansion, as well as the *Posten* and its downtown office building, to a new institution to be called the American Institute of Swedish Arts, Literature and Science (later shortened to its current name). The deal was struck just two months after Christina Turnblad died, at age sixty-eight, in September of 1929. A year later, the mansion was open to the public. Turnblad, meanwhile, remained as the *Posten*'s publisher and also served on the institute's board of directors.

Over the next fifty years, the mansion underwent some internal changes to accommodate the institute and its programs, but otherwise retained its original features. In 1983 the mansion received its first major addition—an auditorium at the rear. By the early 2000s, however, the institute clearly needed more room for its programs than the mansion could

Scandinavians in Minnesota

Long before Swan Turnblad built his elaborate Minneapolis home as an homage to his native Swedish culture, fellow Scandinavian immigrants had become enamored with Minnesota as well. Social, political, and economic forces had caused both Swedes and Norwegians to flee to America in search of better lives during the first half of the nineteenth century. The Swedes gravitated to the farmlands of the Midwest, taking advantage of increasingly attractive homestead benefits as they plowed new farms in Minnesota and South Dakota. Norwegians were often drawn to the burgeoning lumber business in the Upper Midwest and the fishing in Lake Superior. Danes brought their expertise in dairy farming to both Minnesota and Wisconsin. Finns, Icelanders, and Greenlanders followed, albeit in smaller numbers. In fact, Minnesota's population has been dominated by Germans, Swedes, and Norwegians since the 1880s.

As the earliest Scandinavians wrote home about new opportunities in the American Midwest, their family members were enticed to join them. Here they embraced an American social structure that was far less restrictive than that of their homeland.

Norwegian contributions to the state included the establishment of Concordia College in Moorhead, St. Olaf in Northfield, and Augsburg in Minneapolis. Norwegian writers Ole E. Rølvaag (*Giants in the Earth*, 1924–1925) and Thorstein Veblen (*The Theory of the Leisure Class*, 1899) penned American classics, and Norwegians have always been active in local and state politics.

The Swedish migration to Minnesota came in several waves, but the general pattern was to cross the Atlantic by boat, arrive in New York, go out to Chicago by rail, and then boat up the Mississippi River to travel by wagon throughout the Midwest. In addition to farming and lumbering, many of the later Swedes worked in the iron mines of the Mesabi Range and on the burgeoning Minnesota-owned railroad lines. Swedes tended to be Lutherans but also numbered among Baptists and Methodists. It was these Minnesotans of Swedish descent who avidly read Turnblad's *Svenska Amerikanska Posten*.

Third- and fourth-wave Swedish immigrants moved into more urban areas of Minnesota. They established the still-standing Southern Theater in Minneapolis and founded Gustavus Adolphus College in St. Peter and Bethel University in St. Paul. Notable Minnesota Swedes include aviator Charles Lindbergh, sculptor Paul Granlund, and many governors, senators, and congressmen. Writer and conservationist Sigurd Olson was born in Chicago to Swedish parents and was instrumental in designating Minnesota's Boundary Waters Canoe Area Wilderness. The 2010 census reported 586,507 people of Swedish ancestry living in Minnesota, more than in any other state.

Some of Ulrich Steiner's most magnificent carved woodwork, in oak and mahogany, adorns the dining room. The table at center was reputedly carved in place.

Master craftsman Ulrich Steiner earned forty cents an hour carving the Honduran mahogany woodwork in the music room. His creations include fifty-two cherubs who reside in a frieze band at the top of the walls.

The library's furnishings include an ornate *kakelugn* (tiled stove) imported from Sweden. The mansion has eleven such stoves, each of a different design.

provide, and planning began for a large addition, which opened in 2012. Known as the Carl and Leslie Nelson Cultural Center, the 34,000-square-foot addition includes a cafe, a museum shop, meeting spaces, a gallery, a studio workshop, and offices. It's linked via a passageway to the rear of the mansion, where a new elevator tower was built as part of the project. Designed by HGA Architects of Minneapolis, the addition is unabashedly modern in style but features gray-slate siding that echoes the mansion's roof.

At the same time the addition was under way, the institute—which has long worked to preserve the mansion in all of its splendor—began a new round of restoration and renovation. Two impressive fruits of this work were completed in 2011 with the installation of a custom-made replica of the grand hall's original carpet and the restoration of the ornamented plaster ceiling in the basement. The mansion's kitchen was restored in 2013, and projects will continue as the budget allows.

Turnblad himself left the mansion as soon as he turned it over to the institute. But he didn't go very far, moving with his daughter, who never married, to an apartment building on Park Avenue directly across from the mansion. He lived there until his death of heart failure on May 17, 1933, at age seventy-two. With characteristic Scandinavian reserve, the *Posten* said in its obituary, "An unusually capable American-Swede has departed this life. His work shall long be remembered."

Perhaps the most pointed obituary of all, however, can be found on the large granite cross that marks Turnblad's grave at Lakewood Cemetery in Minneapolis. Three Greek letters inscribed in the granite form an abbreviation for the words "I Am Who I Am," which was God's proclamation to Moses from the burning bush. Turnblad presumably didn't think of himself as God, but by all accounts he was a man who took on the world in his own way, for his own purposes, as the mansion he left behind—at once magnificent and peculiar—so perfectly demonstrates. ❧

William Lightner House
St. Paul, 1894

William Lightner, 1916. He enjoyed a long career as one of St. Paul's most successful lawyers.

Opposite: The William Lightner House is among the most beautifully designed homes on St. Paul's Summit Avenue. Architect Cass Gilbert combined rigid front symmetry with elements of the Richardsonian Romanesque style to make an impressive statement.

I N 1891 A RISING YOUNG ST. PAUL LAWYER NAMED WILLIAM LIGHTNER hired architect Cass Gilbert to design a new bluff-top home at 318 Summit Avenue, just two blocks west of the James J. and Louis Hill mansions. At about six thousand square feet, Lightner's house, completed in 1894 as a deep depression gripped the nation, was much smaller than either Hill mansion. Size, however, isn't everything in architecture, and the house is now justly regarded as one of the finest works of Gilbert's long career. Shedding the last vestiges of busy Victorianism, he created a stunning architectural hybrid that mixes classical restraint and symmetry with the bold forms of the Romanesque Revival style. Although Gilbert designed many wonderful homes in St. Paul, none can match the Lightner House's aura of dense, impervious heft. Built largely of ultrahard quartzite stone from South Dakota, it projects a sense of permanence beyond the vagaries of fashion or the nagging reach of time.

The home also offers a remarkable lesson in the possibilities of renewal. After the deaths of Lightner and his wife, the mansion was subdivided and turned into a rooming house. It remained so, in various combinations, for more than a half century. Beginning in 2006, it was meticulously restored and renovated, and today once again functions as a single-family home. Like its neighbors along Summit, the house is part of St. Paul's Historic Hill District, which was added to the National Register of Historic Places in 1976 and forms Minnesota's finest collection of late nineteenth-century architect-designed homes.

Although Lightner was only in his midthirties when he built the house, he was already a prominent figure in St. Paul legal circles. Born in 1856 to a well-off Pennsylvania family—his father was an Episcopal clergyman, his mother the daughter of a lawyer—Lightner moved to St. Paul in the late 1870s after graduating from the University of Michigan. He was admitted to the state bar in 1880 and a few years later joined George B. Young, a former associate justice of the Minnesota Supreme Court, to form a prosperous legal partnership that lasted for more than twenty years.

Cass Gilbert, seated at center, and his office staff during construction of the Minnesota State Capitol, circa 1900. Gilbert won a competition to design the capitol in 1895, catapulting him to a national career.

Cass Gilbert's design for the Lightner House is virtuosic in its powerful simplicity, balance, and scale.

Three windows above the arched front entry look out from behind squat sandstone columns with cushion capitals. Both the columns and the entry arch are distinguishing features of the powerful late Victorian style pioneered by Boston architect Henry Hobson Richardson.

Lightner was active, too, in civic and cultural affairs, serving for a time as an assemblyman on the St. Paul Common Council and as president of the Minnesota Historical Society, among other positions. He also married well. His wife, Carrie, was the daughter of Elias F. Drake, a St. Paul business and political leader whose résumé included an instrumental role in building the first ten miles of railroad track in Minnesota, for the St. Paul and Pacific Railroad, in 1862.

Like his client, Gilbert was among St. Paul's up-and-coming figures in the early 1890s. Raised in St. Paul, he had gone to the East Coast to study and then worked for the celebrated New York firm of McKim, Mead and White before returning home to form a partnership with a boyhood friend, James Knox Taylor. Tremendously talented, iron willed, and intensely ambitious, Gilbert would become an architect of national renown after winning a competition to design Minnesota's new state capitol in 1895. At the time the Lightner House was built, however, Gilbert's fortunes were at low

Cass Gilbert's Remarkable Career

After designing the William Lightner House, Cass Gilbert went on to become a national figure and to this day remains Minnesota's best-known architect. Although he produced many fine buildings during his early years in St. Paul, he lacked anything beyond a regional identity until 1895. That year, a competition was held to select an architect to design a new Minnesota state capitol in St. Paul. The existing capitol had been built just twelve years earlier but was already seen as small and antiquated. The new capitol promised to be a far grander building, and the kind of luscious architectural plum that doesn't come along very often.

After much behind-the-scenes maneuvering (not all of it seemly), Gilbert won the competition. He was just thirty-six years old and had never designed a building of such size and grandeur before. It was the kind of big, showy project that could make an architect's name, and Gilbert—a relentless self-promoter—seized the opportunity. Although the Renaissance-inspired capitol, with its famous white-marble dome, wasn't completed until 1905, Gilbert's plans drew national attention and proved to be a launching pad for his dreams of a national practice.

Gilbert maintained an office in St. Paul while work progressed on the capitol, but by 1898 he was also pursuing projects in New York City. There, in 1899, he won another important competition, for the design of a new U.S. customs house. It probably didn't hurt Gilbert's chances that his former partner in St. Paul, James Knox Taylor, was in charge of the competition by virtue of his recent appointment as supervising architect of the U.S. Treasury.

In 1900 Gilbert sold his house in St. Paul and moved with his family to New York City, where he'd also received a commission for an office building. New York was a tough environment for any architect, with numerous prestigious firms competing for commissions, but Gilbert—whose enormous drive was matched by his talent—soon managed to carve out a place for himself. He specialized in office towers and public and institutional buildings and also undertook urban planning projects.

By 1910 Gilbert's practice was truly national in scope, with projects extending from Connecticut in the east to Oregon in the west. Like other architects of his era, Gilbert worked in a range of styles, although he favored grand Beaux-Arts schemes for his public buildings. These would eventually include two other state capitols, in Arkansas (1917) and West Virginia (1932), libraries in Detroit (1921) and St. Louis (1912), and the U.S. Supreme Court Building (1935) in Washington, D.C. One place where Gilbert failed to secure any more commissions of note was St. Paul, although he prepared a number of plans (never built) for approaches to the capitol.

The summit of Gilbert's career, quite literally, came in 1913, when his magnificent Woolworth Building opened in lower Manhattan. Built for Frank C. Woolworth, owner of the immensely successful dime-store chain that bore his name, it was the tallest skyscraper in the world, rising to a height of nearly eight hundred feet. Although taller buildings appeared by 1930, the Woolworth is still regarded as among the jewels of New York's skyline, and of Gilbert's extraordinary career.

Cass Gilbert's magnificent Woolworth Building, which still stands in lower Manhattan, was the world's tallest skyscraper when it opened in 1913.

The quirky east facade showcases the mansion's superb stone walls, which are built of ultrahard Sioux quartzite from southwestern Minnesota trimmed with soft red sandstone quarried near Lake Superior.

ebb. With only a handful of new commissions coming in to pay the bills, he'd fallen nearly $1,000 behind on his office rent in the Endicott Building in downtown St. Paul. This shortfall was particularly galling given that he had designed the building, to much acclaim, only a few years earlier.

When Lightner commissioned his new house, at a cost of about $27,000 according to the building permit, he was already intimately familiar with Gilbert's work. In 1886 Lightner and his longtime law partner, George Young, had hired Gilbert to design a Romanesque Revival brownstone double house at 322–324 Summit Avenue. The double house's curious design—the west side is symmetrical and restrained, whereas the east side is quite picturesque—presaged what Gilbert would accomplish next door at 318 Summit. Lightner and his family, which ultimately included two sons and a daughter, lived in the east side of the double house and so had a prime view of the construction of their new home next door.

Gilbert was fanatically meticulous about his work, as his contractors well knew, and little escaped his attention. His specifications for the Lightner House, now at the Minnesota Historical Society, run to forty-eight typed pages, many with additional handwritten notes. The specifications cover everything from the kinds of stone, brick, iron, and wood to be used to detailed instructions as to how workers should plaster the walls and varnish the floors. Gilbert brooked no deviation from his plans, and the house as built reflects the great care he took in every aspect of its design and construction.

The main facade of the Lightner House shows Gilbert at the top of his game. The arched entrance and its outsized voussoirs are very much in the manner of Henry Hobson Richardson, the Boston architect who in the 1870s developed a distinctive style based on medieval Romanesque architecture. The three inset windows above the arch, with their thick cushion capitals and squat proportions, are also Richardsonian. Yet the overall composition, which features four perfectly symmetrical windows beneath a hip roof, evokes the quiet dignity of classical design. Richardson himself had begun moving in a similar direction before his untimely death in 1886, but none of his late houses is as classical in spirit as Gilbert's design for Lightner. Gilbert in fact prepared an early sketch that shows the house as entirely Classical Revival in style, complete with a prominent front portico sporting Corinthian columns.

The house's east facade, which originally was to have an arched porte cochere (never built), offers a striking contrast to the balance and regularity of the front. Here, Gilbert took a bit of a walk on the wild side, animating the facade with three unusual window openings. The largest, which brings light to the main staircase landing within, rests in part on a massive lintel supported by a single column of sandstone that also serves to divide two

The rear of the mansion, which overlooks the city, includes a pair of porches converted to year-round use as part of an extensive remodeling project that began in 2006.

The entry hall and main staircase make extensive use of quartersawn oak. One of the home's peculiarities is that the inner vestibule door is much taller than the outer door.

smaller windows. One historian has called this facade "the most imaginative and quirkiest of Gilbert's career," and it's hard to disagree with that judgment.

Much of the house's sense of rugged monumentality comes from the stone used to build it. Gilbert offered Lightner the option of constructing his house out of brownstone, red Lake Superior sandstone, or Sioux quartzite with sandstone trim. Lightner chose the most expensive option and, probably, the one Gilbert favored as well—Sioux quartzite. Quarried primarily in southwestern Minnesota and eastern South Dakota, the pinkish quartzite (also called Jasper stone after the Minnesota town where it was mined) is exceptionally hard, capable of bearing five tons per square inch, and virtually impervious to wear. The difficulty of extracting and working the quartzite made it costly, however, and it never enjoyed widespread popularity as a building stone beyond the Dakotas and Minnesota.

The Lightner House is one of only a few in Minnesota built of Sioux quartzite (another notable example is the George Van Dusen Mansion, completed in 1893, in Minneapolis). To accent the quartzite, which was laid up in eight-inch-thick blocks of varying size, Gilbert employed bands of red Wisconsin sandstone that wrap around the entire house. All of the home's subtle exterior ornament, which includes geometric patterns as well as stylized acanthus leaves, is carved into the soft sandstone.

The house's beautifully detailed interior has undergone significant renovation but still retains many original features, particularly on the main floor. A small vestibule adorned with leaded and stained glass (which incorporates the home's address over the front door) leads to a compact central hall finished in quartersawn oak. The hall opens to a large west-facing living room, a much smaller library to the east, a staircase and side hall that also face east, and a dining room and kitchen to the rear. Like other Summit Avenue houses of its time, Lightner's didn't take full advantage of the magnificent views to the south and east afforded by its bluff-top location. Even so, there was an open rear porch that must have been a lovely place in summer.

The living room, which like the main hall is overseen by an elegantly stenciled ceiling, features a marble fireplace with a carved-wood mantel, built-in mahogany bookcases, and a charming polygonal bay that breaks up the otherwise foursquare regularity of the floor plan. This bay includes one of the home's most peculiar features—a floor-to-ceiling double-hung window that seems to have originally served as an access to a narrow side porch (now gone).

The superbly detailed dining room, finished in mahogany, is even more impressive. Its chief wonder is a wood, leaded-glass, and mirrored sideboard modeled on one owned by the family of Lightner's mother. Light-

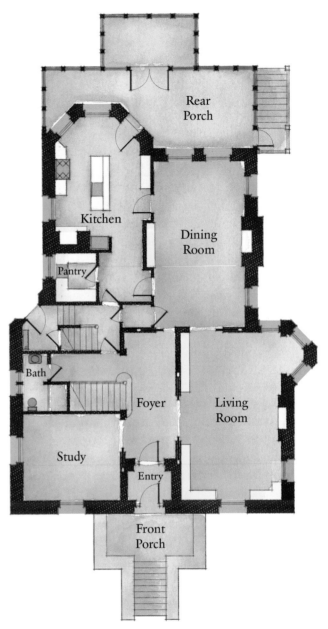

The first-floor plan of the Lightner House originally featured a billiards room, which has been replaced by a modern kitchen.

ner paid $200—no small sum at the time—to have the sideboard custom made. Flanking the sideboard are two doors with patterned stained-glass windows. One of these doors once led to a pantry, and the other, to a large billiards room (now the kitchen). Originally, the kitchen was located in the home's spacious walkout basement, which has been extensively remodeled to accommodate a new rathskeller-type recreation room, a wine cellar, and a one-bedroom apartment.

Another of the home's outstanding features is the main staircase, built of quartersawn oak. It's positioned unusually far forward, an arrangement that left limited space for the library/music room at the front of the house. Colonial Revival in character, the staircase includes distinctive spindled balusters and carefully detailed side paneling. Illuminating the landing is a six-part window notable for its intricate leaded glass—a feature often found in Gilbert-designed homes. A narrow side hall next to the stairs is something of a puzzle. It feels as though it should lead to an outside door, as would usually be the case, but instead it exists solely to provide access to a bathroom tucked under the stairs.

The house originally had five bedrooms on the second floor. Portions of this floor were altered during the 2006 restoration to provide a master bedroom suite and other modern amenities. The home's surprisingly large attic, as built, contained servants' rooms and an unfinished space that presumably was intended to be a ballroom. The depression that struck as the house was being completed may well have convinced Lightner to eliminate the ballroom as a cost-cutting measure.

During his long life, Lightner displayed a deep interest in history, as befitting the owner of a home on one of St. Paul's oldest and most storied avenues. In addition to his service with the Minnesota Historical Society, he was said to have worked for forty years on a book on French history, although it apparently was never finished. In 1930 he even became a proto-preservationist, fighting to save Christ Episcopal Church, of which he was a longtime member, from the wrecking ball. His efforts on behalf of the historic downtown St. Paul church failed: it was razed to make way for an expansion of the city's auditorium. It wouldn't be until the 1970s that a well-organized preservation movement in the city began to take hold.

Lightner lived at 318 Summit (except for winter visits to Arizona) until his death, at age seventy-nine, in 1936. Carrie Lightner stayed on in the house by herself and died eight years later. None of the couple's three children wanted to purchase the mansion, and it stood vacant until a new owner converted it to a rooming house in 1947. The main floor was left largely

The well-appointed living room, on the west side of the house across from the main staircase, features a stenciled ceiling and built-in mahogany bookcases.

Minnesota Stone

When Cass Gilbert selected Sioux quartzite for the walls of the William Lightner House, he chose from a broad menu of readily available stone types. Had the home been designed just fifteen years earlier, however, Gilbert would have had far fewer options. Until around 1880, only locally quarried stone was used for building throughout Minnesota because importing stone from faraway places was costly and difficult. In the Twin Cities, this meant architects and builders had only one choice—gray Platteville limestone, which was quarried extensively in both St. Paul and Minneapolis—if they wanted to use stone for a home, church, school,

mill, office, or public building. A few monumental buildings from this early stone era still survive, including Assumption Church (1874) in St. Paul and the Pillsbury A Mill (1881) in Minneapolis, but most are now gone.

It was the arrival of the railroads, which by the late 1880s had spread to virtually every corner of Minnesota, that brought an end to the reliance on local stone. Even so, architects and builders usually didn't have to go far to find what they needed, since Minnesota is rich in high-quality building stone of all types. Granite was quarried in the St. Cloud area as early as the 1860s and remains an important industry there today. Farther south, around Mankato and nearby Kasota, quarries still produce high-quality dolomitic limestone with a distinctly golden hue. Buff-colored sandstone from the Kettle River region in east-central Minnesota was also coming on the market in the 1890s, as was reddish sandstone from Fond du Lac, near Duluth. These once widely used stones are no longer quarried.

Although Sioux quartzite first appeared on buildings in the late nineteenth century, its history of human use goes back much further. A soft stone known as pipestone, or catlinite, is occasionally found in bands amid the quartzite. This stone was quarried as early as 900 BCE by Plains Indians, who used it to carve pipes and other objects. Pipestone National Monument in southwestern Minnesota marks the site of the most famous of these Indian quarries.

One of the first commercial quarries for mining Sioux quartzite in Minnesota opened in 1876 in Jasper, but it wasn't until about 1890 that the stone began to be used in the Twin Cities, Chicago, and elsewhere. Because of its extreme hardness, the stone was difficult to quarry and cut, and it never achieved the widespread popularity of St. Cloud granite or Mankato limestone, both of which can be found on buildings across the United States.

Today, most of the best buildings constructed from Sioux quartzite can be found in communities near where the stone is quarried. Pipestone has a beautiful historic district that includes seventeen quartzite buildings, mostly dating to the 1890s. The nearby towns of Luverne and Jasper are also well represented. Perhaps the most monumental of all Sioux quartzite buildings is the old Minnehaha County Courthouse (now a museum) in Sioux Falls, South Dakota. Completed in 1893, it was designed by Wallace Dow, who was also the architect of the George Draper Dayton House in Worthington, Minnesota.

Completed a year before the Lightner House, the George Van Dusen Mansion in Minneapolis is also built of Sioux quartzite. The mansion's sheer heft is evident in this 1894 winter view.

intact as a single apartment, but the second floor was subdivided into ten furnished rooms. A rental space was also carved out of the basement.

Although the conversion was almost surely illegal—zoning codes at the time permitted no more than four units in any home on Summit—it was hardly unusual. Other mansions on the avenue were also subdivided into multiple units in the years immediately after World War II in response to a monumental housing shortage that developed as veterans returned home and started families.

In the 1950s, the house saw more changes. It was used for five years as a music studio as well as apartments. Later, it became home to a catering business and also functioned as a guesthouse. By the 1970s, it had reverted to apartments, and it remained in that condition until 2006, when Richard and Nancy Nicholson, owners of the nearby Louis Hill House, acquired the property and set about a lengthy process of restoration under the direction of St. Paul architect Thomas Blanck. It was a complex and daunting job, given the home's history of remodeling and subdivision.

One of Blanck's goals, as he puts it, was to "try to turn the house around" to better exploit the splendid views available from its rear-facing rooms. To accomplish this, Blanck converted the open back porch into a year-round room that now serves as one of the house's most pleasing spaces. Blanck, an expert on Gilbert and his work, also took great care to preserve as much of the original design as possible. Today, the main floor of the house is much as it was in 1894, with only the billiards-room-turned-kitchen and the porch significantly altered.

Upstairs, three bedrooms remain in their original places, but the Lightners' old bedroom at the rear was combined with another bedroom to form a large suite that includes a sitting room, closets, and bath. The suite's chief delight, however, is an old open sleeping porch (probably added to the house around 1910) that now serves as a year-round room with gorgeous views of the city and the Mississippi River Valley. Blanck and his builders also remodeled the attic, turning the never-finished ballroom into a vaulted recreation room lit in part by a stained-glass skylight.

Because of the steep slope behind Summit Avenue, carriage houses and garages for the mansions there were usually built along Irvine Avenue, a narrow alley-like street halfway down the bluff. Lightner apparently intended to build a "barn," as he called it, with one of his neighbors along Irvine but never went ahead with his part of the project.

To provide parking for the property, Blanck designed a pair of pagoda-like two-story garages that each provides parking for two cars on the upper level and a multi-purpose room below. A series of terraces, gardens, pools, walkways, and steps fill the space between the garages, creating a gracious setting for outdoor events or for simply enjoying the expansive views.

An archway with subtle decorative touches opens into a small polygonal bay off the living room.

The dining room is finished in mahogany and includes a mirrored sideboard specially built to resemble one owned by the family of William Lightner's mother. Lightner's sentimental gesture cost $200, a considerable expense in the 1890s.

Now owned by businessman John Fallin, the Lightner House appears set for a long third act as a private home that combines the rich qualities of the past with a full array of modern conveniences. Cass Gilbert, who lavished so much attention on its design and who understood the power of architecture to shape lives, would undoubtedly be pleased. ♈

The staircase's lovely spindled balusters are in the Colonial Revival style, which architect Cass Gilbert introduced to St. Paul in the 1880s.

The second floor, which was once subdivided into ten rental rooms, now includes a large master bedroom suite.

Benjamin and William Goodkind Double House

St. Paul, 1910

Benjamin Goodkind, circa 1915. He was president of the Mannheimer Brothers Department Store in St. Paul.

Opposite: The Goodkind Double House seems to stretch out forever across the top of Grand Avenue Hill in St. Paul. The east end (foreground), built for William and Tillie Goodkind, is only about half as large as the west end, which was occupied by Benjamin and Adelaide Goodkind.

IN THE EARLY 1900S, BROTHERS BENJAMIN AND WILLIAM GOODKIND acquired three acres of prime land atop what is now known as the Grand Avenue Hill in St. Paul. Located in a portion of the Historic Hill District just south of Summit Avenue and its fabled mansions, the property—easily one of the finest building sites in the city—combined panoramic views of the Mississippi River Valley with a surprising sense of quiet and privacy, all within a five-minute drive from downtown. It was here in 1910 that the brothers began building a sprawling half-timbered double house the likes of which had never been seen before in Minnesota. Featuring wood shake roofs curled at the eaves, the connected homes resembled something out of a fairy tale, and so they were, for the Goodkinds had risen to their hilltop dream only after a long ascent from humble beginnings.

The Goodkind family arrived in St. Paul in 1871, when the fast-growing young city of twenty thousand people was the largest in Minnesota. The head of the family was German-born Louis Goodkind, who had immigrated to the United States in the 1850s and settled in Michigan with his wife, Mina. He later moved to Chicago, where he became involved in what was at that time called the dry goods business.

After relocating to St. Paul in 1871, Louis Goodkind opened a small department store with the help of Benjamin, his oldest son, and his brother-in-law, Jacob Mannheimer. Within a few years, other members of the Goodkind and Mannheimer families joined the business, called Mannheimer Brothers, which in 1881 moved into a large new store on Third Street (now Kellogg Boulevard). Twelve years later, the store expanded again into a new five-story building at Sixth and Robert Streets in the heart of downtown St. Paul's department store district. Louis Goodkind, meanwhile, became a leading figure in St. Paul's Jewish community, serving on the board of Mount Zion Temple and as president of the Minnesota Lodge of B'nai B'rith.

Seen from the backyard, the west end of the house seems to tower over its hilltop grounds. With its roof of steamed-and-bent cedar shakes that curl around the eaves in imitation of thatch, the house is an early Minnesota example of the highly picturesque Cotswold Cottage style.

Between 1899 and 1904, all of the founding members of Mannheimer Brothers, including Louis Goodkind, died. Benjamin Goodkind and other members of the two families then assumed control of the business, which continued to prosper. By 1910, Mannheimer Brothers—along with such competitors as the Emporium, the Golden Rule and Schuneman's—was securely established as one of the city's most successful retailers.

The Goodkind and Mannheimer families lived for many years in close proximity, reflecting their strong business ties. During the 1880s, Louis and Mina Goodkind and their younger children resided in one side of a double house (gone) on West Seventh Street in St. Paul, while Jacob Mannheimer and his family occupied the other half. Family compounds of this kind were a common arrangement in the Victorian era and well into the early twentieth century. Large side-by-side double houses—usually built for a father and son or two brothers, or in a few cases for business partners—were especially popular in the Twin Cities, and a dozen or more outstanding examples were built between about 1885 and 1910.

Even among its deluxe peers, the Goodkind Double House stands out by virtue of its size, style, and location. The ten-thousand-square-foot west side was built for Benjamin Goodkind, who was president of Mannheimer Brothers, and his wife, Adelaide. The smaller, six-thousand-square-foot east side became the home of Benjamin's younger brother, William, the department store's secretary and treasurer, and his wife, Tillie. The two brothers were close, having lived in neighboring homes on nearby St. Albans Street before moving into the double house. Although a portion of the double house's original three-acre site was sold in the 1950s to permit construction of two new homes, the property still retains its feel of a country estate in the city—a private realm of walls, terraces, plazas, and gardens built for St. Paul's very own merchant princes.

To design their twin house, the brothers turned to Allen Stem, who with his partner, Charles Reed, had been the architect for the Mannheimer Brothers store on Robert Street. Although not as well known today as fellow St. Paul architects Cass Gilbert and Clarence Johnston, Stem was in their class as a designer. Born in Ohio in 1856, Stem was the son of an architect and began working in his father's office at age twenty after studying at the Indianapolis Art School. The tremendous building boom of the 1880s in the Twin Cities drew him to St. Paul in 1884, and six years later he and Reed, an engineer, established what would be a long and successful partnership.

Reed and Stem designed a broad range of buildings not only in St. Paul but also across the United States. The firm was especially well known for planning railroad stations (Reed's specialty) and in 1903 secured a fabulous plum—the commission for Grand Central Terminal in New York City, one of the biggest projects of its kind in American history. Reed moved to New York to take charge of the massive project, which required more than a decade to complete, while Stem remained in St. Paul to work on other commissions, including the Goodkinds' double house.

Like other architects of his period, Stem did not design in a single style. His houses, in particular, show a wide range. In the late 1880s he turned out at least three superb Shingle-style homes in St. Paul and later worked in a variety of classical and period revival styles. Among the most popular of these period styles in the early 1900s, especially for mansions, was Tudor Revival, a catch-all term that roped in a variety of design typologies loosely based on late-medieval English architecture. Wealthy families of English descent, or families who simply wanted to live like English lords of old, were especially attracted to Tudor Revival. In St. Paul, Tudor Revival

Set beneath an overhead passageway that connects the two sides of the house, the front door of the Benjamin Goodkind home leads into a paneled, barrel-vaulted entry hall. The hall serves as an apt introduction to the home's storybook interior.

Double Houses

The Goodkind Double House is the finest example of its kind in the Twin Cities, and probably all of Minnesota. Although twin homes, as they're often called today, are still being built, most modern versions are far removed in size and quality from their Victorian and early twentieth-century ancestors. Before the introduction of the up-and-down duplex, a building type that became widespread in the early 1900s, most two-family homes were of the side-by-side variety. It's likely such houses were built as early as the 1860s in the Twin Cities, but the biggest and most elaborate examples, usually designed for members of the same family, date from between 1880 and 1910. Less fancy double houses, often of wood-frame or brick-veneer construction, tended to be speculative rental properties.

St. Paul, which has more Victorian-era homes than Minneapolis, is the state's largest repository of historic double houses. Many of the best, including the Goodkind Double House, are located in the Historic Hill District along and around Summit Avenue. Two of the most peculiar, designed in 1888 by architect John Coxhead, are at 524–526 and 534 Laurel Avenue. Queen Anne in style, both feature angled corner towers with roofs as precipitous as church steeples. The Dayton's Bluff neighborhood, just east of downtown St. Paul, is also rich ground for double houses from the 1880s and 1890s.

Two historic double houses of particular note are elsewhere in St. Paul. The Pierce and Walter Butler Double House, at 1345–1347 Summit Avenue, was designed by Clarence Johnston and built in 1900 for prominent brothers. Pierce was an attorney who went on to serve as a justice of the U.S. Supreme Court, while Walter founded a successful contracting firm. It's a very large double house—more than twelve thousand square feet—and an excellent specimen of the Jacobethan Revival style. Another prominent double house (now divided into additional units) is situated on Eagle Parkway opposite the Science Museum of Minnesota. Known as the Armstrong-Quinlan House, it was originally built in 1886 as a rental property on Fifth Street at the western edge of downtown. In 2001, after years of debate over its fate, the ten-thousand-square-foot house, which had been vacant for years, was moved to its current location and then renovated into condominiums.

Most modern-era double houses, including the numerous double bungalows of the 1950s and 1960s, feature mirrored plans with one side basically the same as the other. Some nineteenth-century double houses were also designed in this fashion. But larger examples generally featured two different facades as well as different floor plans. It was also not uncommon for one side to be considerably larger than the other, thereby confirming the hierarchy of its occupants, as was the case with the Goodkind brothers.

Some of the grandest double houses in the Twin Cities are gone. In St. Paul, the Blood-Hardenbergh House, a sturdy essay in the Richardsonian Romanesque style from 1887, stood just south of the state capitol until it was razed in 1956. Built for two sisters and their husbands, the house cost the equivalent of at least $1 million today. In Minneapolis, the Frank W. and Frank B. Forman Double House, home to father and son businessmen and their families, was part of the Park Avenue mansion district for many years. Built in 1888, it came down in 1953.

The Pierce and Walter Butler Double House at 1345–1347 Summit Avenue was built in 1900 for prominent St. Paul brothers.

mansions began appearing on Summit Avenue in the 1890s. Later, in the 1920s, simplified "Tudor cottages" became a favored design for tract housing in the Twin Cities and across the United States.

For the double house, however, Stem chose an especially exotic and picturesque form of Tudor Revival usually called Cotswold Cottage. Based on sixteenth- and seventeenth-century thatched-roof homes found in the Cotswold Hills region of west-central England, the style in its American manifestation was, more often than not, far from cottage-like. The first American homes in the Cotswold style, including some mansions, were constructed on the East Coast around 1900. The Goodkind Double House shows off the style's key identifying feature—a roof made of steamed and bent cedar shakes that curl around the eaves in imitation of thatch.

Why the Goodkinds and Stem opted for the Cotswold style is unknown. It's possible the Goodkinds had seen a similar house elsewhere and found the style fetching, or Stem himself may have suggested it as an alternative to the more standard Tudor Revival designs common at the time. In either case, the double house is very probably the first example of the Cotswold Cottage style in Minnesota. Because of the cost and complexity of constructing their roofs, Cotswold houses never achieved great popularity, and only a handful exist in the Twin Cities (the 1922 Mervyn H. Amsden House on Lake of the Isles in Minneapolis is another outstanding example).

One of the first public images of the Goodkinds' twin house was a drawing, by Reed and Stem, published in the *St. Paul Dispatch* on January 15, 1910. The drawing shows the house as seen from a vantage point on Grand Avenue (known then as Oakland Avenue) and also depicts the limestone staircases and retaining walls that are among the property's defining features. The main retaining wall along Grand, which stretches for more than one thousand feet around the corner to Grand Hill, is unmatched in length among residential properties in the Twin Cities. A caption with the drawing in the *Dispatch* said the twin house would cost $60,000, a figure that seems far too low, given the size of the project.

Much of the area just north of the house, in what is known today as the Summit Hill neighborhood, had been developed in the late nineteenth century with fine homes. Some of the largest were along the street now called Grand Hill. Among its residents was lumber tycoon Frederick Weyerhaeuser, whose 1908 mansion is about a block east of the Goodkind homes. Another of the neighborhood's most prominent homeowners was Cass Gilbert. In 1890 he completed a house (now considerably modified) at 1 Heather Place, directly across from where the Goodkinds would build twenty years later.

The double house, however, was like nothing else in the neighborhood. Built with walls of limestone, stucco, and half-timbering, it consists

William Goodkind, 1925. He served as the department store's secretary and treasurer.

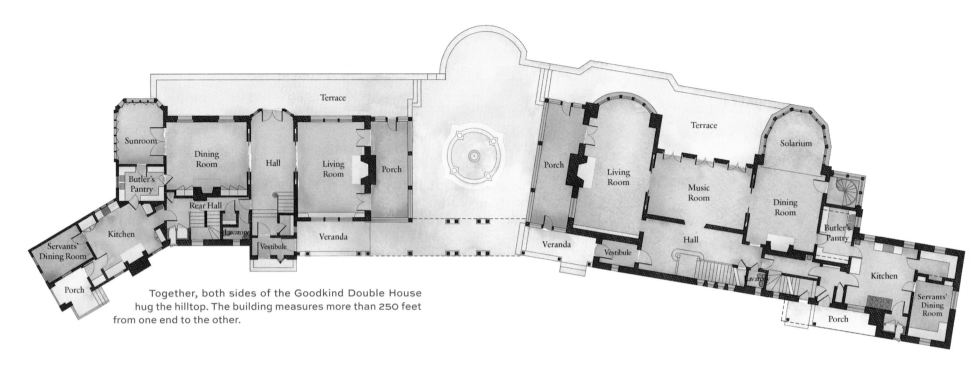

Together, both sides of the Goodkind Double House hug the hilltop. The building measures more than 250 feet from one end to the other.

of two distinct sides connected only by a bridge-like second-floor passageway. A brilliant idea, the passageway links the two sides while allowing them to maintain a clear sense of separation.

Both sides are reached from a circular drive off Heather Place, a short alley-like street that forms a tight loop south of Grand Hill. The driveway leads up to a plaza that extends beneath the overhead passageway to form an elegant outdoor space between the homes. The plaza includes a small fountain—one of the property's many attractive landscaping features.

The house is a grand English ramble, measuring more than 250 feet from one end to the other (counting the overhead passageway). Despite its historic references, the house isn't an authentic vision of *ye olde* England. Instead, it's a modernized dream of the past, perhaps closer to Hollywood in spirit than to the Cotswolds. Stem did all he could to give the house a visual narrative befitting its storybook quality. The walls switch from stone to half-timbered stucco and then back again, windows rise at varying levels and in all manner of shapes, the roof swoops up into gables and then dips down into curled corners, and bays and dormers erupt here and there with well-studied casualness. It's all architectural theater of a wonderful kind.

Inside, the two sides—both beautifully kept by their current owners—are quite different in feel but have similar in-line plans designed to take full advantage of the site's superb views. William Goodkind's home at 5 Heather Place, now owned by Mary McLean Donnelly, is organized around a broad first-floor stair hall that features birch woodwork, a tile floor, and a beamed ceiling. The staircase, on the north side above the front door, leads up to a handsome landing illuminated by a wall of casement windows with leaded glass.

Living and dining rooms flank the main hall. The living room's most prominent element is a large fireplace with a carved mantel featuring delicate classical motifs. A screened porch off the living room overlooks the central plaza. The walnut-paneled dining room is more ornate and has a Tudor-style strapwork ceiling. Connected to the dining room is a pleasant, airy sunroom. A remodeled kitchen takes up much of the home's angled east end, where servants' quarters were originally located.

Like the downstairs rooms, the two original bedrooms on the second floor are oriented toward the south and its expansive views. A utility room on this floor has a door that once provided access to the "pass-over," as the Goodkinds called it, and there was a similar arrangement on Benjamin's side. It does not appear, however, that the pass-over was ever used to go from one residence to the other, and the doors at either end have been closed off for many years.

Benjamin Goodkind's home, though considerably larger than his brother's, has a more discreet entrance, set beneath the overhead passageway. The front door leads through a paneled, barrel-vaulted entry into a hall oriented in an east-west direction rather than north-south, as in William's home. Much of the hall's north side is devoted to a long staircase that climbs up to the second floor beside four stepped-up windows with diamond-shaped panes and stained-glass shields. This staircase is paralleled by another above it that ascends to the third floor. Both staircases are open to the floors below, creating a strong sense of vertical circulation. The walls around the two staircases appear to be limestone but are actually made of golden-toned plaster scored to resemble blocks.

The major downstairs rooms are arranged in line along the south side, beginning with a library on the east, a music room, and a dining room (which includes a solarium). A large kitchen and what were once connected servants' quarters form the west end of the home. The music room, at the center of the house, includes wainscoting, a beamed ceiling, and French doors opening out to a terrace. The paneled living room originally featured a strapwork ceiling like the one in the luxuriously appointed dining room. But the most charming room of all, a step up from the dining room, is the solarium, which spreads out in a circling wall of windows to capture copious southern light.

William Goodkind's home features a welcoming tiled entryway that opens into the living room, which includes a large fireplace and carved mantel.

The music room at the center of the Benjamin Goodkind home includes wainscoting, a beamed ceiling, and French doors opening out to a terrace.

Upstairs, the home offers nine bedrooms on the second and third floors, three of which were in the servants' wing. Benjamin and Adelaide Goodkind had three children—a twenty-year-old son and two teenage daughters—when the house was built, so it's likely some of the bedrooms were initially used for other purposes. Many of the upstairs rooms have a straightforward Arts and Crafts look typical of the period.

The home's current owners, David Duddingston and Clayton Halunen, remodeled the basement to create a large entertainment room in what had long been storage space. They also filled in a small side porch off the dining room to provide space for a new spiral staircase down to the basement. Two other features—a well-equipped basement "fallout" shelter

An Architectural Scandal

When Allen Stem designed the Goodkind Double House, he and his partner, Charles Reed, were at work on numerous other buildings, including the St. Paul Hotel. But their biggest project by far was Grand Central Terminal in New York City. The terminal, completed in 1913 at a cost of about $2 billion in today's dollars, was a colossal undertaking that required the demolition of 200 buildings, the construction of a tunnel beneath Park Avenue, and the creation of a complex network of tracks, roadways, and ramps to serve both long-distance and commuter rail lines. Yet the project never brought Reed and Stem the recognition they deserved, largely because much of the work was stolen from them by a New York architectural firm later found guilty of unethical and illegal conduct.

The New York Central Railroad held an informal design competition for the terminal in 1903. The competitors included such architectural powerhouses as McKim, Mead and White of New York and Daniel Burnham of Chicago. But much to the surprise of the New York architectural community, the commission went to Reed and Stem of St. Paul. The firm had an inside track because Reed was the brother-in-law of William Wilgus, chief engineer of the New York Central. Even so, it was not a selection driven by nepotism. Reed, a brilliant engineer with a degree from the Massachusetts Institute of Technology, had extensive experience planning rail stations, and Stem was a highly capable architect.

It wasn't long, however, before Reed and Stem's prestigious commission began to slip from their grasp. New York architect Whitney Warren was the chief culprit. A practiced maneuverer, he paid a visit to his cousin William K. Vanderbilt, chairman of the New York Central's board, and suggested that Reed and Stem were hardly up to the job of designing the terminal. He scoffed at the St. Paul architects' proposal, calling it "a grocery store plan," and claimed he and his partner, Charles Wetmore, could do much better. Vanderbilt agreed, and in 1904 Warren and Wetmore joined the design team. The shotgun marriage between the two firms was formalized with the creation of a partnership called Associated Architects, with Reed acting as chief executive.

It was not a happy collaboration. Although Reed and Stem were largely responsible for the terminal's intricate circulation system, Warren and Wetmore seized control of the architectural design. The size and complexity of the project took a tremendous toll on Reed, and he died suddenly in November of 1911 at age fifty-three. While Stem was attending his partner's funeral in Rochester, New York, Warren and Wetmore secretly changed the contract for the terminal project, making them the exclusive architects.

When Stem found out what had happened, he sued. In 1916 a New York court issued a scathing decision in which it found that Warren and Wetmore had not only violated their partnership agreement but also tried to take unfair credit for Reed's "masterful work" in planning the terminal. The case went through two appeals, but the decision was upheld, and in 1920 Reed and Stem were awarded $500,000 in damages (about $6 million today). Not long thereafter, Warren was expelled from the American Institute of Architects. Despite his disgraceful behavior, Warren continued to win commissions, including one in 1924 for the design of the baldachin (canopy) over the altar at the St. Paul Cathedral, just a few blocks away from the Goodkind Double House.

Architect Allen Stem, who designed the Goodkind Double House, won the commission for Grand Central Terminal in New York, shown here under construction, circa 1910. Unscrupulous New York architects later wrested control of the gigantic project from Stem and his partner, Charles Reed.

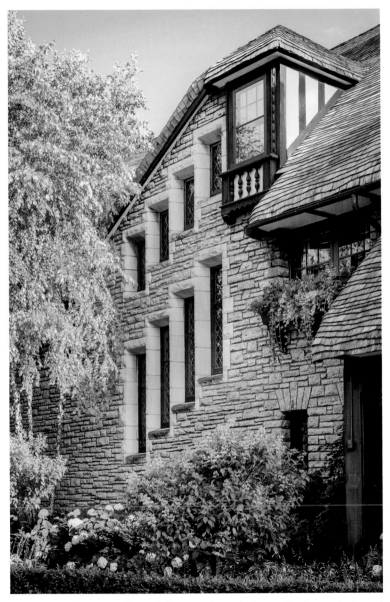

Two rows of parallel stepped-up windows with diamond-shaped panes and stained-glass shields flank the double staircase inside the Benjamin Goodkind home.

complete with a toilet and sleeping cots, and a greenhouse—were added in the 1950s by the home's then owners, Thomas and Frances Daniels, who also maintained a spectacular country estate called Worsted Skeynes in the St. Paul suburb of Gem Lake.

Only a few years after Benjamin and William Goodkind moved into their homes, probably in 1911, their firm became enmeshed in one of the largest failed building projects in St. Paul history. In 1913 Mannheimer Brothers announced plans to erect a huge new downtown department store at Sixth and St. Peter Streets on the site of the old St. Paul Cathedral, which was soon to be replaced by the present cathedral. Work on the $1 million store began amid much fanfare in late 1914, only to come to an abrupt halt less than a year later after the steel superstructure—but nothing else above ground—had been completed.

It's not clear why the project collapsed, but the Goodkinds were never able to resuscitate it. The structural frame remained in place like a giant sculptural insult to the city's business community until St. Paul brewer William Hamm and a group of partners finally came to the rescue in 1919. They put together a new development plan to use the steel skeleton for a combination office building and theater. The Hamm Building, completed in 1920, still stands, but the 2,200-seat Capitol (later Paramount) Theater, the Twin Cities' first true movie palace, was destroyed in 1965.

The strain of the botched building project, which caused Mannheimer Brothers to lose a great deal of money, may have contributed to Benjamin Goodkind's sudden death at age sixty-three in 1919. Adelaide moved out of the double house after her husband's death and later went on to marry Julius Rosenwald, longtime president of Sears, Roebuck and Company. It was a family wedding in every sense, since one of Adelaide's daughters, Edith, was already married to Rosenwald's son, Lessing. William Goodkind also left the double house in about 1920 to live elsewhere. He died in 1938, twelve years after Mannheimer Brothers had merged with Schuneman's. The combined firm was later folded into the now-vanished Dayton's Department Store empire.

The double house, meanwhile, continued to be one of St. Paul's most desirable addresses, attracting a succession of owners, some of whom stayed for many years. Donnelly has lived in the smaller side at 5 Heather Place since 1993. The home was in solid shape when she moved in, but she did undertake two big projects. She remodeled the kitchen to restore its original layout and created a new master bedroom suite upstairs by combining two former servants' rooms. Donnelly's family has deep roots in St. Paul—her grandparents once operated the landmark Lexington restaurant—and she cherishes the home in part for its rich history. But she also loves the quiet and privacy of the home's setting, as well as the light that pours into the many south-facing rooms.

The double stairway in the Benjamin Goodkind home leads to nine bedrooms on the second and third floors, including what were once servants' quarters.

Opposite: The second-story connection between the two houses, dubbed the "pass-over" by the Goodkind families, bridges the entry to a shared fountain and patio.

The current owners of the Benjamin Goodkind home added a small outdoor swimming pool on the south side after purchasing the property in 2004.

Duddingston and Halunen, longtime partners who married in 2013, bought Benjamin Goodkind's side of the house in 2004. Halunen is a Minneapolis employment attorney who grew up on the Iron Range. Duddingston, who was raised in St. Paul, owns his own business. The two men share a deep interest in design and are well aware that their home is one of St. Paul's treasures. They worked with an interior designer to restore key interior features, such as the scored plasterwork around the staircase, and also added new touches, including a hand-painted frieze in the dining room. They have also joined with Donnelly to make landscape improvements. One major addition is a small outdoor swimming pool on the home's south side.

The Goodkinds are now long gone. So, too, is the department store to which they devoted their lives. But the great Cotswold fantasy they inhabited for less than a decade lives on as a unique and remarkable legacy. ❧

James J. Hill and Louis Hill Houses
JAMES J. HILL HOUSE
St. Paul, 1891

James J. Hill, 1902. He was usually photographed from the left so as not to draw attention to his right eye, which was blinded in a boyhood accident.

Opposite: The largest private home ever built in St. Paul, the James J. Hill House stands like a mighty boulder at the head of Summit Avenue. At right is the somewhat smaller house completed twelve years later by his second son and business successor, Louis Hill.

AT THE HEAD OF SUMMIT AVENUE, ACROSS FROM THE COLOSSAL dome of the St. Paul Cathedral, stand a pair of mansions, built more than a century ago, that are rooted like ancient oaks in the history of the city. One was built at 240 Summit for James J. Hill. The other, at 260 Summit, became the home of his son and successor, Louis Hill. Together they form an architectural set piece that speaks not only to the wealth of their original owners but also to the rapid shift in taste that occurred at the end of the nineteenth century as Victorian heft and flamboyance gave way to the quiet proprieties of the Classical Revival. They also remain, more than a century after their construction, the two largest private homes ever built in St. Paul, and without them Summit Avenue would feel as incomplete as a diamond necklace stripped of its most glittering stones.

James J. Hill's mansion, a mighty hunk of red sandstone now owned by the Minnesota Historical Society and open to the public as a house museum, is the larger and older of the two. With its rockbound solidity and sense of aggressive purpose, the mansion, which was designated as a National Historic Landmark in 1961, is very much a reflection of its tough, flinty builder. Completed in 1891 at a cost of nearly $1 million (equivalent to at least $20 million today), it was Hill's official residence for the last twenty-five years of his life.

Although he lavished a fortune on the mansion, Hill actually spent much of his time elsewhere, either on the road attending to his many business interests or summering at his beloved North Oaks farm just north of the city. Perhaps Hill's numerous absences help explain why the mansion, despite its wealth of gorgeous detail and many practical amenities, has always had the chilly air of a place built, above all else, as a show of strength. Yet it was a true family home, where Hill and his wife, Mary, raised their five youngest children, who ranged in age from six to sixteen when the mansion was completed. (The Hills had ten children in all, including a daughter who died in infancy.)

Massive porches at the rear of the James J. Hill House allowed the Empire Builder and his family to gaze down on the city below. The mansion seems particularly powerful, if a bit forbidding, in the deep chill of winter.

How Hill came to occupy the greatest house on St. Paul's greatest avenue is very much the saga of a self-made man. Born in 1838 on a hardscrabble Ontario farm (where he lost sight in his right eye at age nine after an accident with a bow and arrow), Hill made his way to St. Paul in 1856, began working along the busy waterfront, and later formed his own freight-transfer business. Hardworking, fiercely ambitious, and gifted with tremendous intelligence and physical endurance, Hill quickly made a name for himself in St. Paul as an up-and-coming businessman. But it was his acquisition, with several partners, of the bankrupt St. Paul and Pacific Railroad in 1879 that set him on a course toward fabulous wealth as the owner of what would become, in 1893, the Great Northern Railway.

Two years before his initial foray into railroading, Hill had built his first St. Paul mansion, a conventional French Second Empire–style brick home in the Lowertown neighborhood. By then, he had been married for ten years to the former Mary Meghan, the daughter of Irish immigrants, and like Hill from very modest circumstances. Hill's decision in 1888 to build a new, and much larger, mansion on Summit Avenue was not unusual at the time, since a number of St. Paul's most prominent families had by then already left Lowertown because railroad expansion there made it increasingly undesirable as a residential district.

Hill planned well in advance for his new mansion. In 1882 he acquired two choice lots on Summit that offered superb views of downtown St. Paul and the river valley beyond. Both lots were occupied by houses dating to the 1850s and 1860s. Once he was ready to build, Hill had the houses demolished, an early example of the kind of teardowns that still occur today in high-demand neighborhoods.

Hill considered a number of architects, none of them from the Twin Cities, when it came time to plan his new mansion. Why he showed no interest in such local design luminaries as Cass Gilbert and Clarence Johnston isn't known, but it's likely he thought he could achieve greater effect by using an outside architect. Henry O. Avery of New York was among the candidates, submitting a French Gothic design in 1887 that Hill ultimately rejected. Perhaps the most intriguing architect on Hill's list was Frank Furness, based in Philadelphia. A Civil War veteran who earned a Medal of Honor for gallantry, Furness was a volcanic character who routinely manhandled the conventions of Victorian Gothic design to produce some of the most strange, powerful, and distinctive buildings in all of American architecture.

A Furness-designed mansion on staid Summit Avenue would indeed have been a remarkable sight. Hill, however, finally chose to hire the more conservative Boston firm headed by partners Robert Peabody, John Stearns Jr., and Pierce Furber. The firm's résumé included a wide range of commissions, from office buildings to schools to private homes. Most of these works were in New England, but the architects also maintained an office in St. Louis, where Furber was based. Hill knew Furber's father, and it's likely that relationship led to Hill's hiring the firm.

Stearns came out to St. Paul in 1887 to meet with Hill and look at the building site. By that July, the architects had produced a number of possible designs, ranging from what was described as "an old time English mansion" to a French chateau. Eventually, however, the architects and their client settled on the Richardsonian Romanesque style, which suited Hill's taste for monumentality combined with limited doses of ornament.

Construction began in 1888. The work proceeded smoothly enough

The main split staircase, finished in dark oak, ascends past a landing illuminated by stained-glass windows. A portrait of Hill hangs nearby.

The St. Paul Cathedral, which Hill had a hand in building, creates a grand spectacle framed through one of the porte cochere's arches.

until August of 1889, when Hill had a blowup with his architects. The problem occurred when someone from the firm, without Hill's permission, tried to change how the sandstone used for the mansion's walls was to be cut and carved. Hill's reaction to this affront was swift and decisive. In a bluntly worded letter, he fired the architects, warning them that "hereafter I will not allow you to come near the building, or have anything to do with it, directly or indirectly." But the most telling sentence in Hill's letter of dismissal came at the end: "I regret to be compelled to take this course, but it appears to be the only one that will enable me to keep you in your proper place." The new King of Summit Avenue had spoken.

The letter was in every way characteristic of Hill, a man who was born to be in charge and who brooked no challenge to his authority. Stocky and powerful, he was "built like a buffalo," said one writer, "with a prodigious chest . . . truly a massive, imposing figure of a man." Yet the roughhewn "Empire Builder," as he came to be known (or as his servants more irreverently called him, "the Big Bug"), was far from one dimensional. He was a self-taught engineer, a highly knowledgeable farmer, a clever financier, a voracious reader, and a true visionary in the development of what was then known as the Northwest. He was also, of course, a railroader, and as his

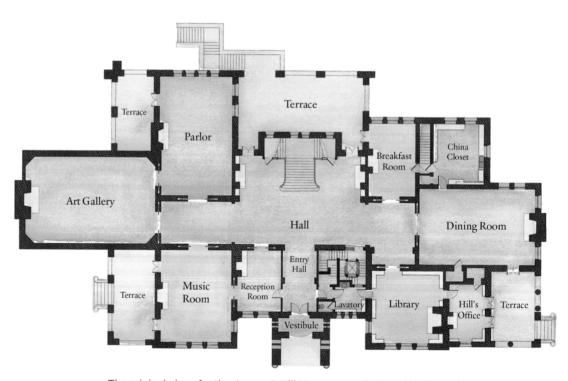

The original plans for the James J. Hill House were designed by the architectural firm of Peabody, Stearns, and Furber. The main hall alone is long enough to accommodate two railroad boxcars.

mansion rose on Summit, he was in the midst of the biggest project of his life, pushing his Great Northern Railway to the West Coast.

Despite so many other demands on his time, Hill paid very close attention to the building of his new home. He personally reviewed and approved every feature of the work, rejecting many sketches and plans he didn't like. Hill insisted that his mansion include a large art gallery to show off his connoisseur's collection of paintings from the French Barbizon school.

After dismissing Peabody, Stearns and Furber, Hill turned to his in-house architect, James Brodie, to oversee work on the mansion. He also hired Irving and Casson, a prestigious Boston firm of decorators and furniture makers, to complete the interior design. Founded in 1875 by Charles R. Irving and Robert Casson, the firm employed numerous skilled craftspeople, among them Johannes Kirchmayer, who was put in charge of the mansion's wood carving.

As the mansion was being completed in 1891, the *St. Paul Pioneer Press*, no doubt seeing considerable benefit in saying nice things about the richest man in town, averred that the new home made "no attempt at display" and showed "no desire to flaunt an advertisement of wealth in the eyes of the world." Just the opposite is true, of course. The three-story mansion, which has changed little since it was built, is nothing if not a proclamation of Hill's worldly success and a demonstration of his power.

The mansion's size alone is impressive. It stretches for 187 feet along Summit, from its skylit art gallery on the east end to a terrace and dining room on the west. Its 36,000 square feet and thirty-two rooms (not counting various servant and utility spaces) were unprecedented in Minnesota at the time and still have few equals in the state. Often referred to as "forbidding" or "overpowering," the mansion is uncommonly well made, as is true of everything Hill built. As a result, his mansion conveys, more so than perhaps any other of the state's great houses, a sense of implacable permanence, and it is hard to imagine it could ever be dissolved by time.

Although the mansion's overall profile is irregular, much of the front facade is symmetrical, with identical three-story hipped-roof pavilions flanking a central section set behind a massive arched porte cochere. Entirely clad in stone, the mansion's walls offer very little in the way of ornament except for a few carved column capitals and some decorative flourishes around the porte cochere. Even the windows, mostly simple

Hill was a man who believed in big gestures, as demonstrated by the mansion's one-hundred-foot-long main hall lit by a row of chandeliers. Hand-carved pilasters add a decorative touch.

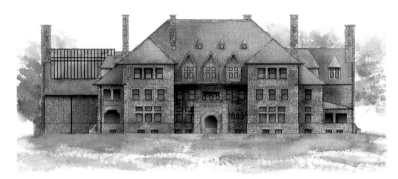

The Hill House's front facade is symmetrical at the center, with balanced pavilions flanking the porte cochere in front of the main entrance.

Constructed of red Massachusetts sandstone that has darkened over the years, the Hill House exemplifies the Richardsonian Romanesque style. The cleaned stonework of the port cochere suggests the original coloring.

double-hungs, are very plain, and the only stained glass is at the rear above the main staircase landing.

The walls are actually built of brick, which is overlaid with rough-faced blocks of red Massachusetts sandstone arranged in a random ashlar pattern. The choice of sandstone from Massachusetts, rather than from much closer quarries along the south shore of Lake Superior, was very unusual in Minnesota at the time. The Massachusetts stone darkened over the years, losing much of its luster, although efforts have been made to restore the original color to the porte cochere. Steel beams, some big enough for a railroad bridge, support the roof and tile floors. Legend holds that the mansion was designed to withstand a direct hit from a tornado, and there's little doubt it would do so quite nicely.

Inside, the mansion is a vastness of wide halls, great rooms, and sumptuous expanses of hand-carved oak and mahogany woodwork. The intricate wood carving, especially in the dining room, is in many ways the mansion's glory and does much to humanize its overwhelming scale. And even if the mansion doesn't always feel like home—the place is simply too big to be anything like "cozy"—there's no denying Hill created a residence in every way worthy of his status as the state's dominant business figure.

The mansion's front door, a thick slab of oak sheltered by the porte cochere, opens into a small vestibule and then into a hall with a reception room to one side. This rather quiet entry sequence serves as prelude to the mansion's most imposing feature—a one-hundred-foot-long main hall so high and broad it could comfortably accommodate a pair of railroad boxcars. Lit by five magnificent crystal chandeliers, the hall is the largest domestic space of its kind in Minnesota. As such, it makes quite a first impression, although not necessarily of the most welcoming sort, as a magazine writer noted in 1889: "There is a freezing politeness about the hall which acts as a barrier to the stranger until it is decided whether or not to admit him to the grateful warmth of the interior apartments."

Directly across the main hall from the entry is the mansion's grand staircase, which sweeps up in a single flight to a landing illuminated by a dozen stained-glass windows and then splits in two before climbing to the second floor. During daylight hours, the landing windows glow like fire against the backdrop of the staircase's dark oak woodwork. Past the staircase, doors lead out to the rear terrace, where Hill and his family could relax during the summer months and take in the panoramic views.

The mansion's two-story art gallery, which includes a 1,006-pipe tracker organ built by George Hutchings of Boston, is at the far east end of the main hall. Hill was a an avid collector, spending close to $2 million on fine art during his life, and the gallery, which he opened to the public, was where he displayed the best of it. The French artist Jean-Baptiste-Camille

Corot (1796–1875) was one of Hill's favorites. Much of Hill's collection eventually ended up at the Minneapolis Institute of Arts.

All of the major downstairs rooms, located in conventional fashion along the main hall, spotlight different styles of period decoration, a common practice at the time. Most of these rooms feature dark-stained woodwork and dark walls—not the cheeriest of arrangements—but the music room and parlor were given a lighter "French" touch. The main floor's standout space is the dining room, at the west end of the house. Here, Kirchmayer's wood carving, executed in luxurious St. John's mahogany from the Virgin Islands, reaches its swirling apogee in a stunning fireplace mantel. The dining-room table, made by Irving and Casson from the same exotic wood, is equally fine.

The second floor, part of which is now used for offices, includes James J. and Mary Hill's bedroom suite, at the southeast corner of the house. There were also five bedrooms for the family's at-home daughters arranged around a central hall, two guest bedrooms, and plenty of bathrooms (the mansion as built had thirteen in all). The Hills' suite is nicely detailed, with many built-ins, but it's not especially lavish. Hill in general did not favor fancy design, and the relative simplicity of his bedroom may tell more about his true taste than all of the ornamental flourishes downstairs.

The third floor, which is nearly as large as the second, provided bedrooms for the family's three sons, two of whom—James and Louis—were already in college by the time the mansion was completed. There was also a schoolroom where the younger children received their lessons. The rest of the floor was taken up by quarters for some of the dozen or so servants—most of them young, unmarried women—who typically worked in the mansion.

Visitors to the mansion often find its huge basement to be especially fascinating. Here was the home's working heart—a kitchen, a laundry that included eighteen cedar drying racks for clothes, a wine cellar, and fourteen metal-lined rooms equipped with ceiling-mounted radiators that served as heat chambers to send warm air up through the mansion. The heat was supplied by coal-fired furnaces in the mansion's impressive two-level boiler room, which looks as if it could pump out enough heat for an entire office building. A storage room next to the boiler room held fifty tons of coal.

The mansion was among the first homes in Minnesota to employ electric lighting (provided by on-site generators), although gas was also used for this purpose. The mansion included a security system, an elaborate bell system for summoning servants, and two safes to protect the family's valuables. A total of 473 numbered keys, all kept in a second-floor closet, were required for the mansion's array of doors, windows, chests, cupboards, and cabinets. Key number one was for the door to Hill's bedroom.

A pair of swans inhabits one of the landing's stained-glass windows, designed by A. B. Cutter of Boston. Hill rejected glass designs offered by the more famous Tiffany firm of New York.

The dining room, finished in St. John's mahogany from the Virgin Islands, features especially elaborate wood carving. German-born master carver Johannes Kirchmayer did much of the work.

Johannes Kirchmayer

If the white oak carvings adorning the interiors of the James J. Hill House in St. Paul seem church-worthy, it's no surprise. They were created by master wood-carver Johannes Baptist Kirchmayer, one of the nation's foremost ecclesiastical designers/carvers of his time (1860–1930).

Kirchmayer (originally spelled Kirchmayr) was born in Oberammergau, Germany, a Bavarian village known for its elaborate Passion play

productions. The play has been staged nearly every decade since the Middle Ages as a thanksgiving to God for sparing the villagers from the bubonic plague. Kirchmayer learned modeling techniques under his grandfather's tutelage as he prepared first pottery, then wood figures for the beloved play. He thus learned biblical stories and characters and secured a foundation for his career designing church interiors in the United States.

Armed with remarkable skill and poised for adventure, the young artisan traveled to Paris and London and, finally—at age twenty—to New York City, where he began to meet architects and designers. He signed on with the Boston architectural woodworking firm of Irving and Casson and worked on many buildings designed by an architect who specialized in Gothic Revival churches, Ralph Adams Cram. Kirchmayer was equally proficient with wood, stone, ivory, wax, and plaster and often left a cheeky self-portrait among his designs.

Most of his church, school, museum, and home commissions centered in New England, New York, and Pennsylvania, but as his fame spread, Kirchmayer was called upon for projects farther afield. In Minnesota, there was the Hill commission in St. Paul in 1891, St. Mark's Episcopal Cathedral in Minneapolis (1911–1915), and House of Hope Presbyterian Church in St. Paul (1914).

The Hill House was a formidable commission that included all of the elaborate woodwork, staircases, railings, ceilings, and much of the furnishings throughout the house. Kirchmayer figured he spent 1,470 hours on the home, and Hill paid him a dollar an hour, making Kirchmayer the highest-paid worker on the project.

Johannes Kirchmayer left a fanciful image of himself in one of his wood carvings for the main hall of the James J. Hill House.

Hill spent what would amount to $5 million or more today to furnish his new mansion, although he also brought along many items from his former home in Lowertown. Once the move was complete, Hill had the Lowertown house demolished, possibly because he could not bear the thought of another family living there. If so, it was a rare instance of a sentimental gesture on his part, since the home was only thirteen years old.

When Hill and his family moved into their new mansion in August of 1891, they became part of a phenomenally wealthy residential precinct. Their next-door neighbors, lumber baron Frederick Weyerhaeuser and all-purpose capitalist Amherst Wilder were, like Hill, among the richest of all Minnesotans. Wilder's mansion, to the east of Hill's, had been the largest and most lavish home on Summit when it was completed in 1887, but Hill managed to outdo it, at least in size. The demolition of the Wilder property in 1959 was a tremendous blow to St. Paul's architectural heritage, and deprived the Hill House of a truly splendid companion piece.

Hill died in his bedroom at the mansion, at age seventy-seven, in 1916, leaving behind no will and therefore plenty of room for dispute among his heirs. The mansion itself went to his widow, and Mary lived there until her own death in 1921. A devout Catholic, Mary had indicated she wished to give the mansion to the Archdiocese of St. Paul, but she, too, failed to prepare a will.

For the next four years, the fate of the mansion remained uncertain as Hill's heirs squabbled in court. There was talk that the mansion and its art collection would be donated to the City of St. Paul as a museum. One overly excited proponent of this idea claimed that such a museum "would be renowned; where art is spoken of, St. Paul would flash into the mind along with the Louvre and the Metropolitan."

A judge finally decided in 1925 that given all of the disagreements among the heirs, the best course would be to sell the mansion at a public auction. Lawyers representing four of the Hills' daughters, who knew their mother's wishes, made the only bid at the auction, for $90,300. After completing the purchase, the daughters donated the mansion to the archdiocese along with furnishings not already claimed by family members. Over the next half century, the archdiocese (which by the early 1900s also owned the neighboring Wilder property) used the mansion for a variety of purposes while doing little to alter its essential character.

With the help of state and federal funds, the Minnesota Historical Society acquired the mansion in 1978. Initial renovation work began the next year. Another large round took place in 1983–1984 and included upgrading the mansion's mechanical and electrical systems, restoring the art gallery, installing replicated light fixtures, and painting or recovering interior walls to bring them back to their original appearance. Exterior work included restoring roofs, driveways, and terraces.

A 1,006-pipe tracker organ built in Boston occupies one end of the mansion's skylit art gallery. Hill opened the gallery to the public to show off his collection of French Barbizon–school paintings.

Today, about fifty thousand visitors a year come to the mansion for tours, special events, and art shows. For many first-time visitors, the home's size and splendor evoke genuine awe, but nothing in the mansion is quite as astonishing as Hill himself, a farm boy with one good eye and a far-ranging mind who grabbed hold of the world with an iron grip and made it do his bidding.

Movable drying racks in the basement laundry were among many practical devices Hill incorporated into the mansion.

The industrial-strength boiler in the basement serves as an impressive testament to how well Hill built every part of his home.

LOUIS HILL HOUSE
St. Paul, 1903, 1913

WHEN JAMES J. HILL DIED, LOUIS HILL ASSUMED CONTROL OF HIS father's business empire. Slender and bespectacled, Louis wasn't the elemental force his father had been. Although he could be imperious and demanding—traits he definitely inherited—he was an altogether smoother operator than his father. A bon vivant who enjoyed the pleasures of wealth, Louis Hill possessed a wide array of talents. He was an exceptionally canny investor, an accomplished painter and photographer, a lover of the American West (he played a central role in establishing Montana's Glacier National Park in 1910), a civic leader in St. Paul, and a great philanthropist.

Much more so than the family's other two sons, Louis stayed close to his father, and that was the case after his marriage to New York–born Maud Van Cortlandt Taylor in 1901. A year after the wedding, the couple built a magnificent home directly west of James J.'s mansion. Louis's suave new residence, much more understated than his father's gigantic Victorian, aptly expressed the differences in temperament and style between the two men.

The elder Hill had acquired the property at 260 Summit, which included an 1850s-vintage house, at a cost of $20,000 in 1899. A platted but never built street separated Hill's mansion from his new acquisition, but in 1901 the city agreed to vacate the street provided Hill build a staircase in its place. Those public steps are still in use today. Well before the street was vacated, Louis Hill hired St. Paul architect Clarence Johnston to design his new mansion. Johnston was then the city's leading society architect and had already designed thirty homes on Summit, far more than anyone else.

By the early 1900s in Minnesota, and most of the nation, a wide range of classically derived styles had become fashionable for mansions of all kinds. One popular variant was Georgian Revival, based on American

Louis and Maud Hill with their oldest children, Louis Jr. and Maud, 1903. Two other children were born later.

Colonial models, and it was this kind of home that Johnston designed for Louis and Maud Hill. The broad-fronted Georgian style also fit well on Hill's property, which was much larger than the standard forty-foot-wide lot found in St. Paul. As completed in 1903, the mansion incorporated a full range of Georgian Revival features—red-brick walls, a two-story front portico with paired Ionic columns, a gambrel (two-sloped) roof with side gables, simple rectangular windows, and sparingly applied ornament.

The mansion's floor plan, however, was highly unorthodox. To take advantage of views from the home's bluff-top site, Johnston placed the living and dining rooms at the rear, along with a semicircular conservatory. A reception room, coatroom, butler's pantry, and servants' staircase were at the front. This unusual plan was evident on the home's original front facade, where two small windows illuminating the staircase interrupted the otherwise standard Georgian symmetry.

The living room (which also serves as a library) and the dining room both feature exquisitely carved woodwork by William Yungbauer. Born in what is today the Czech Republic, Yungbauer had worked on the James J. Hill House with master carver Johannes Kirchmayer before establishing his own business in St. Paul. An overmantel above the living-room fireplace shows off Yungbauer's skills. The dining room, which includes a table and two John LaFarge–designed stained-glass windows from James J. Hill's former Lowertown mansion, is also exceptional. The conservatory, located between the living and dining rooms, is adorned with art-glass windows designed by Louis Millet. The Chicago-based Millet also designed windows for the St. Paul Cathedral and for Louis Sullivan and George Elmslie's renowned National Farmers Bank (1908) in Owatonna, Minnesota.

Overall, the Louis Hill House was brighter and homier than James J.'s mansion. As originally built, it was also much smaller—perhaps a third the size of its massive neighbor. Louis and Maud Hill settled into their new home in December 1903, although a few finishing touches remained. The family ultimately included four children, the last born in 1906. Louis Hill had carefully supervised construction of the house, no doubt making life difficult for Johnston, who had to sue his wealthy client to collect the last of the money owed him for his work. This disagreement may explain why Hill chose a different architect when he decided to greatly expand his mansion less than a decade after its completion.

In 1912 Louis succeeded his father as chairman of the Great Northern Railway, and with this new position came added responsibilities for entertaining guests. To meet these needs, Louis decided he needed a much bigger

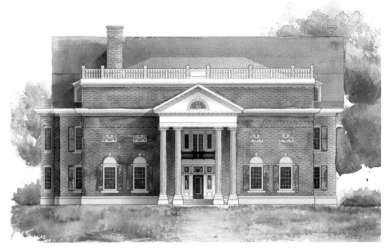

This elevation shows the Louis Hill House as it is today, with the front addition designed by Chicago architect Charles Frost.

The Louis Hill House in 1905, before a large front addition altered its appearance.

Summit Avenue and Its Mansions

Summit Avenue in St. Paul constitutes Minnesota's greatest gathering of mansions, but there was a time when other parts of the city actually had far larger concentrations of wealthy residents. Although the first mansions appeared on Summit in the 1850s, the avenue at that time was difficult to reach from the downtown core because of its location atop a high bluff. As a result, the earliest mansion district in St. Paul developed in the Lowertown neighborhood just east of downtown. It was there, in 1877–1878, that James J. Hill built his first mansion, on Canada Street. His neighbors within a radius of a few blocks included such luminaries as Henry Sibley (Minnesota's first governor), Horace Thompson (founder of the First National Bank of St. Paul), and Amherst Wilder (one of the city's most successful businessmen).

But the Lowertown mansion district, which was centered just northeast of today's "spaghetti junction," where Interstates 35E and 94 meet, began to fall out of favor not long after Hill built his mansion. It was Hill's own business—railroading—that led to the district's demise as a desirable residential area. As rail lines expanded through the Trout Brook corridor along the district's eastern edge in the 1880s, they brought noise, smoke, and industry with them, none of which appealed to wealthy homeowners. Change came so rapidly that by the early 1900s almost all of Lowertown's well-to-do residents, including Hill, were gone.

Summit Avenue offered many advantages over Lowertown, including splendid views and a lack of nearby railroad tracks or industry. It was also close to downtown. But getting up the big hill remained a problem, and only about twenty-five houses were built along Summit before 1880. By comparison, there were at least twice as many mansions in Lowertown by that time.

It was during the boom years of the 1880s, when St. Paul's population exploded from 41,000 to more than 133,000, that Summit Avenue swept away all competitors to become the city's most prestigious residential address. More than sixty mansions were built on Summit in the 1880s and another fifty appeared over the next decade. The arrival of good mass transportation in the form of a cable car line in 1887 (soon replaced by streetcar service) helped make these mansions readily accessible. Another 250 or so homes—many of mansion quality—were constructed along the westerly portions of the four-and-a-half-mile-long avenue between 1900 and 1930.

What is most remarkable about Summit is how many of its landmark homes still stand. Summit's favored location—less than a mile from the heart of downtown, yet sharply separated from it by a bluff too steep to build on—helped preserve the most historic portions of the avenue from urban renewal, freeway building, and other modern-era intrusions that decimated mansion districts in many other American cities.

In his wonderful book *St. Paul's Historic Summit Avenue*, Ernest Sandeen called Summit "the best-preserved American example of the Victorian monumental residential boulevard." He was right, and today Summit remains not only St. Paul's most famous street but also a true national treasure.

James J. Hill bought land adjoining his mansion to provide a homesite for his son Louis. The house Louis built for himself and his family is less monumental than his father's.

house, and early in 1913 he hired Chicago architect Charles Frost to design the addition. Frost by then had already received a much larger commission from Hill, to design a huge new headquarters building for the Great Northern in downtown St. Paul (known as the Railroad and Bank Building, it was completed in 1916). Although Frost was primarily a railroad architect—he designed more than two hundred stations during his long career, including St. Paul's Union Depot and the Milwaukee Road Depot in Minneapolis—he produced a handsome addition to Hill's mansion.

Because the mansion as built sat well back from Summit at the edge of the bluff, the addition had to be placed on the front. Completed in 1913, the addition, which doubled the home's size to over twenty thousand square feet, features a flat balustraded roof but otherwise follows the Georgian style of Johnston's design. The addition also made use of the home's original portico, which was disassembled and moved to the new front facade.

Inside, the addition continued Johnston's reversed plan by placing four bedrooms at the front of the first floor to either side of a large entry hall. Frost also redesigned the main staircase, which became the double set of stairs that now form one of the home's outstanding features. The addition's second floor was devoted entirely to a music room, as the Hills called it, complete with a pipe organ. Here the Hills were able to host all manner of large gatherings, including a dinner and reception in 1926 for Queen Marie of Romania, a granddaughter of England's Queen Victoria.

Maud and Louis Hill remained together in the mansion until 1934, when they separated. Maud then

A lovely double staircase was among many features added to the house in 1913.

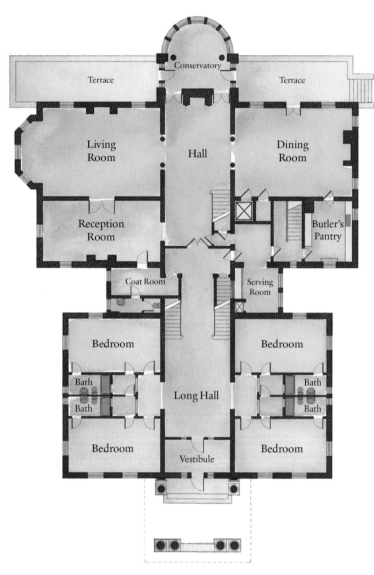

The main floor plan shows how the front addition extended the line of the house. The plan's orientation is unusual in that the living and dining rooms are at the rear and the bedrooms are at the front.

The home's elegant portico, part of the original 1903 design, was disassembled in 1913 and then reattached to the front of the addition.

Louis Hill's mansion dates to 1903 and is an excellent example of the quietly dignified Georgian Revival style. What is now the front portion of the house was added a decade later and includes a large second-floor ballroom.

moved into a home a few blocks away. Louis stayed on in the mansion, with only a few servants as company, until his death in 1948. Six years later, the mansion, like its two neighbors to the east, was donated to the Catholic Church. The mansion was first used as offices for the *Catholic Digest*, a quarterly magazine, but later became a residence and retreat center for the Daughters of the Heart of Mary, a Catholic religious society for women. Significant alterations were made to the mansion's interior during this time. After the Daughters moved out in 1998, a group attempted to establish a pediatric hospice in the mansion, but that venture failed.

After nearly a half century of institutional use, the mansion finally became a home again in 2001, when it was purchased by Richard and Nancy Nicholson. Working with architect Gar Hargens of Close Associates in Minneapolis, the Nicholsons undertook extensive restoration and renovation of the mansion both inside and out. Many of the changes made to the house in the 1950s and 1960s, such as the conversion of the music room to a chapel, were undone as part of the project.

Today, the mansion and its lovely grounds form one of St. Paul's finest residences. The Nicholsons, who renamed the mansion Dove Hill, generously share their home with the public, hosting numerous events in the beautifully restored music room. They are also active in historic preservation and in 2006 bought and restored another superb Summit Avenue property—the William Lightner House. ༄

Architect Clarence Johnston broke from tradition by placing the living room at the rear of the house to take advantage of views from the Summit Avenue bluff tops.

VICTORIANS

✒ William Windom/Abner Hodgins House

Winona, 1869, 1890

William Windom, circa 1867. He served as a congressman and U.S. senator from Minnesota and as secretary of the treasury under two presidents.

Opposite: The Queen Anne–style Abner Hodgins House is the product of a remarkable makeover in 1890. It was originally built in 1869 as a French Second Empire–style home for William Windom, a prominent Winona lawyer.

THE RECLAMATION OF A HISTORIC HOUSE CAN BE THE WORK OF months, years, or in the case of Dave and Kathy Christenson, decades. The Christensons—he a family physician, she an artist and photographer—found the house of their dreams at 275 Harriet Street in Winona in 1977. It was a towered, richly detailed, but well-worn Victorian that had long been one of the city's landmarks. The house had everything they wanted but also needed virtually everything they could give it, from painting and roofing to chimney and porch repair to a complete restoration of the interior. The Christensons, with plenty of help from their three sons, took on what was to be the project of a lifetime, slowly and meticulously uncovering and restoring the home's long-hidden beauty. Today, after more than thirty years of work, the Christensons' historic home is once again one of Winona's architectural jewels.

The story behind the house, which was listed on the National Register of Historic Places in 1984, is as complicated as its design. With its irregular profile, varied wall surfaces of shingle and clapboard, and free use of classically inspired ornament, the house appears to be an excellent example of the Queen Anne style, which was especially popular in Minnesota from the mid-1880s through the early 1890s. Yet the house didn't begin its life draped in Queen Anne finery.

It was originally constructed in 1869, in the French Second Empire style, for William Windom, a prominent Winona lawyer and politician (and the namesake of a small park across the street from the home). By the time Windom built the house, he had already served five terms as a congressman and would soon be appointed to the U.S. Senate. Later, he became secretary of the treasury under presidents James Garfield and William Henry Harrison. Windom even made a bid for the presidency as one of six announced candidates at the 1880 Republican National Convention in Chicago, but he received only ten votes (all from the Minnesota delegation), and the nomination finally went to Garfield after an exhausting thirty-six ballots.

Windom's house was a plain example of the Second Empire style. Built of wood, with clapboard-sided walls, it lacked the weighty presence of the towered stone and brick mansions popular at the time, such as the nearby Henry Huff House, completed in 1858. The Windom House—foursquare except for a rear extension—featured the usual mansard roof, a tall front porch with attenuated columns, and window hoods in the prescribed manner. It was probably designed by a local master builder rather than an architect.

Windom lived in the house until 1883. By then, he was spending most of his time on the East Coast, so he sold the house and moved to New York City. The second owner stayed until 1889, when he, too, left Winona. Abner Hodgins, a partner in a large lumber company, then bought the home and immediately set about rebuilding and enlarging it. By the time he was done, the home's appearance had been transformed so completely that few of its Second Empire roots were visible.

A Tennessee native who'd grown wealthy in Winona's booming lumber trade of the 1870s and 1880s, Hodgins was one of many taste-conscious Victorians who drastically altered older homes to give them a more up-to-date look. Such rebuilds became particularly common in the 1880s, when the nation's rapidly expanding rail network made it possible to deliver a cornucopia of building materials to almost any location. Numerous academically trained architects were also available by then to take on the task of redesign. In Hodgins's case, the reconstruction was done exceptionally well under the direction of longtime Winona architect Charles Maybury, who by 1890 operated in partnership with his oldest son, Jefferson.

The painted-wood decorations around the third-floor Palladian window and on the pediment above the front door were painstakingly hand restored by the current owners, Dave and Kathy Christenson.

Abner Hodgins bought the French Second Empire house William Windom had built and hired Winona architect Charles Maybury to transform it into a Queen Anne Victorian.

Abner Hodgins was one of Winona's wealthiest lumbermen.

Maybury refashioned Windom's old house by extending its overall length, adding a pair of towers along with a wraparound front porch and a side porch, squaring up the original rounded windows, and replacing the mansard with a steeper, more picturesque roof garnished with dormers, gables, and balconies. Inside, the house also took on a new appearance. Maybury reconfigured the floor plan, designed a gorgeous new oak staircase, and added a variety of decorative features, including carved woodwork, tile fireplace surrounds, stained-glass windows, and ornamental plaster ceilings. Only a few items from the 1869 house, such as nine arched doors on the second floor, were reused. When the overhaul was finished in 1890, Hodgins was the proud possessor of a Queen Anne home as stylish as any in Winona.

The Queen Anne style has always been hard to define because it was more an amalgam of architectural gestures than a carefully prescribed system of design. Its name is also a misnomer, since the average American Queen Anne house bears no resemblance to the chaste, symmetrical architecture favored by the British queen in the early 1700s. The Hodgins House—with its festival of forms, piling on of parts, decorative detailing, and incorporation of classical features (such as the three-part Palladian window in the attic)—brims with the sort of freewheeling architectural energy that characterizes Queen Anne design. Even so, the house is actually quite staid compared with five-alarm examples of the style, where variety for its own sake seems to have been the guiding principle.

Hodgins had more than sufficient means to undertake the rebuilding project, which cost an estimated $10,000, enough to construct several standard homes at the time. He'd arrived in Winona in 1856, a year before it was formally incorporated as a city. Because of its proximity to huge pineries along the nearby Chippewa River in Wisconsin, Winona quickly became a hub for milling and shipping lumber, and by the 1870s the city was home to four large lumber companies. Hodgins was a partner in one of them—Youmans Brothers and Hodgins—formed in 1871. By the late 1880s, the company's Winona sawmill produced forty million board feet of lumber a year.

The business peaked just about the same time Hodgins moved into his rebuilt mansion. He was sixty-five years old, married to his third wife (the first two died), and the father of ten adult children when he began living in the house, located in a neighborhood where many of Winona's business elite already lived. It's not known why Hodgins chose to rebuild Windom's house rather than construct an entirely new home. He may simply have liked the neighborhood. It's also possible that he wanted to save money, although Hodgins's wealth appears to have been such that he

Winona Architecture

An architectural divide runs down the middle of Minnesota. The eastern half of the state—from Duluth to St. Cloud, through the Twin Cities and farther south to communities like Owatonna, Rochester, Red Wing, and Winona—was generally settled before the western half and is far more populous. Because its cities are older and larger than those on the western prairies, eastern Minnesota is home to most of the state's landmark historic architecture. One city—Winona—has an especially rich architectural environment, unmatched in Minnesota outside of the Twin Cities and Duluth.

Founded in 1851 by, fittingly enough, a steamboat captain, Winona developed quickly as a major shipping point for wheat and lumber on the Upper Mississippi River. By 1857 it was the third-largest city in Minnesota, and as many as 1,300

The grand hall of the Paul Watkins House, 1928. Now a senior residence, the mansion is one of many exceptional works of architecture in Winona.

riverboats a year docked at its levee. Later, manufacturing added to Winona's wealth, especially after it became headquarters for the J. R. Watkins Company in the 1880s. At its height the company, which is still in business, commanded an army of salespeople who peddled items ranging from health remedies to spices all across the United States.

Between 1911 and 1913 the Watkins Company constructed a huge office and manufacturing building to the designs of Chicago architect George Maher. Mixing elements of Frank Lloyd Wright's Prairie school with Austrian Art Nouveau, the building remains one of Winona's great monuments. So, too, is Maher's Winona Savings Bank (1916), a strange architectural outlier that somehow succeeds in blending Art Nouveau and Egyptian Revival features into one unlikely, if undeniably impressive, package.

Winona's early twentieth-century masterpiece, however, is the Merchants National Bank of 1912, designed by Minneapolis Prairie school masters William Purcell and George Elmslie. The bank incorporates some of Elmslie's most glorious terra-cotta ornament as well as two walls of art-glass windows. Purcell and Elmslie also designed a house in Winona that dates to 1913.

Because it came to maturity in the late nineteenth century, Winona also possesses a superb stock of Victorian-era buildings, many of them in a historic preservation district that encompasses eleven downtown blocks. Chief among these Victorian delights is Charles Maybury's massive Winona County Courthouse (1888). Maybury also designed the Basilica of St. Stanislaus Kostka (1894), a domed and twin-towered church that was built to serve Winona's large Polish community.

The city's collection of architectural treasures includes many homes in addition to the Windom-Hodgins House. The Huff-Lamberton House (1857 and later) is one of Minnesota's premier examples of the Italian Villa style, although its interior has been compromised. Winona's most magnificent mansion (now a nursing home) was built in 1927 for Paul Watkins, then president of the family company. It was designed by Ralph Adams Cram, a prominent Boston architect best known for his ecclesiastical projects, among them the gigantic Cathedral of St. John the Divine (1912 and later) in New York City. For Watkins, Cram designed a Jacobethan Revival mansion centered around a great hall the size of a small church, and as is the case with so much of Winona's best architecture, it's as good as anything of its kind in Minnesota.

could easily have afforded a larger mansion. If nothing else, Hodgins's line of work ensured that he had ready access to all manner of fine woods for his home.

In Winona, as was the case elsewhere in the Upper Midwest, sawmilling in the nineteenth century was a fast-burning fire that eventually became starved for fuel. As the pineries were cut to stubble, one sawmill after another shut down in the 1890s and early 1900s. When Hodgins died in 1896, his mill was already nearing its end, and it closed two years later.

Another lumberman, William Tearse, purchased the home in 1896 and remained there with his family until his death twenty years later. Tearse's widow, Harriet, stayed on until she died in 1934, when the Catholic Diocese of Winona purchased the house to serve as a bishop's residence and chancery offices. The home then became known locally as the Bishop's House. In 1949 the bishop established his residence in another mansion next door, after which the Hodgins House was used exclusively as church offices. At some point, an unsympathetic brick addition holding a large vault was added to the north side of the house. The diocese decided to relocate its offices elsewhere in 1976, and the house went up for sale.

Enter the Christensons, who'd attended college in Winona and returned once Dave completed his medical studies. After helping to defeat a proposal that would have rezoned the house for use as law offices, the Christensons bought the property in 1977 and began the demanding task of restoration. "We knew we were committing to a lifetime project," Kathy recalls. The couple did much of the work themselves, with sons Mike, Tom, and Charlie joining in as soon as they were able. "The house," Kathy says, "became our sixth family member." However, the couple hired skilled workers to undertake such large and difficult jobs as replacing the roof.

Architect Charles Maybury artfully changed the home's original mansard roof to its current steep roofline in 1890, adding dormers, gables, and balconies. The Christensons preserved Maybury's design when they had the home reroofed in 2006.

The graceful wraparound porch was added when Maybury redesigned the home. It had begun to sag and move away from the house by the time the Christensons moved in, so the couple had the porch reinforced and rebuilt.

Charles Maybury

By the time Charles Maybury undertook his Queen Anne transformation of the Windom-Hodgins House, he was well established as Winona's most successful architect. As such, he was one of the few architects in Minnesota in the late nineteenth century who managed to flourish away from the main population centers of Minneapolis–St. Paul and Duluth. Architecture has always been an urban profession, and in Minnesota—a state with one dominant metropolis—the vast majority of architects are to this day based in the Twin Cities.

Maybury hailed from New York state, where he was born in 1830, the son of a stonecutter who worked on the Erie Canal. After apprenticing with a builder for five years, Maybury struck out on his own for awhile before moving to Winona in 1856.

He quickly established himself as a contractor and builder in the growing riverfront community. Along the way, he learned how to design buildings as well as construct them. In 1865, Maybury gave up contracting in favor of architecture, and over the next forty years he designed scores of schools, churches, houses, commercial blocks, and public buildings in southeastern Minnesota and neighboring portions of Wisconsin.

One of Maybury's earliest designs in Winona, the Anger's Block (1872) on Walnut Street, still stands. Most of his surviving works, however, are from the 1880s and 1890s, a period when Winona and other Minnesota cities experienced rapid growth, providing plenty of work for architects. It was also in the early 1880s that his son, Jefferson, joined him as a partner.

Maybury's best known building is the Winona County Courthouse, a three-story monument in the Richardsonian Romanesque style completed in 1888 for the then-substantial sum of $120,000. Built with walls of locally quarried Dresbach limestone trimmed with red sandstone from the Lake Superior region, the courthouse is one of the finest of its era in Minnesota. It features a pair of towers, the tallest of which reaches to 136 feet, along with richly decorated interiors. In 1970, the courthouse became the first in Minnesota to be placed on the National Register of Historic Places. It was nearly lost in 2000 after a ceiling collapse and subsequent water leak caused massive interior damage. A $7 million restoration brought the building back to life, and it was rededicated in 2003.

Two of Maybury's other most notable designs in Winona are churches—the Basilica of St. Stanislaus Kostka (1894) and Central Methodist (1896). A fire in 1961 destroyed much of Maybury's work at Central Methodist, but the Romanesque Revival stone tower that remains is one of the most romantic pieces of architecture in Minnesota. Outside of Winona, Maybury's historically significant Minnesota buildings include the Houston County Courthouse (1885) in Caledonia. He also designed a pair of homes (both gone) for brothers William and Charles Mayo in Rochester.

The firm of Charles G. Maybury and Son remained in operation until 1905, when the elder Maybury retired and his son moved to Seattle to work as an architect. Maybury lived in Winona until his death in 1917 at age eighty-seven, leaving behind an enduring architectural legacy.

Charles G. Maybury, circa 1902. He practiced architecture in Winona for forty years and designed several of the city's most prominent buildings.

The front parlor in the base of the tower features a beamed ceiling, an angled picture window, and one of three downstairs fireplaces decorated with tiles made by the J. and J. G. Low Art Tile Works of Chelsea, Massachusetts.

Although the house was in generally sound structural shape, its long use as diocesan offices had led to partitioning and other interior changes, and much of its glorious cherry, maple, oak, pine, and walnut woodwork had been painted over more than once. Other decorative features were also in need of restoration. Exterior projects, in addition to the new roof, included chimney cleaning and repairs, fixing wall damage caused by an invasion of hungry carpenter ants, and a complete repainting. The front porch, which had begun to sag and move away from the house, demanded attention as well.

Kathy's photographic skills came in handy as she documented every stage of the work when she wasn't busy stripping wood, removing old

Across the hallway from the front parlor is another sitting room, with double doors that connect to both the hallway and the dining room. All of the main-floor rooms are trimmed with carved oak woodwork.

asbestos tile, or painting walls. The couple learned by doing. Dave turned himself into an expert wood refinisher, working on weekends and evenings or whenever he could find time away from his busy medical practice.

Nothing came easily, and Dave says even a seemingly simple task such as removing and cleaning brass door hinges took hours of effort. Restoring the home's decorative details was also a challenge. Two intricately carved wood pieces—a pediment above the front porch and an arched surround over the Palladian window in the attic—required particular care. Carpenters replaced damaged portions of the woodwork while Dave meticulously stripped old paint. Kathy then repainted the pieces to restore their original look. The couple's last big project—building a new bathroom on the second

The fireplace surround in the dining room is especially beautiful, with red-and-gold tiles and warm woodwork. The ornate oak staircase across the hallway is one of the home's loveliest features.

floor—was completed in 2009. "There's nothing definite to do now," Dave says, although maintenance is an eternal chore with a historic home.

In addition to her photographs, Kathy compiled a list of all of the work done at the house over a span of thirty-two years. Here's a sample entry covering the summers of 1989 and 1990:

Painted house.
Repaired north side, 3rd-floor balcony.
Replaced front porch floor—removed railing, stored in garage, removed pillars.
Supported roof.
Rebuilt foundation piers.
Placed 2 30-foot I beams under porch floor.
Removed pediment triangle over front entry; Dave began stripping it indoors in December 1990.
Opened semi-circle in south 2nd-floor porch.

Was it all worth it? The Christensons' answer is a resounding *yes*. "We never felt like abandoning it," Dave says, and one especially sweet fruit of their labors was the way it brought the family together. Their boys not only took on all manner of work but also learned so much in the process that one went on to become an architect. The family's preservation effort has produced a house that not only is beautiful inside and out but also shines with a pride of ownership borne of hard work.

The home's many charms begin at the double front doors, which lead into a vestibule, where stained- and beveled-glass transoms bring in welcome light. Past the vestibule is a long central hall defined by buttery oak wainscoting. Like many large Victorians, the house has a surprisingly open feel, its downstairs rooms connected to one another and the hall via broad openings outfitted with pocket doors. Two front parlors flank the hall, with a dining room farther down on the right. The main staircase is across from the dining room, while a kitchen and a billiard room occupy the rear of the house.

All but one of the four bedrooms on the second floor feature restored etched- and beveled-glass double walnut doors that were salvaged from the old Windom House and used as part of the 1890 rebuilding.

Like many large Victorians, the house has a surprisingly open feel, its downstairs rooms connected to one another and the hall via broad openings outfitted with pocket doors.

One of the most delightful rooms is a front parlor that takes in the base of the tower at the southeast corner of the house. It features a beamed ceiling (as does the dining room), an angled picture window, and one of three downstairs fireplaces decorated with gorgeous tiles made by the J. and J. G. Low Art Tile Works of Chelsea, Massachusetts. The company, which flourished in the late nineteenth and early twentieth centuries, made a variety of tiles and also became known for its design of elaborate tile soda fountains (one of which sold for $17,000 at auction in 2011).

The second front parlor includes a semicircular bay with three windows (a feature that appears to have been retained from the Windom House) and ornate plasterwork around the ceiling. Double doors connect this parlor to the dining room, which features an especially striking fireplace surround made of gold-and-red tile. All of the chief rooms on the first floor are trimmed with crisply carved woodwork that displays delicate beads, dentils, and other ornamental motifs.

The home's woodwork reaches its apogee at the main staircase, which is all oak. Elegantly turned balusters set between grids of chunky posts form the distinctive rail, while paneled wainscoting lines the walls opposite. Stained-glass windows illuminate a wide landing at the turn of the stairs and create different patterns of light throughout the day. There are four main bedrooms on the second floor, all but one of which feature double walnut doors with etched- and beveled-glass windows. These doors came from the old Windom House and were salvaged as part of the 1890 rebuilding.

One of the many stories the Christensons tell about their long years of work concerns a finial that crowns the steep roof atop the home's octagonal tower. When the time came to put another new roof on the house in 2006, the finial was removed and then later reinstalled. But as the reroofing job was about to wrap up, Kathy dreamed one night that the finial was crooked. The next day, she went out for a better look. "It *was* crooked," she says. The Christensons had gotten to know all of the roofers, and one of them quickly agreed to shinny up the tower roof. He adjusted the finial ever so slightly, and all was right with the world.

Out of such small details, and such deep caring, come great houses. ❧

The French Second Empire–style William Windom House before its transformation in 1890.

Opposite: A second-floor bedroom nestles into the tower. Throughout the house the Christensons have appointed the rooms with original antiques and artful replicas to preserve its turn-of-the-century charm.

WILLIAM WINDOM/ABNER HODGINS HOUSE ℚ 107

William and Mary LeDuc House

Hastings, 1865

Colonel William LeDuc in his Union army uniform, 1863. Away at war, he faced many challenges in building his new home in Hastings.

Opposite: "A Cottage in the Rhine Style" is how Andrew Jackson Downing, author of *Cottage Residences,* described the Gothic Revival design William and Mary LeDuc chose for their house. They built it out of limestone quarried in nearby Red Wing, Minnesota.

I N OCTOBER OF 1863, AS COLONEL WILLIAM GATES LEDUC, A QUAR- termaster in the Union's Army of the Cumberland, worked furiously to supply forty thousand troops besieged by Confederate forces in Chatta- nooga, Tennessee, he was in the midst of a far more personal campaign back home in Minnesota. He was trying to build a new house in the grow- ing young town of Hastings. It promised to be quite the place, and in the end it was—a pure Gothic Revival fantasy with no equal in Minnesota. But the work wasn't progressing as quickly or affordably as LeDuc had hoped, and each week seemed to bring some new construction crisis.

The outlook in Tennessee, by contrast, soon brightened. LeDuc and his men transformed an old wooden scow into a makeshift steamboat, loaded it with provisions, and in the dead of night ran it past Confederate lines. The Union army went on to win a dramatic victory at Chattanooga, but LeDuc would have to wait until war's end to see his house brought to completion.

LeDuc was used to waiting. A powerful belief in the possibilities of the future had always been his strong suit, and even in old age he never aban- doned his hope of better days to come. Protean and restless, he lived his long life as a series of improvisations, caroming from one money-making scheme to another. Success more often than not eluded him, however, and for many years he and his family teetered at the brink of insolvency. One of the chief wonders of his four-thousand-square-foot stone mansion is how he managed to pay for it, since it ultimately cost $30,000, a fortune in Min- nesota in the 1860s. LeDuc was far from possessing such riches at the time, and on several occasions he sought to sell the house as his finances grew ever more precarious.

LeDuc was forty-five years old when he and his family moved into the house in 1865, and he had already led a variety of lives by then. Born in 1823 in Ohio, he was the only child of Henri LeDuc, a onetime French army officer who had fought in the American Revolution, and Mary Sumner LeDuc, also from a military background. After graduating from Kenyon

With its high-hatted tower, curling wood trim, arched and trefoil windows, side porches, and pleasing ramble of gables and dormers, the house has the exotic look of old-world Europe.

College—where he met his wife to be, Mary Bronson—he studied law for a time in Mt. Vernon, Ohio, Mary's hometown. But he wasn't ready to settle down there, and in 1850 he headed off to St. Paul, then the largest city in the recently created Minnesota Territory.

In 1851 LeDuc started his business career by opening the first bookstore in St. Paul. That same year, he returned to Ohio to marry. Back in St. Paul with Mary, LeDuc soon took on a variety of business ventures that included railroading, construction, land development, and bridge building. Farming, however, eventually proved to be his steadiest source of income. In 1854, while still living in St. Paul, LeDuc made an investment that would change his life. For $4,000, he acquired a quarter stake in the new town site

Mary LeDuc, 1863. Like her husband, she was not in Hastings during much of the time the home was under construction, living instead with her mother in Ohio.

of Hastings. The town, which offered a good location on the west bank of the Mississippi River about twenty miles south of St. Paul, was named after its most prominent backer, Henry Hastings Sibley, who in 1858 became the newly minted state of Minnesota's first governor.

Early in 1856, LeDuc also acquired a flour mill in Hastings at the falls of the Vermillion River. The next year, LeDuc and his family moved to Hastings so he could tend to his business interests there. A substantial plot of land had come with the flour mill, and it was on this property at 1629 Vermillion Street that the LeDucs later built their new home. Because the property was a mile and a half from the center of Hastings, which clung to the Mississippi River in its early days, the mansion was quite isolated, especially during the snowbound winter months.

When the LeDucs began planning their home in about 1860, they already had three children—daughters Elizabeth and Florence and son Willie—the oldest of whom was eight. A fourth and final child, Alice, was born in 1868. The size of the family dictated a house big enough to accommodate four bedrooms while providing an ample attic for servants' quarters and storage.

Like so many other couples of the time, they found their domestic dream in Andrew Jackson Downing's *Cottage Residences*, one of the most influential books of its kind in American history. A native of the Hudson River region in New York, Downing started out as a gardener and nurseryman, but his interests soon extended to architecture. In 1841 Downing published his first book, on landscape gardening. *Cottage Residences*, written in collaboration with architect Alexander Jackson Davis, came out the next year and went through multiple editions. The LeDucs owned a copy of the third edition, which was published in 1851, a year before Downing died heroically at age thirty-six while trying to rescue victims of a steamboat accident on the Hudson.

Downing's chief purpose was to spread a gospel of good design in the building of rural houses, or "cottages," as he preferred to call them. In the book's introduction, he wrote: "I wish to inspire all persons with a love of beautiful forms. . . . I wish them to appreciate how superior is the charm of that home where we discover the tasteful cottage or villa, and the well designed and neatly kept garden or grounds, full of beauty and harmony . . . not the less beautiful and harmonious, because simple and limited; and to become aware that these superior forms . . . may be had at the same cost and with the same labor as a clumsy dwelling and its uncouth and ill-designed accessories."

To illustrate his theme, Downing offered twenty-five examples of what he considered to be well-designed country homes, all in picturesque styles—Italianate, French Second Empire, and Gothic Revival—that by

Minnesota Gothic

Although the style of William LeDuc's Gothic Revival house can ultimately be traced back to the architecture of medieval Europe, its most influential ancestors are of later origin. What is generally regarded as the earliest Gothic Revival house dates to 1749, when Horace Walpole began remodeling his large estate, known as Strawberry Hill, in Twickenham, England, just outside London. Walpole was a rich dilettante who in 1764 wrote *The Castle of Otranto*, considered to be the first Gothic novel, a literary genre whose later practitioners included Edgar Allan Poe. Walpole spent decades transforming Strawberry Hill into a Gothic fantasy complete with towers and battlements. It wasn't long before other members of the English aristocracy followed suit by building Gothic estates of their own.

In the United States, churches displaying Gothic features were built as early as the 1700s, but it wasn't until the 1830s that a simplified version of the style was applied to houses. Alexander Jackson Davis, coauthor of *Cottage Residences*, source of the LeDuc House's design, was an early proponent of the Gothic style. His first Gothic Revival design was Glen Allen, a country estate built near Baltimore in 1833 and razed in 1929. But it was Davis's book, written in collaboration with Andrew Jackson Downing, that popularized the so-called Gothic cottage, a modest middle-class house sporting pointed-arch doors and windows, steep roofs, decorative bargeboards, and in some cases, towers. In its simplest form, this type of home was built of wood in a style that is sometimes called Carpenter Gothic. Another highly decorated variation is known as Steamboat Gothic, after the gaudy paddle-wheelers that once plied American rivers.

Davis and Downing emphasized "rural cottages" in their works, and as a result Gothic Revival never became an especially popular urban style. Nor did it gain wide currency in Minnesota, in part because the style was already becoming passé by the time much of the state was settled, as other picturesque styles, such as Italianate and French Second Empire, grew more fashionable.

Even so, Minnesota retains a small number of high-quality Gothic Revival houses, both in the Twin Cities and outstate. Minneapolis's best-preserved Gothic Revival home is the Cutter-Gilfillan House (now occupied by a fraternity), located on Tenth Avenue Southeast near the University of Minnesota campus. The oldest portion of the house, which is of wood-frame construction, dates to 1856. Across the river in St. Paul, the Knox House of 1860 in the Irvine Park neighborhood features vertical board-and-batten siding, a hallmark of the Carpenter Gothic style. St. Paul was also once home to a peculiar pair of small Gothic houses known as Dodge's Alpine Cottages. They were built in 1866 by a man with the wonderful name of Ossian Euclid Dodge, on property overlooking Rice Park where the St. Paul Hotel now stands. The cottages, alas, were torn down in 1915.

A few notable Gothic Revival homes also survive in greater Minnesota. Among them is the Willard Bunnell House of 1858 in Homer, not far from Winona. Another outstanding example is the E. St. Julien Cox House in St. Peter, which was built in 1871 and includes a corner tower. Both the Bunnell and Cox homes are today maintained by county historical societies as museum houses and are open for public tours.

The St. Julien Cox House, St. Peter, 1975. Built in 1871, it's one of only a small number of Gothic Revival–style homes remaining in Minnesota.

At the heart of the home's simple but sturdy interior is a graceful staircase with spindled banisters.

The wood-clad carriage house/barn complements the family mansion on the LeDuc Historic Estate, which is now owned by the City of Hastings and managed by the Dakota County Historical Society.

the late 1830s had begun to challenge the long reign of Greek Revival in America. One of Downing's featured designs, number fourteen, was called "A Cottage in the Rhine Style," and it was this plan the LeDucs decided to build, with one key change. Mary LeDuc wanted to reorient some of the rooms, so she traced the home as shown in Downing's book, put her tracing against a window, and then redrew the image on the back of the paper so it came out in reverse.

The "cottage" the LeDucs decided to construct had actually been designed and built for Joel T. Headley, a popular author of the day and one of Downing's neighbors in New York. In style, it was pure Gothic Revival, featuring steep gables and dormers adorned with lacy bargeboards, bracketed eaves, front and side porches, a pointed-arch entry, and a three-story central tower culminating in a flared saddle roof. Inside, the house offered a pinwheeling floor plan reflecting its irregular profile. The first-floor plan included an adjoining library and dining room (both sixteen by twenty feet) to one side of a central hall and staircase, with a slightly larger drawing room on the other side and a kitchen at the rear. There were four bedrooms, a bathroom, and a small dressing room on the second floor.

An arched bay in the stately front parlor brings copious natural light into the mansion's most robust room.

The simple dining room originally boasted pine woodwork, floors, and fireplace surrounds. The painting above the soapstone fireplace, which was added by a later owner, depicts two of the LeDucs' daughters, Florence and Alice.

"Though spirited and irregular in composition, it is simple in details," Downing wrote of the house, the "object being to erect a picturesque rural home . . . without the least unnecessary outlay for decoration." Headley's house, which still stands in what is today New Windsor, New York, was built of brick, but for their version the LeDucs chose limestone quarried from nearby river bluffs. It's not known how many of Downing's Rhine-style cottages were built, but the Headley and LeDuc houses are believed to be the only surviving examples in the United States.

Today, the house is known as the LeDuc Historic Estate. Owned by the City of Hastings and managed by the Dakota County Historical Society, it's open for public tours and special events from May through October, offering visitors an opportunity to see the best and most intact example of a Gothic Revival country estate in Minnesota. Set amid four-and-a-half-acre grounds that include a historic carriage barn and icehouse, the mansion could hardly be more picturesque. With its buff walls of Red Wing limestone, high-hatted tower, curling wood trim, arched and trefoil windows, side porches, and pleasing ramble of gables and dormers, the house has the exotic look of a small piece of the Old World magically transported to Minnesota. At night, preferably with a full moon posted overhead, it may also be the state's spookiest-looking house.

Inside, the show isn't quite as spectacular, simply because the LeDucs lacked the wherewithal to create the kind of epic sumptuousness found in later Victorian mansions. The main entrance, at the base of the tower, opens into a vestibule with double inner doors and a pointed-arch fanlight. The hall beyond holds a staircase that rises in a single flight to the second floor. As built, all of the downstairs rooms featured pine woodwork, floors, and fireplace surrounds, and the decorative details throughout are quite modest. A stately front parlor with an arched bay that brings in copious natural light is the mansion's most robust room. The south-facing library, where LeDuc spent much of his later years, is also impressive. Many of the home's windows are equipped with an ingenious feature—interior shutters that fold into side pockets when not in use.

The four family bedrooms upstairs are good sized, averaging about sixteen by twenty feet. The second-floor bathroom in its original form was literally just that—a room used for bathing. There was no running water, so a maid had to bring up buckets of heated water to fill the zinc-lined tub. The attic was used mostly for storage but did include an observation room in the tower where LeDuc could survey the town site he partially owned.

Although the house is not exceptionally large, its construction was an ordeal that consumed nearly four years. The LeDucs began by hiring St. Paul architect Augustus F. Knight to draw up plans based on those in Downing's book. Work got under way in 1862, just as William volunteered to serve in the Civil War. Mary and the couple's three children were soon gone as well. Lonesome without her husband, Mary decided to live out the war with her mother in Ohio. With no one from the family on site to oversee construction, the LeDucs were asking for trouble and they got it. Their first contractor abruptly quit the job in 1863, forcing LeDuc to make a quick trip home. He then hired a young master carpenter from Hastings named Eri Cogshall as the new contractor.

The south-facing library, where Colonel William Gates LeDuc spent much of his later years, is a masculine room, from which he launched his many ill-fated money-making schemes.

George Washington Daniels

George Washington Daniels was born in Georgia about 1845 to slaves Moses and Amanda Daniels. As a slave, he was conscripted into the Confederate army during the Civil War, but at the end of one particular battle, he feigned death and later escaped to the Union army, where he served for the remainder of the war. There, he worked diligently for Colonel William Gates LeDuc in the Quartermaster Corps, and the two men formed a bond of mutual trust.

After the war, LeDuc hired Daniels to transport his horses from Washington, D.C., to Hastings. Once that mission was accomplished, Daniels moved into the carriage barn behind the LeDuc home and began work as a hired hand on two nearby farms owned by the family. William LeDuc mentioned Daniels often in his diaries and clearly held his employee in high esteem.

Daniels married Georgia-born Chloe Hudson in 1872 at the Methodist Episcopal Church in Prescott, Wisconsin, and they took up residence in a small home on the LeDuc property. The Danielses were one of only a few black families in Hastings at the time.

LeDuc and Daniels eventually came to an agreement in which Daniels would manage both farms. According to the Dakota County Historical Society's publication *An American Gothic* (2004), the arrangement was this: "On the Four Mile Farm [Daniels] had full use of the existing livestock and equipment in exchange for half the produce at the end of the three-year lease. On the Six Mile Farm, two miles further west of Hastings, Daniels was paid for his labor."

In 1884, Daniels and his family set out to homestead their own farm in Brookings County, South Dakota, where they thrived. There, they were active in local churches and schools and raised a large family (reports vary as to how large). They eventually sold the farm in 1912 and attempted to reestablish roots in Georgia. But within a few years racism drove them back to South Dakota, where they remained until Daniels's death in 1921 at over ninety years of age. Chloe died in 1929 and was remembered fondly in the *Brookings County Press*.

George Daniels, who escaped from the Confederate army as a slave, managed LeDuc's two farms and later established a homestead in South Dakota.

Cogshall quickly discovered that Knight's plans were so poorly detailed that, as he put it in a letter to LeDuc, "No mechanic could build from them unless he went . . . upon his own judgement." Another architect, Abraham Radcliffe, was called in to redraw the plans, at a cost of twenty dollars. Cogshall had to cope with numerous other predicaments, including a shortage of building stone, unexpectedly high costs for some materials, and a potential strike by laborers. All through construction, LeDuc maintained a three-way correspondence with Cogshall in Hastings and Mary in Ohio. Mary was very involved in the process, sometimes urging her husband to reject cost-saving measures sought by the contractor.

The family finally moved into the unfinished house in August of 1865, following LeDuc's discharge from the Union army. By then, the home's initial cost estimate of $5,000 was a nostalgic fiction, leaving the family house rich and cash poor. The home's high cost was a constant worry. At one point, LeDuc wrote to Mary, "I see very plainly that the house will take all I can earn." He added that if "everything goes well in our farming we may get through without embarrassing ourselves with debt of which we cannot yet entirely clear."

The house was complete by January of 1866, but the LeDucs weren't able at first to fully furnish it. The front parlor and one bedroom were left bare until late that year, when Mary inherited many fine items from her late mother's estate. Although often hard up for cash, the family remained in the house for the next eleven years, as LeDuc continued to try his hand at one scheme after another, including a mining venture in Utah.

The four family bedrooms are good sized and furnished appropriately with antique pieces.

All the while he was also maneuvering for a position with the federal government. He succeeded in 1877, when he was named U.S. commissioner of agriculture by his old military friend and fellow Ohioan President Rutherford B. Hayes. The LeDucs moved to Washington, D.C., for the next four years and closed up their mansion. They briefly returned in September of 1878 to host an event for the president, who visited Hastings as part of an agricultural tour. Hayes "partook of splendid collation" at the mansion, as a local newspaper quaintly described the event, before continuing his tour.

The family returned to Hastings in 1881 after LeDuc lost his position in Washington. The years that followed were difficult, with money constantly in short supply. Mary, in particular, was anxious to move elsewhere. In an 1885 letter she wrote that the family had to "get out of Hastings—we are all going to waste." LeDuc, too, was unhappy, and like many another Minnesotan, he entertained California dreams. "How I wish we were all planted there," he wrote in 1893, "and rooted so as to make a living from the fruit-producing soil under the shadow of our own vines and fig trees."

Although the dream faded over time, LeDuc continued his incessant travels in pursuit of the one new thing that would at last secure his fortune. In 1904 the eighty-one-year-old LeDuc was still on the road, chasing a coal deal in Tacoma, Washington, when Mary died. He didn't make it back to Hastings for the funeral, perhaps not all that surprising in view of how much time over the years he and his wife had spent apart.

By the time of Mary's death, most of LeDuc's income still came from a pair of farms he owned a few miles west of Hastings. The farms had been run since 1874 by another remarkable character, George Daniels, a former slave who had accompanied LeDuc back to Hastings after the Civil War. Another source of family income was Hastings Needle Work, a company founded in 1901 by two of LeDuc's daughters, Florence and Alice. The company made high-quality hand-stitched items prized by customers as far away as Boston and New York.

In a startling bit of good fortune that could also be regarded as a cruel irony, LeDuc's long financial struggles abruptly ended in 1916 when he received a $100,000 bequest from the estate of Julia Butterfield, widow of General Daniel Butterfield, a Civil War hero best known for composing "Taps," the most famous of all bugle calls. In his postwar business career, however, Butterfield was a notoriously shifty customer who, his widow believed, badly cheated LeDuc in a railroad scheme. The $100,000 bequest was thus a form of atonement. LeDuc was ninety-three when he received the money, and it allowed him to pay off all of his debts and help provide for his children and grandchildren before his death in 1918.

After LeDuc's death, Florence and Alice stayed on in the house, but by the 1920s they were using it only as a summer residence because it was

The authentic period stove in the kitchen emphasizes the old-fashioned lifestyle of Minnesota in 1865, when the LeDucs moved into their still-unfinished house.

so hard to keep warm during the winter months. Florence died in 1929, leaving Alice as the sole owner. By the late 1930s, however, the hard-to-maintain old house appeared headed for tax forfeiture. A Hastings man named Carroll Simmons was renting the house at that time as a seasonal home for his antique business, and in 1940 he bought the place.

Dubbing his new acquisition Chateau LeDuc, Simmons gradually upgraded the home's mechanical, heating, and electrical systems and made other improvements. He also altered the interior by installing new chandeliers and wood flooring in some rooms and replacing three pine fireplace mantels with soapstone surrounds, all the while operating his antiques business from the home.

By the 1950s, as Hastings gained population, a developer voiced interest in buying the mansion and tearing it down to make way for a shopping center. The idea sparked opposition because of the house's exceptional historic and architectural significance, and the shopping center plan failed to advance. Instead, in 1958, the year of Minnesota's centennial, Simmons agreed to donate the home to the Minnesota Historical Society but retained the right to stay in the house as long as he wished. It was the first historic home acquired by the society.

Today, the house remains a much-loved landmark along busy U.S. Highway 61 in Hastings. It's also a testament to the enduring power of a dream that came to life more than 150 years ago when Mary LeDuc, longing as so many still do for a beautiful place to call home, put a sheet of tracing paper against a windowpane and began to draw. ⌇

Mary LeDuc saw the plan for "A Cottage in the Rhine Style" in *Cottage Residences,* a book by Andrew Jackson Downing and Alexander Jackson Davis. She put the plan up to her window and traced it, thereby reversing the layout.

William Sawtry House and Recreation Hall

Stillwater, 1881, 1902

William Sauntry. Born in Ireland and raised in Canada, Sauntry became a partner in a lumber company five years after moving to Stillwater.

Opposite: William Sauntry enlarged his Victorian home several times until it became a twenty-eight-room mansion. He also built a magnificent recreation hall at the rear of the property.

M ORE SO THAN ANY OTHER CITY IN MINNESOTA, STILLWATER HAS THE feel of a Victorian time capsule, a place still saturated in its history as a logging boomtown where fortunes flowed down from the pineries of the St. Croix River Valley. The lumbermen who consumed the valley's treasure within a span of fifty years were a roughhewn lot, and their names—Staples, Hersey, Bean, and McKusick, among many others—still resonate in Stillwater by virtue of their association with the numerous mansions strung along the city's high, steep hills. In many ways, the most fascinating home of all, which includes a grand folly that evokes the exotic architecture of Moorish Spain, was built by William Sauntry, who at the height of his career in the 1880s was said to be worth a tidy $2 million.

Sauntry, whose relatives included a crooning first cousin named Bing Crosby, was one of six children born to an impoverished farm family in County Cork, Ireland. His father died when he was very young, and his mother—who must have been a woman of remarkable strength—managed to immigrate with the entire family to New Brunswick, Canada. There, Sauntry gained his first experience as a lumberjack. In the late 1860s Sauntry and other members of his family relocated once again—this time to Stillwater. Sauntry, who was then in his early twenties, soon found employment in the woods, where he handled teams of oxen and was also a river driver, extremely perilous work that required maneuvering logs through fast-flowing water.

Physically strong, hardworking, and eager for advancement, Sauntry within five years became a partner in a lumber company. Later, he branched out into other enterprises, including part ownership of the Stillwater Boom Company, which managed a site just north of the city where logs coming down the St. Croix were sorted and then sent on to their ultimate destinations. By the 1880s Sauntry was associated with Frederick Weyerhaeuser,

Current owners Thomas and Sandra Lynum have turned the mansion into a welcoming bed-and-breakfast. Their dedication to authentic restoration is reflected in the home's finely detailed front entry.

Minnesota's Victorian City

The William Sauntry Mansion is one of hundreds of nineteenth-century homes that line the streets of Stillwater, which might well be called Minnesota's Victorian City. No other community of its size in Minnesota comes close to matching Stillwater as a place to experience the colorful gamut of Victorian styles embodied in houses large and small. Many of the biggest homes are located in the North Hill and South Hill neighborhoods, which rise to either side of long ravines that lead up from the downtown riverfront. All told, the city has more than one hundred designated "heirloom" homes, including a half dozen listed on the National Register of Historic Places. Vintage brick buildings in the downtown area further reinforce the city's appeal to history-minded residents and visitors.

The stellar quality of Stillwater's architectural legacy is a direct result of the city's prosperity as a lumbering center during the second half of the nineteenth century. Minnesota had no gold rush to speak of, but its virgin stands of timber attracted numerous fortune seekers from the 1830s onward. It's hard now to appreciate just how vast and lucrative the lumbering business was in the days of the great northern pineries, but a man like Sauntry, at his peak, was worth upwards of $30 million in today's dollars, and he was not Stillwater's wealthiest citizen. By the 1850s, timber money wafted through Stillwater like sawdust, supporting not only a bevy of millionaires but also a well-off middle class who built fine homes. The presence of a major public institution—the state prison—helped enrich the community as well.

Founded in the 1840s, Stillwater grew steadily until 1900, when its population approached thirteen thousand, making it the state's fourth-largest city. Because new houses were being built in Stillwater during much of the nineteenth century, the city's residential neighborhoods today offer a bit of everything: small Greek Revival cottages from the 1850s, Italianate and French Second Empire homes from the 1860s and 1870s, and many ornate Queen Annes from the 1880s and 1890s. Several lumber barons, including Sauntry, built costly homes in North Hill, but the South Hill neighborhood also attracted wealthy builders. Albert Lammers, another lumberman, completed a mansion on South Third Street in 1893 that remains one of Stillwater's chief Queen Anne landmarks. Not surprisingly, most of the city's Victorian houses are built of wood, a material that—to say the least—was readily available.

There's one other factor that helps explain why Stillwater retains such an outstanding collection of historic homes. As the forests north and east of the city were cut down, a task largely completed by the early 1900s, the city's boom days abruptly ended. Between 1900 and 1920, Stillwater's population plummeted by a third, to just under eight thousand people. The population would remain stagnant for the next forty years. No growth meant little development pressure, and so Stillwater simply sat, an old logging town where little changed. A few historic mansions were lost to demolition or fire, but most of the city's housing stock—like old logs preserved at the bottom of a deep, cold lake—proved indestructible.

Once Stillwater began to grow again in the 1960s, much of the new development occurred in the western part of the city well beyond the older neighborhoods. Then came the historic preservation movement of the 1970s, which found fertile ground in Stillwater as a new generation discovered its magnificent Victorian legacy.

The Albert Lammers House, Stillwater, 1965. Completed in 1893, it's one of many mansions built by Stillwater's nineteenth-century lumber barons.

This elevation shows the Sauntry House as it now stands, after Sauntry's two decades of expansion and remodeling.

As befitting the lumberman who built it, the Sauntry Mansion is filled with fine woodwork, including red birch, walnut, cherry, and oak. The music room's patterned wall coverings, like those throughout the house, are replicas of originals from the same time period.

the richest of all lumbermen, managing his interests in and around Stillwater for many years.

In 1881 Sauntry married Eunice Tozer, who was related to his first partner in the lumber business, David Tozer. Sauntry by then had completed a new house on a block-deep lot at 626 North Fourth Street in Stillwater's North Hill neighborhood. He was in good company. Just two blocks away, on North Second Street, the city's wealthiest pioneer lumber baron, Isaac Staples, resided in a towering French Second Empire home (gone) that was considered to be the city's most magnificent mansion. In its initial form, Sauntry's house hardly qualified as magnificent. It wasn't especially large—about two thousand square feet—nor was it very distinctive. Like many houses of the time, it offered an unabashed mélange of styles, incorporating elements of Eastlake, Italianate, and Gothic Revival into its overall composition.

Over the next two decades, however, Sauntry transformed his once-modest dwelling into one of Stillwater's largest homes. He pushed out walls here and there, enlarged the front porch to become a sweeping wraparound, and literally raised the roof in 1893 to create a new attic after a fire burned through the old one. He also undertook numerous interior renovations.

By the time Sauntry was done, the house had ballooned to a seven-thousand-square-foot mansion with twenty-eight rooms spread over three floors. The house's complex construction history is evident in its rambling profile of bays, towers, porches, gables, and dormers. An ornamental panel beneath the front gable, bands of dentil work, and a pair of carved pediments over the front porch provide a limited amount of exterior adornment. Over the years the house has shed a few decorative features, including a small balcony above the porch and all of its roof cresting, but it was never as ornate as some of Stillwater's other Victorian-era homes.

Sauntry was still fiddling with the house in the early 1900s when he made his most significant addition to the property in the form of a recreation hall, or "gymnasium," as the newspapers of the day described it. Built at 625 North Fifth Street in what had once been the property's rear yard, it quickly became more of a landmark than the mansion itself. Today, the house and recreation hall, which has been converted into a residence, are under separate ownership, as they have been for many years. Both were added to the National Register of Historic Places in 1982.

The main house, now formally known as the William Sauntry Mansion, has been owned since 1999 by Thomas and Sandra Lynum, who operate it as a bed-and-breakfast inn. Under their stewardship, the sprawling house has been what every big Victorian always seems to be—a work in progress. Performing much of the work themselves, the Lynums have renovated the downstairs rooms one at a time while refashioning those upstairs

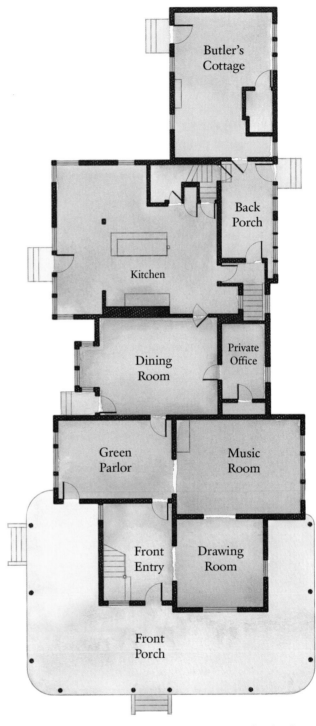

In its initial form, the Sauntry House measured only about two thousand square feet. By the time Sauntry was finished expanding the home, it had ballooned into a seven-thousand-square-foot mansion.

Lumber Kings of the St. Croix Valley

In a shockingly short amount of time—between 1840 and 1914—the white pine forests of northeast Minnesota and northwest Wisconsin were devoured by an explosive lumber industry, changing the region forever. The St. Croix River Valley, thick with white pine and threaded with tributaries, provided lumber companies with both resources and direct shipping access to the Mississippi, and therefore to all U.S. markets. So it was along the St. Croix's banks that the industry flourished, creating instant millionaires and ecological disasters.

One of those lumber barons was William Sauntry, who, through a complicated arrangement, hitched his wagon to the most powerful name in the business, Frederick Weyerhaeuser, a German immigrant and corporate genius. Well before Sauntry's arrival, pioneer foresters made treaties with the native Ojibwe and Dakota to begin acquiring logging rights. These early lumbermen devised methods of hauling felled trees from the forests along ice roads by ox- or horse-driven sleds and floating them downriver to pop-up sawmills, where they were turned into lumber and rafted down the Mississippi to St. Louis.

Earliest reports of the seemingly inexhaustible pine forests came by word of French explorer and scientist Joseph N. Nicollet, who ventured up the St. Croix in 1837. Joseph Renville Brown, a former fur trader, was already busy there, more than willing to switch from fur to lumber. After the Treaty of 1837, logging began in earnest. Most of the lumbermen came from New England and Canada, where the industry had already taken root. Franklin Steele and John McKusick were among the first, establishing Stillwater as their base. Isaac Staples, a seasoned lumberman from Maine, coaxed Samuel Freeman Hersey to join him in a Stillwater endeavor. Others, including Orange Walker and Asa Parker, came up from the Lower Mississippi to claim land that would become the town of Marine on St. Croix.

McKusick's mill was powered by water wheel, but Staples brought steam engines into the mix. Other innovations rapidly followed, as axes were replaced by crosscut saws, gang saws, circular saws, and steam-driven saws. Staples ventured into associated businesses such as distribution, wholesaling, retailing, banking, and eventually railroads. He also owned large farms that provided food for his logging camps. Supplying alcohol—lots of alcohol—was another camp-related business.

The log prospectors were a world unto themselves. River-based log-sorting, log-holding, and log-channeling activities gave rise to companies such as the St. Croix Boom, just north of Stillwater. By 1890 the boom had sent 452,360,890 feet of logs to sawmills downriver. The lumber barons, meanwhile, built elaborate Victorian mansions, such as Sauntry's, in and around Stillwater.

Yet the lucrative lumber industry came at a heavy price. The pine forests were depleted, replaced by fast-growing pulpwood. The piles of branches left in the wake of logging caused forest fires to break out on a lethal scale, including the horrendous Hinckley Fire of 1894, which claimed more than four hundred lives.

Logs piled up at the Stillwater levee, 1904. Within a few years the city's once booming lumber trade would come to an end.

to serve as guest bedrooms and suites. Thomas says the goal has always been "to maintain the historic integrity of the house," a tricky proposition given the home's tangled history of remodeling and the fact that no original floor plans are known to exist.

In addition to renovating the house inside and out, the Lynums have landscaped its spacious grounds along Fourth Street. A small pool and fountain, retaining walls, walkways, and gardens combine to create one of Stillwater's prettiest yards. During Sauntry's tenure in the house, the grounds included a tennis court, built in 1889, but it was long gone by the time the Lynums acquired the property.

The home's interior, which embraces every kind of surface except a plain one, perfectly expresses the Victorian love of visual plenitude. The first floor—which includes a front entry hall with staircase, two parlors, a dining room, a music room, and a kitchen—features stained- and beveled-glass windows, parquet floors, four tile fireplaces with elaborate carved- and turned-wood mantels, stenciling, and richly patterned replica period wall coverings. Sandra handled many of the redecorating chores, a long and exacting labor that has brought the home's once-faded interiors back to vibrant life. As befitting the lumberman who built it, the house does not stint on woodwork. Red birch, walnut, cherry, and oak are among the species represented. The dining room offers some of the finest woodwork, with paneled wainscoting and a built-in red birch sideboard.

Upstairs, the house is something of a puzzle, reflecting its longtime use as apartments, starting in the 1930s, well after the Sauntrys were gone. The long hallway here takes an unexpected jog, and the Lynums aren't sure exactly how all of the bedrooms were originally arranged. There are now four guest bedrooms and a suite on this floor. The Lynums occupy the home's enormous attic, where Sauntry once had a billiards room.

The house, however, wasn't sufficient to fulfill all of Sauntry's dreams, and in about 1900 he began laying plans for the recreation hall. Buildings like the hall were not unheard of at the time—another Stillwater lumber baron, George Atwood, had a gymnasium in his house—but they were very rare. In the Twin Cities area, at least one other private recreation hall of comparable size was built, but not until 1914, as part of the Charles Wales estate in suburban Bloomington. That building, demolished in 1933, was far more utilitarian than Sauntry's 4,800-square-foot structure, which drew its inspiration from the last and greatest of Spain's Moorish palaces, the Alhambra.

Sauntry's decision to model his recreation hall on a fourteenth-century Moorish palace seems today like an odd choice. It was, but it's also worth noting that by the time Sauntry built his fanciful structure, the Moorish Revival style, as it's usually called, already had a long history in the

The home's elaborately carved stairway is surrounded by the lush details of restored Victoriana: stenciled ceilings, patterned wall coverings, parquet floors, and a unique, stepped-up radiator.

This beautiful red-tile fireplace, located in what was originally the mansion's billiards room, typifies the Victorians' love of decorative surfaces.

United States. Washington Irving's *Tales of the Alhambra*, published in 1832, helped popularize the style, and in 1848 showman P. T. Barnum built the nation's first Moorish Revival mansion in Connecticut (the house stood for only ten years before burning down). In Minnesota, Moorish Revival made its debut in the 1880s via the work of Minneapolis decorator John Bradstreet. A few homes, most notably the Bardwell-Farrant House (1890) in south Minneapolis, also adopted the style, which enjoyed another revival in the 1920s.

It's likely that Sauntry visited the Alhambra before ordering up his own mini-version, since he was known to have traveled widely. Some sources say he even sent craftspeople to Spain to make molds from portions of the Alhambra's ornament. Regardless of whether that happened, Sauntry must have been a man in the grip of a deep infatuation when he built the recreation hall.

To create his Moorish fantasy, Sauntry hired the Chicago architectural firm of Wilson and Marshall. Why Sauntry selected Chicago architects, as opposed to ones closer at hand in the Twin Cities, is unknown. The firm's junior partner, Benjamin Marshall, probably handled the design work. Marshall, who later formed a successful partnership with Charles Fox, went on to design numerous theaters, hotels, and apartment buildings in Chicago as well as the largest private home ever built in Minneapolis, the short-lived Charles Gates House (1914–1933, razed) on Lake of the Isles.

Completed in 1902, the recreation hall at first glance resembles a park pavilion. Its hipped roof,

Another Moorish-style ballroom was built in 1911 in the attic of the Lewis Gillette House on Lowry Hill in Minneapolis. Both the home and ballroom were demolished in 1935.

Sauntry's 4,800-square-foot recreation hall drew its inspiration from the last and greatest of Spain's Moorish palaces, the Alhambra. Completed in 1902, the hall abounds in exotic details, many of which have been uncovered and brought back to life by current owners Marty and Judi Nora.

The main living area of the recreation hall is furnished with antiques and reproduction pieces from all over the world. Huge wall mirrors create the illusion that the room is even larger than it is.

wide bracketed eaves, and distinctive pebble-embedded stucco walls evoke the Arts and Crafts style. But the doors and windows, which culminate in striped horseshoe arches encircling stained-glass transoms, suggest the exotic wonders within.

A covered, bridge-like passageway (gone) originally led from the house to a balcony on the east side of the recreation hall. From there, visitors descended into a grand entry hall offering access to a tiled swimming pool, a bowling alley, and the building's astounding centerpiece—a thirty-by-forty-two-foot ballroom. Sauntry and his architects designed the ballroom to be a showstopper, and it is all of that: a glittering fantasy of mirrors, chandeliers, arcades, and intricate plaster arabesques. How much this Moorish extravaganza cost Sauntry is anyone's guess. The building permit, which puts the cost of the entire recreation hall at $7,000, is a fiction, but whatever Sauntry paid, he seems to have earned plenty of adulation for his efforts.

A reporter for the *Stillwater Gazette* was certainly impressed. In a story headlined "In Fairy Land," the reporter uncorked a long, if not especially grammatical, sentence to describe the hall's grand opening on September 19, 1902: "The soft, dazzling lights, radiating from the many colored globes of the chandeliers, exquisite in design and workmanship, caught the beauty of harmony and coloring, polished floors and rugs and draperies, all of Oriental design, reflected the scene, radiant with grace and beauty, again and again in the long mirrors extending from floor to ceiling." According to the article, William and Eunice Sauntry and their son, Beltram, greeted guests in a reception room as the Twin City Mandolin Club strummed background music. Dancing presumably ensued, but the article makes no mention of bowling or swimming.

It wasn't long before Sauntry's Moorish extravaganza had competition in Minnesota. In 1911, Minneapolis industrialist Lewis Gillette hired John Bradstreet to produce another salute to the Alhambra in the attic of Gillette's Lowry Hill mansion. Long and narrow, the ballroom wasn't quite as spectacular as Sauntry's version. It was demolished with the Gillette House in 1935.

Sauntry's ballroom didn't survive for long in its original form. A few years after his death in 1914, the house and hall were split into separate properties. In 1920, the new owner of the hall converted it into three apartments. As part of this work, the pool and bowling alley were removed and the ballroom ceiling was lowered, hiding much of its plaster and stained-glass ornament and its twenty-foot-high painted canvas ceiling.

Then, in 1999, Marty and Judi Nora acquired the building and undertook the multi-year task of uncovering the ballroom's hidden beauties as part of an overall renovation aimed at turning the hall into a home for themselves and their three children. "The first time I walked in here," Judi

An intimate corner of the great hall is at once cozy and expansive, its mirrors creating a seemingly endless row of columns and arches.

In 1920 the hall's elaborate arches disappeared beneath a dropped ceiling when the then owners carved out three apartments. Removing the false ceiling to uncover the hall's lost splendors was one of the Noras' first projects.

recalls with a laugh, "I thought I could hear it screaming, 'Help me!'" The Noras listened to that call, and over the span of a decade they brought in skilled craftspeople to restore what they could and renovate where needed to make the old recreation hall work as a single-family home.

Marty, who's a manufacturer's representative, and Judi, a stay-at-home mother, knew the project would be long and disruptive. It was. The renovation took place in stages, requiring the family to move back and forth from one side of the building to the other several times to accommodate the work. At one point, Judi says, the ballroom, which now serves as a living and dining room, was piled almost to the ceiling with salvaged artifacts. "But it was just something we had to do," she says of their long restoration project.

The most intact part of the building when the Noras bought it was the entry foyer—a spectacular space featuring a twenty-five-foot-high vaulted ceiling, ornate ogee arches mounted on slender wood columns, inlaid hardwood floors, and stained-glass windows. The plaster ornament here and in the ballroom includes an array of geometric and botanical arabesques as well as bands of Arabic calligraphy (some of which were apparently installed backward by local craftspeople who didn't know the language).

The ballroom, unlike the foyer, was a daunting restoration challenge. The room's upper walls, with their arches and ornate plasterwork, had long been out of view in an attic space above one of the old apartments. The Noras hired Henning Church and Historical Restoration, a firm based in nearby Forest Lake, Minnesota, to undertake the delicate task of recasting and repainting damaged portions of the plaster ornament. Another big job entailed repairing the ballroom's twenty-foot-high canvas ceiling. A dozen or so large wall mirrors, some fourteen feet tall and weighing 250 pounds, also had to be installed so the room would look as it did in Sauntry's day.

While the ballroom was being restored, the Noras worked with designer Ed Hawkesford to remodel other parts of the building for the family's use. The finished result includes four bedrooms, three bathrooms, and a new kitchen, where tile that once surrounded the swimming pool is still visible on the floor. The Noras also searched out suitably exotic furnishings to complement the ballroom's Moorish decor. The recreation hall is now very much a home, and the Noras hold frequent gatherings in the ballroom where Stillwater's elite once danced the night away. "It's just so much fun to share this place with others," Judi says.

The recreation hall was designed to be a place of entertainment and celebration, but it failed to bring lasting joy to its builder. Sauntry's fortunes

At first glance, the recreation hall resembles a park pavilion, its wide eaves and pebble-embedded stucco evoking the Arts and Crafts style. But the exotic striped arches above the stained-glass windows and doors hint at the wonders inside.

began to decline in the decade after he completed his Moorish folly, and by late 1914 the world he knew was coming to an end. That year, the Stillwater boom site, where Sauntry and other lumbermen had once sorted millions of logs annually, closed for good because the pineries that fed it were gone. Sauntry was also in financial trouble due to failed investments in iron and gold mines, although accounts vary as to just how dire his circumstances were. It's possible, as well, that he was in failing health.

The end came on the afternoon of November 10, 1914. Sauntry, who was invariably identified as a "millionaire lumberman" by the newspapers, left an apartment he shared with his wife in what is now the Blair House on Selby Avenue in St. Paul, and rode a streetcar downtown to the stately old Ryan Hotel (gone) at Sixth and Robert Streets. According to the hotel clerk on duty, Sauntry seemed to be in a perfectly normal state of mind as he requested a room. He was carrying a small package but no luggage and gave his address as Stillwater. When he reached his room on the third floor of the hotel, he carried out his final act. He propped open the room door, sat down in an upholstered chair, took out the revolver he had brought along in the package, and shot himself through the roof of his mouth. Sauntry, who was sixty-nine years old, left no note behind, and his wife later said she did not know why he shot himself.

If Sauntry's death is a mystery, his architectural legacy is not. His mansion and his fabulous Moorish pleasure palace remain essential landmarks in Stillwater from a time when lumber was king and even the most magical dreams could be made real. ꙮ

The hall's Moorish-themed ornament includes intricately carved and painted wood columns.

George Draper Dayton House

Worthington, 1890

George and Emma Dayton and their first two children, about 1885.

Opposite: The George Dayton House introduced the Colonial Revival style to Worthington. Its stylistic details include balustrades, a rooftop widow's walk, classically inspired window crowns, and a handsome Palladian window above the front entry.

THE BEAUTIFULLY RESTORED GEORGE DRAPER DAYTON HOUSE IS the early fruit of one of the most remarkable business careers in the history of Minnesota. Its builder was a New York–born entrepreneur who acquired his first business when he was still a teenager and who initially visited Worthington not to settle but to monitor investments made by wealthy friends. When he finally did move to Worthington, Dayton became a successful banker and real estate agent despite having little experience in either field, and within seven years he was able to build the town's first true mansion. By then, he was already investing in property in Minneapolis, where in 1902 he completed a large new building on Nicollet Avenue. A year later, that building became home to the newly minted Dayton Dry Goods Company, launching its owner on yet another career that would one day make him Minneapolis's most famous retailer.

Dayton was born in 1857 in the Finger Lakes region of Upstate New York. His father, David Dayton, was a doctor turned apothecary. His mother, Caroline, was the daughter of a Methodist minister and, like her husband, very devout. Dayton shared his parents' religious fervor and considered becoming a Presbyterian minister. But he also had a strong head for business, and at age sixteen he went to work for a coal and lumber dealer. The dealer failed to prosper, however, and soon ended up owing Dayton $1,500 in back salary. Flat broke, the dealer suggested that Dayton buy the company in lieu of his salary. In 1874, Dayton, who was all of seventeen and a half years old, did just that. By the time he married Emma Chadwick in 1878, at age twenty-one, and settled down, he had already saved today's equivalent of $100,000.

Three years later, Dayton found himself, one cold November day, in the tiny hamlet of Worthington on the high, rolling prairies of southwestern Minnesota. Founded in 1871 by a group hoping to establish a colony of God-fearing, teetotaling settlers, Worthington—which was soon served by a new railroad line—did not flourish initially, as grasshopper plagues, brutally cold winters, and a severe economic downturn in 1873 took their toll

This drawing shows the Dayton House as it stands today, fully preserved.

The home's wraparound front porch sports simplified Tuscan columns and provides a welcoming entryway to the house.

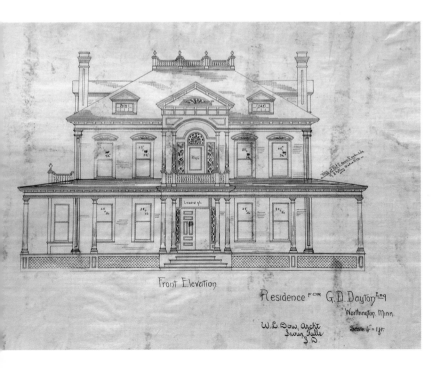

South Dakota architect Wallace Dow drew the plans for the Dayton House, which was the largest home of its day in Worthington.

on farmers. Some of these farmers had taken out mortgages held by wealthy capitalists in and around Geneva, New York, where Dayton lived. Worried about what was happening in Minnesota, investors decided in 1881 to send the reliable and highly respected young Dayton out to the hinterlands to inspect the situation.

Dayton made his first visit to Worthington just after the area had experienced a winter of stunning ferocity that began with a mid-October ice storm and blizzard and continued well into the following April. When spring finally arrived, some settlers gave up and abandoned their farms. Dayton wrote in his autobiography: "The settlers were thoroughly discouraged. One man traded a choice quarter section [160 acres] for a team of horses, harness and buggy. To the farmers the outlook seemed hopeless."

During his visit in 1881, Dayton also discovered that Worthington's only bank was on shaky footing. A year later, he returned and found the

The long front porch of the Dayton House gives it an air of Victorian elegance. The bead-board ceiling and white columns mark it as Colonial Revival.

bank to be all but insolvent. He advised the mortgage holders back in New York, as he later wrote, that "someone must take charge of investments already made to protect the investors. It developed I was the one to do that, so it was arranged that I should buy the 'Bank of Worthington' to take possession the following April 1."

When Dayton moved to Worthington in 1883, the town's population was about 650, but it was beginning to grow quickly as more settlers poured in. German and Irish immigrants, two groups not averse to a drink now and then, were among the newcomers, and the town founders' dream of an alcohol-free village failed to materialize. By 1890 well over a thousand people lived in Worthington, and Dayton flourished with the vibrant young community, becoming its "big" man, even though he stood just five feet four inches. Besides attending to his bank, he invested heavily in real estate, not only in the Worthington area but in Minneapolis as well. Dayton also established several businesses in Worthington, including the town's first flour mill.

Whatever else he may have been, Dayton certainly proved to be tolerant of the cold, and unlike those overmatched settlers who fled Minnesota after a winter or two, Dayton found the rigorous climate to his liking. In a letter to a newspaper back in New York, he wrote: "Friday, January 4th, was quite cool here. In the morning, the mercury was 34 below zero; at five p.m. it was 30 below zero. . . . I am wearing this winter the same pants as last summer, and nearly all the time a light spring overcoat. The great secret of it all is that our air is drier than with you, and we have no dampness. . . . Some may prefer to go to Florida, but if you want to inhale air that will do you good, give you an appetite, make you feel fresh and vigorous and give a healthy glow to your countenance, come up here and take in these fresh breezes and feed on the pure, dry atmosphere of the prairies."

Whether a breeze at thirty-four degrees below zero can best be described as "fresh" is open to debate, but Dayton clearly had no trouble adjusting to his new circumstances. He ended up staying in Worthington for nineteen years, even as his business interests in Minneapolis continued to expand. His family also grew, with the last of four children born in 1889. A year earlier, the Daytons had moved into a new Queen Anne–style house on the north side of town. The house must not have been satisfactory, however, because Dayton and his wife soon began planning a new and considerably larger home to be located on a double lot they owned about five blocks away at 1311 Fourth Avenue. When it was completed in the fall of 1890, it was the grandest house Worthington had ever seen.

The ornate dining room, its walls and ceilings covered with period reproduction wallpapers, boasts a large picture window with a beveled-glass transom and a beautifully carved wood fireplace surround.

Porch

Dining
Room

Kitchen

Bath

Nursery

Library

Conservatory

Sitting
Room

Hall

Parlor

Porch

To design his mansion, Dayton called on Wallace Dow, an architect based in nearby Sioux Falls, South Dakota. It was in some ways a surprising choice, given Dayton's connections to the Twin Cities, where any number of architects were available, but it also made sense to hire someone close at hand who could oversee the work as needed. Today, Dow is little known outside of South Dakota, but he was a skilled designer whose work includes the old Minnehaha County Courthouse in Sioux Falls, completed in 1893. That same year, he also designed South Dakota's pavilion at the Chicago World's Fair.

The Dayton House is a solid example of the Colonial Revival style, which was introduced in the early 1880s by the trendsetting New York architectural firm of McKim, Mead and White. Based on the rectilinear, British-inspired homes built in the United States in the 1700s and early 1800s, the style quickly gained popularity, and examples are still being built today in exclusive suburban communities. The style reached the Twin Cities in the mid-1880s—mainly through the work of St. Paul architect Cass Gilbert, who'd worked for McKim, Mead and White—but it was quite a novelty in a prairie town like Worthington, where the busy Queen Anne style remained popular well into the 1890s.

In fact, what's most striking about Dow's design is how sophisticated it was for its time and place. Worthington in 1890 wasn't far removed from its frontier days, and an early photograph of the house shows open land extending just behind it all the way out to the horizon. Some accounts claim that buffalo still roamed the prairies outside of town, although that seems unlikely given how many farms had been settled by then. In any event, Dayton's stylish new house, described by one writer as "a mansion among shacks," clearly made an impression in town, as a local newspaper noted in July of 1890: "Mr. Dayton's new residence . . . will be an ornament to the village,

The floor plan is organized in a traditional fashion around a central hall and staircase. Unusual, however, is the placement of a nursery (playroom) on the main floor.

The Glory Days of Dayton's Department Store

If Donaldson's was the first major department store in the Twin Cities (1883), Dayton's (1902) was by far the most stylish. Its haute-couture Oval Room brought the latest in European and New York fashion to the fast-growing Midwest. Jeanne Auerbacher, a native of Strasbourg, France, presided over the Oval Room for more than thirty years and came to be known as Madame A, the quintessential arbiter of elegance and taste. No longer did fashionistas on the prairie need to travel to Chicago or New York in order to be chic. Dayton's was a fashion destination for nearly the entire twentieth century.

The store was the result of George Draper Dayton's entrepreneurial strategy. Having become successful as a banker, agriculturalist, and real estate broker in Worthington, he began investing in commercial real estate in the heart of Minneapolis. His first dry goods tenant was Goodfellow's, which he promptly bought and renamed Dayton Dry Goods Company. Dayton's business acumen, strict adherence to Presbyterian morals, and high ethical standards contributed to his success, and the Dayton name was soon behind much civic activity, including the Minneapolis Aquatennial, the Guthrie Theater, the Walker Art Center, the Minnesota Symphony Orchestra, and the Minneapolis Institute of Arts.

Dayton was a master of public relations. In 1920, for example, he arranged for a cargo plane to land in Minneapolis's Parade Stadium and, with wings removed, proceed down Nicollet Avenue to Seventh Street to deliver coveted goods directly to Dayton's from high-fashion sources in New York. The department store's other promotions included elaborate Christmas window displays—occasionally featuring live lions and bears—Breakfast with Santa, the annual Daisy Sale, and the Bachman's Flower Show. Santa Bear became Dayton's hallmark of the season, the chubby plush toy selling thousands of limited-edition copies each year.

Within the walls of Dayton's rapidly expanding flagship store could be found the finest of amenities. Like Donaldson's, Dayton's included several tearooms, the most popular being the clubby Oak Grille and the twinkling Sky Room on the twelfth floor. The bridal shop rivaled any local specialty shop, and the lower-level Marketplace gave birth to Dayton's bridal registry. Hudson's Jewelry of Detroit joined the Dayton fold as a store-within-a-store, and the Looking Glass Salon provided elegant personal services. And of course, the fur sales and storage department were big successes in Subzero Land.

Eventually, Dayton's anchored the nation's first enclosed shopping mall, Southdale, which opened in 1956, followed soon thereafter by replicas named Ridgedale, Brookdale, and Rosedale in other suburbs.

In 1962, the firm opened its first Target discount store, and in 1966, its first B. Dalton's Bookseller. Target would become an international force in the retail industry, flourishing today around the world.

The Oval Room at Dayton's Department Store in Minneapolis, circa 1956. The room was for many years a high fashion destination.

and marks a new epoch in our village history, where progress and prosperity is evinced in structures of elegance, taste and comfort." Perhaps more important, the house was also said to have Worthington's first indoor bathroom.

Records indicate that the house was built in a span of only about four months (furnishing it undoubtedly took more time) and at a cost of no more than $20,000. By 1890 two different railroads ran through Worthington, so Dayton would have had no trouble obtaining anything he wanted for his house, from decorative glass to fireplace mantels to carved-wood paneling. It appears local workmen built the house, which is about five thousand square feet in size. That would be small for, say, a Summit Avenue mansion in St. Paul, but in Worthington the house easily qualified as a mansion. Dayton, however, never referred to it as such. To him, it was always simply "home."

It's likely that Dayton himself specified the home's style, which was familiar to him because of his origins in Upstate New York, a region well stocked with colonial-era buildings. Dow was also a New Englander, born in New Hampshire, and the style would have come naturally to him, as well. The Colonial Revival label takes in a broad spectrum of houses, most of which are not historically "correct" but instead mix modern elements with a variety of forms and decorative motifs that evoke early American architecture.

So it is with the Dayton House, which has the overall feel of a large Victorian home but offers authentic Colonial exterior details such as balustrades, a rooftop widow's walk, bracketed eaves, and window crowns with classically derived ornament. The house's boldest Colonial feature, above the front porch, is a handsome Palladian window (an arrangement of three windows, the middle one arched,

The second-floor hallway ends in an intimate alcove framed by a Palladian window and door. The gorgeous leaded glasswork allows sunlight to pour in from the south.

Worthington

In the 1830s, a half century before George Draper Dayton appeared on the scene, French explorer Joseph Nicollet became the first European to visit the region in southwestern Minnesota, situated between the Mississippi and Missouri Rivers, which eventually became Worthington. He mapped the area, calling it Sisseton Country after the Sisseton Dakota people who lived there. He named Lake Okabena for the Dakota word that translates to "nesting place of the herons."

After the U.S.–Dakota War of 1862, waged in the southwestern part of the state, few white settlers chose to live in what had been renamed Nobles County. But by the end of the nineteenth century, a mismatched group of French Canadian trappers, land-grant pioneers, Ohio teetotalers, Civil War veterans, railroad magnates, and poor immigrants from Ireland, Scandinavia, and Germany ended up living there together—if not always in peace. The widely differing lifestyles of these groups caused many a local battle, especially where alcohol was a factor.

In 1871 the Saint Paul and Sioux City Railroad Company launched a railway to connect its two namesake cities diagonally across the prairie. The railroad's steam locomotives had to take on water at various points along the way, and Lake Okabena seemed perfect for this purpose. This stop became known as the Okabena Railroad Station.

Meanwhile, a group of evangelical Protestant Christians from Ohio formed the National Colony Company and decided to locate a temperance village along the promised tracks. The group included Dr. A. P. Miller, editor of the *Toledo Blade*, and Professor Ransom Humiston of Cleveland, who together acquired land the railroad would need. All parties came to a mutually profitable agreement, made the land transfers and all the ensuing side deals, and decided to rename the station Worthington, the maiden name of Dr. Miller's mother-in-law.

When the railroad opened, the National Colony launched an aggressive advertising program to promote Worthington and bring in citizens, who soon came in droves on the train. But the teetotalers weren't prepared for the onslaught of hard-drinking settlers, and the town's July 4, 1872, Independence Day celebration turned temperance advocates against their foes, resulting in poor Prof. Humiston being burned in effigy. By the time George Dayton first visited Worthington nine years later, however, the temperance battles were over, and the town was ready to embark on a long period of steady growth that has continued to this day.

The George Dayton House is at the center of a panoramic view of Worthington taken in the 1890s. The large brick school building nearby, which Dayton helped to build, is now gone.

Pocket doors open into a parlor on the east side of the house. The parlor features parquet floors and a reddish-gold tile fireplace.

named after the enormously influential sixteenth-century Venetian architect Andrea Palladio). The middle part of this window is actually a low door that opens out to a balcony above the porch.

The home's Colonial Revival touches coexist with many Victorian elements, most notably a wraparound front porch that sports simplified Tuscan columns. A large dining-room picture window along the southwest of the house is another feature that would never be found in a true colonial-era home. The columned, projecting dormer that shelters the Palladian window also draws its inspiration from well past the colonial period.

Inside, the house is organized in traditional fashion around a central hall and staircase. The vestibule, reached through a double front door, makes a fine first impression, with leaded-glass transoms and sidelights and a mosaic-tile floor. Another set of double doors leads into the hall, which features a parquet floor and cherry trim. Pocket doors to either side of the hall lead to a pair of spacious parlors. The staircase, also in cherry, is farther down the hall just past one of the home's loveliest bits of decoration—a delicate wood transom screen animated by wavy sunray motifs.

Past the staircase, on opposite sides of the hall, are a library and a children's playroom (called the nursery). The playroom, a feature not typically found on the main floor of a Victorian home, testifies to the Daytons' devotion to family life. A dining room and kitchen occupy most of the rear of the house. There's also a charming alcove between the playroom and the front sitting room that the Daytons used as a conservatory for their plants. With its four south- and west-facing windows, the alcove also offered an excellent view of the towered brick school (now gone) that Dayton, who served as treasurer of the school board, helped build in 1889.

All of the downstairs rooms, with the exception of the modernized kitchen, are richly detailed in a manner typical of the era. Tile fireplaces with mirrored and carved-wood surrounds, leaded-glass windows, parquet floors, and many pieces of fine furniture all combine to create a warm, inviting atmosphere. Much of the home's woodwork, especially around its five fireplaces, features intricately carved scrolls, beads, and swags in a variety of patterns. The ornate dining room offers a particularly fine fireplace, as well as a leaded-glass transom above the home's only picture window.

Upstairs, there were originally four large bedrooms (now combined into two suites), a bathroom, and servants' quarters. But the most striking space of all is the upstairs hall itself, which ends at the Palladian window and door. Here is some of the home's most gorgeous leaded glass, and the southern exposure ensures that sunlight pours through in prismatic patterns for much of the day.

Dayton's career in Worthington hit a rough patch in 1893, when what was up to that point the worst depression in American history caused many banks to fail. One bank in town went under and a panicked run of withdrawals nearly brought down Dayton's Bank of Worthington as well. But he was a cool man in times of crisis, and he managed to get by, though just barely. His methods, however, could be unorthodox. In one case, a woman who had withdrawn a large sum received a surprise visit from Dayton later that day. He later wrote: "I went to her home about six o'clock and said, 'There is no time to talk. You don't need that money and I do.'" After some persuading from her husband, the woman returned the money to the bank.

In 1902, with his numerous business endeavors in Minneapolis taking up ever more of his attention, Dayton decided that the time had come to move there. It is a measure of how much he liked his home in Worthington that he built a similar, albeit less elaborate, home on Blaisdell Avenue in South Minneapolis. Before Dayton left Worthington, he sold his mansion to Charles Smallwood, a business associate. Following Smallwood's death in 1908, his daughter and her husband moved in and stayed for many years. In 1938, however, the house met the fate of many an old mansion when it was turned into a nursing home. More changes came in the 1960s, when an addition was constructed at the rear of the house.

After the nursing home closed in the 1980s, the home fell into tax forfeiture and was later sold at a public auction for $10,000 to a new owner, who used the property as a boarding house. Subdivided and in need of much work, the house by 2000 seemed destined for an unhappy end. But a renaissance was just around the corner. Late in 2001 a nonprofit group called Historic Worthington bought the house with the help of members of the Dayton family, particularly Bruce B. Dayton, one of George's grandsons and his biographer. The house then underwent a two-year, $2 million restoration funded by the Target Foundation, members of the Dayton family, and other donors.

An elegant surround of carved wood frames the east parlor's fireplace and mirror.

A plan prepared by River Architects of La Crosse, Wisconsin, guided the project, which included removal of the 1960s addition as well as many interior partitions. Workers then painted and reroofed the house, repaired numerous broken and leaky windows, upgraded mechanical and electrical systems, and restored the home's major rooms with period wallpaper, drapes, and furnishings. The work revealed a number of long-hidden features, among them the home's ornate cherry staircase banister, which had been encased for decades in wallboard.

Now called the Historic Dayton House, the home functions as a gathering place for special events and offers two guest suites for overnight visitors. Equally important, the house has become a source of pride in Worthington, an elegant monument to the city's nineteenth-century origins and to the man who contributed so much to its development and growth.

George Dayton went on to a long life after leaving Worthington. His new Minneapolis department store flourished, as did his real estate interests, and Dayton became one of the city's most admired businessmen, as well as an uncommonly generous philanthropist. He died just before his eighty-first birthday in 1938, outliving both his wife, Emma, and his oldest son, David Draper. One of his favorites quotations, which he took to heart, came from the French philosopher Jean-Jacques Rousseau: "Every man goes down to death bearing in his clutched hands only that which he has given away." ∾

The dramatic front entry is anchored by massive double doors with sidelights and a beveled-glass transom. The glass creates a prismatic pattern on the porch ceiling.

Opposite: The front hallway makes an exquisite first impression as visitors pass beneath a delicate wood transom screen before reaching the carved cherry staircase. Architect Wallace Dow's design was strikingly sophisticated for its time and place.

ꙮ Alexander Ramsey House
St. Paul, 1872

Alexander Ramsey and his young son, Alexander Jr., circa 1850. The boy died a few months later, at age four.

Opposite: The Alexander Ramsey House in late autumn, after the leaves have fallen. Built of Platteville limestone quarried nearby, the house is one of Minnesota's finest surviving examples of the French Second Empire style.

I N THE SPRING OF 1849, ALEXANDER RAMSEY, HIS WIFE, AND THEIR young son journeyed from their home in Pennsylvania to the newly created territory of Minnesota, arriving in the early morning darkness at the steamboat landing in St. Paul. At first light, Ramsey—whose political connections had won him an appointment as the territory's first governor—stepped on shore to survey his new domain. It was not an impressive sight. St. Paul then consisted of no more than a few dozen log and wood-frame buildings scattered in no apparent order on the bluffs above the Mississippi River. The town was so discouragingly crude that the Ramseys could find no decent place to live and had to move in for a time with another of the state's pioneers, Henry Sibley, at his home in Mendota.

First impressions do not always prove conclusive, however. Ramsey stayed on in Minnesota to become one of its founding figures and also a very rich man in an era when the line between public service and private gain was all but invisible. He and his wife, Anna, celebrated their wealth and status by building, between 1868 and 1872, a mansion in St. Paul that is among Minnesota's finest surviving examples of French Second Empire–style architecture. Costing well over $40,000, including land and furnishings, the mansion was also one of the largest and most lavish homes of its time in Minnesota.

Today, the mansion—more so than any other Minnesota home of its period—remains remarkably intact. Ramsey and his descendants occupied the house for more than ninety years and kept many of its original furnishings in place. When Ramsey's last surviving granddaughter died, she donated the home at 265 South Exchange Street to the Minnesota Historical Society, which maintains it as a historic house open to the public. In 1969 the mansion became one of the first properties in Minnesota to be listed on the National Register of Historic Places.

The "Mansion House," as it was sometimes called, has an especially rich history because Ramsey was such a pivotal figure in the making of Minnesota. Born near Harrisburg, Pennsylvania, in 1815, Ramsey became

The mansion's full-width front porch, with its attenuated pro-portions, has an Italianate feel.

an orphan at age ten. He was then sent off to apprentice as a carpenter but soon became more interested in politics and the law. Shrewd and well spoken, with a broad face adorned through most of his life by mutton-chop sideburns, Ramsey—who was sometimes called "Bluff Alec"—was known to like "jolly company," according to one newspaper sketch, and was also "a capital story-teller and most hearty laugher." Initially a member of the Whig Party, he served as chairman of its central committee in Pennsylvania. After Zachery Taylor, a Whig, was elected president in 1848, Ramsey's reward—which did not initially inspire him with much enthusiasm—was the governorship of faraway Minnesota.

Ramsey's wife, Anna, was eleven years younger than her husband and hailed from a Quaker family in Pennsylvania, although she was ultimately disowned by the sect for failing to attend meetings. Even so, she continued to use the Quaker "thee" in letters, if not in speech. The move to Minnesota, with its climatic rigors, was especially hard on her, as she told her traveling husband in a letter written on Christmas Day, 1849, when the thermometer sunk to twenty-two degrees below zero: "Oh Alex, could thee be here and know how we suffer with cold thee would never want to winter again in St. P[aul]. I know I will not I nearly froze to death in bed . . . and nothing in the house to eat but strong butter and coffee without cream every potato and vegetable is frozen up. . . . I tell thee now thee shall never leave me again so long. I will not stay." There would be deep tragedies in St. Paul, as well—the Ramseys' first-born son, Alexander Junior, died at age four in 1850, and a second son perished that year in infancy. But in the end Anna was able to adapt to her new life in Minnesota.

The Ramseys' first home in St. Paul was a log house covered with board siding. In 1850, however, the couple built a substantial wood-frame house on a large lot (about 150 by 100 feet) at the corner of Walnut and Exchange Streets in the Irvine Park neighborhood. Organized around a New England–style square, the neighborhood—just below the downtown bluffs—was then becoming a fashionable precinct. The Ramseys were living in this house when their only child who survived into adulthood, a daughter named Marion, was born in 1853.

Alexander Ramsey's two terms as territorial governor were momentous, largely because of the Treaty of Traverse des Sioux, concluded in 1851, by which the Sisseton and Wahpeton bands of the Dakota ceded much of what is today southern and western Minnesota to the U.S. government for

Anna Ramsey, circa 1850–1855. She found St. Paul cold and lonely after arriving with her husband but persevered to become one of the city's best-known figures. As the family's new mansion neared completion, she went on a shopping spree in New York to fill it with fine furnishings.

The side door off Walnut Street was the family's private entrance. The house's heavy window hoods and wide bracketed eaves exemplify its blend of Italianate and French Second Empire features.

less than eight cents an acre. Ramsey pushed hard to acquire the Suland, as it was called, within months of becoming governor. He was a key negotiator of the treaty, which proved ruinous to the Indians but very lucrative to traders. Today, an aroma of swindle hangs over the whole enterprise, but what happened at Traverse des Sioux was hardly unique in the nation's long history of dealing with its native populations.

Rescuing Irvine Park

It's easy to imagine the then U.S. senator Alexander Ramsey and his wife, Anna, dressed in summery white linen, circa 1878, stepping out the front door of their elegant new "Mansion House" to cross Exchange Street and stroll through nearby Irvine Park, a white dimity parasol in Anna's lace-gloved hand. The park today is that picturesque, although the scene is perhaps improbable.

The park, one of St. Paul's most charming places, dates to 1849. It was named after John Irvine, who deeded the property to the village of St. Paul, which initially used it as shared grazing land for the early Irish and German settlers in the area. In the early 1870s, Joseph Forepaugh urged the city to improve the park, which was graded in 1871; the following year it was officially named in Irvine's honor. More improvements ensued, with the addition of gaslights, wrought iron fencing and benches, and a stone-and-iron fountain installed at a cost of $900. Wealthy residents began to build or move costly homes around the park, and the neighborhood became very stylish by the time the Ramseys completed their new mansion.

But as local economies rise and fall, so do public amenities, and after its heyday, Irvine Park gradually fell into neglect. In 1917 the park was downgraded to "playground" designation. Ten years later, the fountain was removed, and the metal, scrapped. The once-elegant homes surrounding the park were chopped into flats, and vagrants idled there. By 1970 the neighborhood had hit rock bottom. Enter urban renewal.

Just before the area was to be leveled, neighbors and planners came to their senses and realized the park's historical significance. They nominated the Irvine Park Historic District to the National Register of Historic Places in 1973, saving the park and commencing its renovation. Old homes were restored to their former grandeur, and other historic houses were moved to the neighborhood. Some new homes were also built. In 1978, the Robinson Iron Company of Alabama was commissioned to cast a new fountain, resembling the original. This time the cost was $40,000. St. Paul mayor George Latimer formally dedicated the restored Irvine Park on October 1, 1978.

Today, the beautifully maintained park, with its fountain and gazebo, is the setting for weddings and other events. And it's easy for visitors to daydream about the time the Ramseys entertained President Rutherford B. Hayes and his wife, and perhaps went for a stroll after dinner.

The central fountain at Irvine Park, circa 1888. The small park and its surrounding homes became the scene of a highly successful preservation and renewal project in the 1970s.

Ramsey remained territorial governor until 1853. Two years later, he was elected mayor of St. Paul. He was also adding to what would become a considerable fortune, much of it acquired by investing in land in Minnesota and parts of Wisconsin. By 1855 he was worth $200,000, at least on paper. He also became enmeshed in various railroad schemes, not all of which appear to have been savory, and served as well as a lobbyist in Washington, D.C. He was in every respect what today would be called a well-connected man, a political insider who knew all of the right people.

When Minnesota achieved statehood in 1858, Ramsey ran for governor under the banner of the newly formed Republican Party, but lost to his old friend, Henry Sibley, a Democrat. Two years later, however, Ramsey won the election. In 1861 he became the first governor to offer troops to President Abraham Lincoln when the Civil War broke out. A year later, he had to deal with Minnesota's own bloody conflict: the U.S.–Dakota War. Promising the Dakota would be "exterminated or driven forever beyond the borders of the state," Ramsey sent out forces that soon had the Dakota on the run. The war's aftermath was vengeful, and Ramsey—no doubt expressing the sentiments of his constituency—urged Lincoln to execute more than three hundred men involved in the fighting. Reviewing every single case, Lincoln reduced the number of condemned to thirty-eight, all of whom were duly hanged in Mankato on the day after Christmas 1862.

Ramsey, meanwhile, went on to become a U.S. senator from Minnesota in 1863, serving two six-year terms. His finances were such that by 1868 he and Anna were ready to replace their wood-frame house with a far more splendid home. They decided to build on their existing property, so they had their house moved across the street and lived there while the mansion was under construction.

To design and build their mansion, the Ramseys hired the St. Paul firm of Leonard and Sheire. Monroe Sheire, who handled the design work (for a fee of $250), wasn't formally trained as an architect. Like other designers in Minnesota at the time, he came out of the master-builder tradition, having learned his profession by working for his father, who was a contractor in New York state. Sheire arrived in St. Paul in 1860 and went into partnership with Charles Leonard two years later. Sheire's brother, Romaine, joined the firm in 1865, by which time it had become one of the most successful in St. Paul.

Sheire wasn't the most dynamic of designers, and the Ramsey House—squarish and a bit squat—is typical of his work. Nonetheless, the mansion's heavy stone construction conveys a sense of dignity and mass, as befitting the importance of its owner. Its signature Second Empire feature is a slate mansard roof adorned with elaborate arched dormers. The mansard, which allows for a full third floor, covers only the main body of the house.

The Ramsey House's signature French Second Empire feature is a slate mansard roof adorned with arched dormers, creating a full third story.

The home's front porch looks out onto Exchange Street. Irvine Park, established thirty years before Ramsey built his mansion, is just beyond.

A two-story service wing that extends to the rear has a simpler hipped roof.

Many of the mansion's details, such as its heavy window hoods and wide bracketed eaves, are actually more Italianate than French Second Empire in character. The two revival styles, which were contemporaneous in Minnesota, shared much in common and architects regularly mixed them together. The mansion's full-width front porch, with its attenuated proportions, also has an Italianate feel. One common Second Empire element Sheire left out of his design was a tower, which would have added a note of monumentality to the mansion but also would have pushed up its cost.

Structurally, the house is a mix of masonry and wood-joist construction. The two-foot-thick exterior walls are built of gray Platteville limestone quarried nearby. Harder, smoother building stones, such as granites from the St. Cloud area, didn't became available in the Twin Cities until the mid-1870s, so Ramsey and his builders had little choice but to use the local limestone. A large masonry support wall also extends up through the center of the house. The architects took particular care with the floors, placing three inches of grout between the floorboards and subflooring. This technique, sometimes called sandwich construction, provided both sound and thermal insulation.

Although foundations were laid in 1868–1869, work on the mansion walls didn't begin until May of 1871. It's not certain why the Ramseys were content to leave a hole in the ground for nearly two years. Part of the reason was that they were traveling in Europe, although Ramsey himself returned in 1869. But Anna, who was deeply involved in planning the mansion, stayed on in Europe with daughter Marion until August of 1870, at which point a decision may have been made to delay the start of construction until spring.

The mansion was nearly finished by late November of 1872, when the Ramseys hosted a party for all of the workmen. A month later, Anna staged her first formal social event in the house—a benefit for House of Hope Presbyterian Church. Even so, the task of furnishing the mansion was not yet complete, and some exterior work remained to be done, including installation of the iron fence that surrounds the property. The mansion in its final form was equipped with central heat, hot and cold running water, and gas lighting—amenities found only in the most expensive homes of the day.

Inside, the Ramsey House is notable for the grand scale of its major rooms. The main entrance, at the center of the porch, leads through an elegant vestibule with etched-glass doors to a broad, forty-foot-long hall. A large parlor takes up one side of the hall. The other side consists of a reception room and library. These three rooms all feature fifteen-foot ceilings, elongated windows with built-in shutters, and enormous black walnut and butternut double doors, nearly three inches thick, which swing on brass hinges hefty enough for a bank vault. Few other homes in Minnesota—even the far-larger mansions that began to appear in the 1880s—possess a comparable sense of weight and power.

The twenty-by-forty-foot parlor on the west side of the hall is by far the mansion's biggest room. It includes a central bay and a pair of intricately carved white-marble fireplaces. This room was the mansion's grand formal space, where Anna Ramsey and, later, Marion held parties and entertained a wide range of visitors.

Across the hall from the parlor is a smaller reception room that was used not only to receive guests but also as a comfortable spot for small gatherings. A pair of huge pocket doors connects this room to the library, where Ramsey spent much of his time reading or visiting with friends. It was also here that Ramsey's body lay in state after his death.

The main staircase, finished in black walnut, is located about halfway down the central hall. Rising in one long flight with a short return at the top, it features an ornate, multistage newel post and expertly turned balusters. Past the staircase, a side hall leads to an entrance on the east side of the mansion facing Walnut Street, which was used by the family.

One unusual feature of the home's design is the placement of the dining room, which is in the rear service wing next to the kitchen. In most mansions of the period, the dining room occupied a more prominent position. The mansion also has a third entrance, on the west side just off the kitchen and back stairs, originally intended for servants.

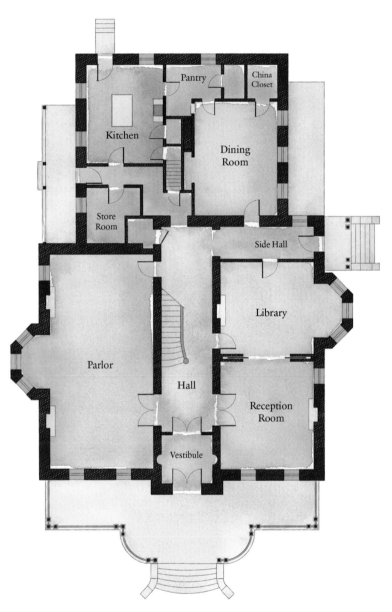

As seen in this floor plan, the twenty-by-forty-foot parlor on the west side of the Ramsey House was designed to be large enough for all of the state and civic gatherings hosted by the prominent family.

St. Paul in 1857, eight years after Alexander Ramsey arrived to become governor of Minnesota Territory. This view looks north toward the first territorial and soon-to-be state capitol building at Tenth and Cedar Streets.

An ornate, silver-plated brass doorknob is one of many superb interior details. The house remains remarkably intact, thanks to Ramsey family descendants who donated the property to the Minnesota Historical Society.

Upstairs, there are four bedrooms in the front portion of the house, plus two others at the rear. Ramsey used one of these rear rooms for many years as his office. Business callers, including tenants of properties Ramsey owned in St. Paul, came in the servants' entrance and then up the back steps to see him. Initially, Ramsey had maintained an office in the mansion's expansive attic, but it became a children's nursery and playroom in the 1880s after Marion moved in with her three young children.

During its early years, the mansion was something like Minnesota's White House, and virtually every important figure in the state stopped by on occasion. William LeDuc was a frequent visitor. Henry Sibley, Archbishop John Ireland, and William Windom were among the other distinguished guests entertained at the mansion.

The most celebrated visitor was President Rutherford B. Hayes, who on September 5, 1878, while on a tour of agricultural lands, had breakfast with the Ramseys before going off to open the Minnesota State Fair. Hayes and his wife, Lucy, were supposed to have a big banquet that evening, but it was canceled at the last moment, and Anna Ramsey suddenly found herself preparing an unexpected presidential dinner. Marion recalled many years later how her mother, "nothing daunted, searched the icebox and found what remained of the breakfast. . . . There were sirloins from which the fillets had been removed and the legs of the prairie chickens, which my mother had the presence of mind to tell the president were considered the most delicate part of the bird. Mrs. Hayes assured us that she had enjoyed the meal much more than she would have enjoyed the banquet." The dinner must also have pleased the president, who later appointed Ramsey as his secretary of war.

All of the mansion's rooms contain historic furnishings—everything from sofas, tables, and chairs to beds and nightstands. Some of these items date back to 1872, when Anna Ramsey went on a mighty shopping spree in New York City. She made the trip in May, well before the mansion was ready for occupancy, and bought what would today be at least $75,000 worth of merchandise. Anna did much of her shopping at A.T. Stewart's department store, then the largest in the country, in Lower Manhattan. She also bought items at Lord & Taylor, another prominent New York retailer. Her haul, which filled two train cars, included furniture, light fixtures, linens, mattresses, drapes, lambrequins, and carpeting.

Although the Ramseys spent a fortune on their St. Paul showpiece, they did not initially occupy the mansion year-round. Alexander Ramsey served in the Senate until 1875, and the couple wintered in Washington, D.C., during that time. Later, they also spent portions of each winter in Philadelphia, where Marion lived after her marriage to Charles Furness in 1875. The Ramseys went back to spending winters in Washington in 1879,

A double parlor occupies the entire west side of the first floor. Two intricately carved mantels are the work of St. Paul stonemason A. J. Tostevin.

Anna Ramsey's reception room, adjacent to the library, is the most elaborately decorated room in the house. It was here, rather than in the huge parlor, that the Ramseys formally received callers.

when Alexander began his two years of service as secretary of war. Later, he served on government commissions that also caused him to spend much of his time away from St. Paul.

The mansion's interior as it exists today reflects two major refurbishings. One occurred in 1881 after the Ramseys returned from Washington. At that time, Anna had many of the downstairs rooms tinted and wallpapered and also installed new carpeting. Another round of work came in 1884, following Anna's death at age fifty-eight. By then, Marion Furness was living in the house with her three young children—a son and two daughters. She had returned to St. Paul to live with her parents because her husband, who suffered from an unspecified mental illness, was committed to an asylum in 1882. He remained hospitalized until his death in 1909.

The Second Empire Style

The monumental Second Empire style of the Alexander Ramsey House takes its name from the sumptuous, classically derived architecture favored during the reign of Napoleon III (1852–1870) in France. There, it was a bombastic style bristling with columns, pediments, garlands, festoons, and other classical devices, often piled up into highly sculptural facades. The style reached its delirious summit in the Paris Opera House, completed in 1875.

In its American version, Second Empire tended to be a bit more restrained, although a few major monuments, such as the Philadelphia City Hall (started in 1871 but not finished until 1901) strove for true French grandeur. Homes displaying at least some Second Empire features, most commonly a mansard roof, appeared on the East Coast as early as 1850, but it wasn't until after the Civil War that the style became widely popular, not only for mansions but also for public and commercial buildings. It was so prevalent during the postwar presidency (1868–1876) of Ulysses S. Grant that it is now sometimes called the General Grant style.

Most Minnesota examples of the style are smaller and less sophisticated than those in the East, primarily because the state was still in its formative years after the Civil War, and the means of architectural expression were limited. Among the most prominent public buildings to adopt the style was the first Minneapolis City Hall (1873–1912), an ungainly stone affair with a mansard roof but few other adornments. Many commercial buildings of the 1870s also donned mansard hats in an effort to appear stylish, usually with indifferent results. The Brackett Block in Minneapolis (1871–c. 1920) was perhaps the most impressive of the lot.

Mansions were another matter. Many of the finest homes built in Minnesota between about 1865 and 1880 followed the Second Empire fashion, often with Italianate features tossed in for good measure, as is true of the Ramsey House. In St. Paul alone, at least fifty Second Empire mansions were built in the 1860s and 1870s. A few of the larger homes—such as those owned by George Becker and John Prince in the city's old Lowertown mansion district—included massive front towers. Second Empire mansions were also built in established river towns like Stillwater, Red Wing, and Winona.

One of Minnesota's last great Second Empire mansions was also its largest—the enormous Norman Kittson House, on the present site of the

St. Paul Cathedral, completed in 1884 and razed just twenty-two years later. Critics lampooned the house for its old-fashioned look when it was built, since by the mid-1880s a variety of new Victorian styles, including the ubiquitous Queen Anne, had all but ended what might be called the Mansard Roof Era.

Part of what makes the Ramsey House so important today is that it is a rare survivor of its kind. The vast majority of Minnesota's Second Empire architecture is gone, swept away by tides of urban change and growth.

The French Second Empire style was popular for a wide array of buildings in Minnesota from the 1860s to the early 1880s. The long-gone Brackett Block in downtown Minneapolis, built in 1871, featured the style's signature mansard roof.

The dining room, presided over by portraits of Alexander and Anna Ramsey, is in the back of the house, an unusual location for its time. The built-in sideboard replaced the original china cabinet in 1888.

Marion became the woman of the house after Anna's death, taking charge of the social calendar and tending to her father. Ramsey lived well into his eighties, becoming the grand old man of Minnesota politics.

After Marion's death in 1935, Laura and her older sister, Anna (usually called Anita), took on the task of running the home. Over the years the sisters, who never married, added new items to the mansion but kept the old furniture. They modernized the kitchens and bathrooms and installed an elevator but otherwise made few changes. The mansion's exterior also remained virtually unaltered. After Anita's death in 1964 (her sister had died five years earlier), the mansion and its contents—fourteen thousand items in all—were willed to the Minnesota Historical Society, which Alexander Ramsey had helped to establish more than a century earlier.

Once it took possession of the mansion, the society set about restoring rooms to their nineteenth-century appearance. Much of this work consisted of rearranging furniture so that items would be located where they had been in the 1870s. The mansion was opened to the public in 1965. In 1970, the society made a significant addition to the property by building a new carriage house similar in design to an earlier one constructed in 1883 and torn down in 1920. The rebuilt carriage house is used as a visitors' center. In addition to regular tours, the mansion hosts special and seasonal events, among them the popular Victorian Christmas at the Ramsey House.

Today, the Ramsey House remains an extraordinary experience, not just because of its imposing architecture but because its history is so intensely palpable in the furniture, fixtures, and everyday objects that fill every room. History is often about big things, but in the Ramsey House it's the little things—the pitcher and soap dish in Alexander's bedroom, Anna's favorite Willcox and Gibbs sewing machine, Marion's childhood tea set, a dollhouse built for Laura by a master carpenter in 1887—that make the past seem most real. ❧

The second-floor hallway provides access to a family bedroom and a front-facing sitting room. The upstairs rooms feature lighter finishes and furnishings than those downstairs.

The third-floor playroom contains a charming dollhouse made for Laura Furness, the Ramseys' granddaughter, by master carpenter Matthew Taylor. It was designed to resemble the family house.

MODERN LIVING

E. S. Hoyt House
Red Wing, 1913

Elmore S. Hoyt. He loved the house and lived in it until his death in 1947.

Opposite: The E. S. Hoyt House, designed by William Purcell and George Elmslie, is one of Minnesota's most exquisite Prairie-style residences. It was built for the longtime president of the Red Wing Union Stoneware Company.

N 1913 ELMORE S. HOYT DECIDED TO BUILD A NEW HOUSE ON A HIGH corner lot at 300 Hill Street in one of Red Wing's most historic neighborhoods. The lot was already occupied by an 1870s-vintage mansion, and the surrounding blocks were then, as now, thick with Victorian homes dating as far back as the 1850s. Hoyt, however, had something novel in mind. After the old mansion was moved away, he replaced it with a house more sleek and modern than anything Red Wing had ever seen before. Today, the house is justly regarded as one of the summits of Prairie-style architecture in Minnesota. It also ranks among the finest works of its architects, William Purcell and George Elmslie, who did more than anyone else to bring the progressive design pioneered by Frank Lloyd Wright to cities and towns all around the state.

E. S. Hoyt, as he was usually called, was by 1913 one of Red Wing's business leaders. Born in Kansas, he'd arrived in Red Wing in 1881 as an eighteen-year-old. A few years later, he began work as a salesman for the recently organized Minnesota Stoneware Company, one of two large potteries then operating in Red Wing. In about 1887 he moved to Minneapolis, apparently still working in sales there for the stoneware company. A year later, he married Florence McCart, whose father had been a veterinarian in Red Wing.

The couple had two daughters before returning to Red Wing in 1893, when Hoyt was named general manager of Minnesota Stoneware. A savvy businessman, he helped engineer a merger in the early 1900s between Minnesota Stoneware and its chief competitor, the Red Wing Stoneware Company. The combined firm was called the Red Wing Union Stoneware Company, and Hoyt became its president, a position he would hold for more than forty years.

Hoyt assumed leadership of the company at a time when the Arts and Crafts movement was sweeping across the United States. The movement promoted a fusion of architecture, craftsmanship, and high-quality ceramics—in the form of tile, terra-cotta, and pottery—that was frequently incorporated into buildings of the period. Although Hoyt's company didn't produce much art pottery, he knew many people in the business, and he may well have come across the work of Purcell and Elmslie, who embraced the Arts and Crafts aesthetic, before he hired them. Even so, it appears that a family connection was the direct source of the commission. One of Hoyt's daughters, Hazel, told an interviewer in 1970 that Purcell had an uncle in Red Wing who recommended his nephew's firm to Hoyt.

When Hoyt reached out to Purcell and Elmslie, they represented the avant-garde of architecture in Minnesota, riding a wave of modernity that had begun to infuse design in both Europe and America around 1900. In Europe the style known as Art Nouveau, which came in many national varieties, sought to replace the tired disciplines of the past. In the United States, however, the early modernist movement turned out to be a special case, largely because of the work of one man—Frank Lloyd Wright—a Wisconsin farm boy possessed of talents so deep and magical that his work still resonates today like that of no other American architect.

Almost entirely self-taught, Wright found a job at age twenty as a draftsman in the offices of Chicago architect Louis Sullivan, whose work, primarily in the form of tall office buildings, presaged the modern styles to come. Five years later, Wright left Sullivan to establish his own home and studio in Oak Park, Illinois, a Chicago suburb. There, he began to develop a new kind of American house with long bands of windows, wide eaves, open pinwheeling floor plans, and fully integrated geometric ornament. Eventually, the term *Prairie style* was coined to describe these remarkable houses, which were often long and low, seeming to evoke the flat midwestern landscape. By the early 1900s, Wright had perfected his new style, producing such masterpieces as the Robie House (1908) in Chicago.

Wright was a magnetic figure, and he soon attracted a group of followers, known today as the Prairie school. Mostly from the Chicago area, they were eager young idealists who shared Wright's dream of remaking American architecture. Among them was William Gray Purcell, who hailed from a wealthy Oak Park family and had a degree in architecture from Cornell University. After his graduation in 1903, Purcell returned to Chicago and there met George Grant Elmslie, a native of Scotland who was Louis Sullivan's chief draftsman. Nine years older than Purcell, Elmslie specialized in drawing the complex, swirling ornament for which Sullivan was famous.

In 1907 Purcell moved to Minneapolis to establish his own firm. Elmslie was still in Chicago, working for Sullivan, but he was making frequent visits to Minnesota, where Sullivan had won a commission in Owatonna to design what would be the first of a series of small-town banks that sustained him during the bleak final period of his career. The lushly ornamented National Farmers Bank of Owatonna, in which Elmslie had a large

The Purcell-Cutts House in Minneapolis, completed the same year as the Hoyt House, is another of Purcell and Elmslie's outstanding designs. It's now owned by the Minneapolis Institute of Arts.

This front elevation gives a sense of the bands of windows and wide eaves typical of the Prairie style.

hand, opened in 1908, and today it remains the most renowned of all Minnesota buildings. Sullivan, however, was nearly flat broke by the time the bank was finished and could no longer afford to pay Elmslie. In 1909 Elmslie finally left Sullivan and became Purcell's partner in Minneapolis. The firm of Purcell and Elmslie (which until 1913 had a third partner, engineer George Feick) would over the next decade design most of Minnesota's outstanding Prairie-style buildings, including a half-dozen banks and more than twenty houses.

The two architects were well-matched partners. Purcell was a solid designer who also acted as the firm's front man, scouring up business, sometimes with the help of family connections, as was the case with the Hoyt House. Elmslie was a brilliant draftsman, gorgeous ornamental motifs blooming like flowers from his pen, but he was also dreamy, reticent, and often sad. Long a bachelor, he had married his one true love, Bonnie Hunter, in 1910, then saw her die two years later after a failed medical operation, and afterward it was only work that kept him going.

The partners reached their apogee in 1913 with the design of three stunning homes—the Edward Decker House (gone) in Wayzata, Purcell's own house (now owned by the Minneapolis Institute of Arts) near Lake of the Isles in Minneapolis, and the Hoyt House, which has always been privately owned. At four thousand square feet, the ten-room Hoyt House is Purcell and Elmslie's largest surviving home in Minnesota and a work that superbly demonstrates their devotion to the tenets of Prairie architecture.

Although Purcell and Elmslie were very much influenced by Wright, their work has its own distinctive qualities. Their houses tend to be more compact than Wright's and more practical as well. The Hoyt House, for example, features a modified T plan that is far less sprawling than Wright's Francis Little House (gone), built about the same time in Deephaven, Min-

A projecting bay at the rear of the house rests on brackets decorated with fret-sawn ornament that combines geometric and botanical motifs in Elmslie's characteristic style.

nesota, on Lake Minnetonka. The Little House's long and narrow profile, with its hundreds of feet of exposed walls and windows, made it incredibly difficult to heat, a problem that also plagued the more famous Robie House. Wright's great Prairie houses were like Italian sports cars—utterly gorgeous, but prone to frequent breakdowns—whereas Purcell and Elmslie worked hard to design homes that were both beautiful and reliable.

The Hoyt House, like many of Wright's designs, is dominated by glass. All told, nearly a hundred diamond-patterned art-glass casement windows, typically arranged in long bands, puncture the walls. Designed by Elmslie in several distinct patterns, the windows feature pale, opalescent colors that create a soothing light throughout the home. The biggest group of windows—eleven in a projecting second-floor bay and another nine below—march across the long north facade of the house overlooking Third Street.

The prominent north-side bay is one of several balconies and overhangs that give the home's stuccoed second floor a sense of floating above its brick base. The rose-colored stucco was an unusual choice for Purcell and Elmslie, who normally opted for earthier tones. They chose the color to blend with the multicolored facing of tapestry (also known as Oriental) brick on the first floor. Purcell later wrote, "The whole color scheme was very carefully related to the Oriental brick, which we had brought from Brazil, Indiana, for both exterior and interior. The selection was similar to that used in the Owatonna bank, and the result was beautiful."

Many of the house's brackets and bays are decorated with delicate fret-sawn ornamental panels featuring Elmslie's characteristic mix of botanical and geometric forms. Elmslie learned this style of ornament from Sullivan, and he delighted in using it—in wood, glass, or terra-cotta—whenever he could. For the Hoyts, he turned out one especially magnificent piece of ornament—a fret-sawn screen mounted along a brick passageway that links the house to a

The front entrance is set well back from Hill Street on the short side of the house, next to a projecting wing that extends over an enclosed porch.

Two fret-sawn ornamental panels serve as grace notes over the front door. The passageway at left connects to a garage that was also designed by Purcell and Elmslie.

garage also designed by the architects. The screen, added in 1915, is unique in Purcell and Elmslie's domestic work, and it indicates just how much care and attention they were able to lavish on the house because of the ample budget provided by the Hoyts.

The house's long front facade has no entrance. Instead, as is often the case in Prairie designs, the main entrance is on the side, set well back from Hill Street at the corner of the broad T that defines the two major sections of the house. Wright was famous for elaborate entry sequences intended to lead visitors on a visual adventure before finally encountering the front door. Purcell and Elmslie rarely went to such lengths, and the entrance to the Hoyt House, reached via a series of low steps flanked by walls, is quite straightforward. It does, however, provide a sense of being enfolded in the

Red Wing Pottery

In the early 1860s, German immigrants who came to farm the fertile soil around Red Wing also discovered high-quality natural clay deposits in the area. Among the Germans were skilled craftspeople who used the clay to make crocks and bowls for food storage and processing on their farms. Salt-glazed Red Wing clay produced light tan or gray finished products, which were often decorated with distinctive cobalt-blue designs of flora or fauna.

Independent potters organized as the Red Wing Union Stoneware Company in the late 1870s. Eventually the company became the country's largest producer of utilitarian ceramic objects for the home and farm, including coolers, milk jugs, and butter churns. The firm spawned several iterations under different names, including Red Wing Pottery.

After stints at Red Wing Furniture and Red Wing Wagon Works, the young Elmore Sherman Hoyt was recruited into the pottery business. In the 1890s he took over as president of Red Wing Pottery, a position he held for more than forty years. He was simultaneously president of the Red Wing Sewer Pipe Company, another manufacturer employing the region's clay.

As new inventions for food storage became available and new methods of production were established, Red Wing Pottery needed to change both process and product. The potteries undertook mass production of Bristol-glazed wares and turned toward fine-art ceramics for the home, such as hand-painted dinnerware and vases, carrying the distinctive "red wing" logo and individual potter's mark.

The manufacturer continued to thrive until a labor strike led to its closing in 1967. But the salesroom remained in operation under the R. A. Gillmer family. In 1996, Gillmer's grandson, Scott, restarted the manufacturing business with an emphasis on the original styles and expanded the retail shops and services. The firm operated until near the end of 2013, when it was acquired by Red Wing Stoneware, which continues to run the historic pottery today. Collectors eagerly seek out original, early Red Wing pottery, prized for its aesthetic simplicity, historic significance, and most of all, dreamy nostalgia.

Pottery workers at the Union Stoneware Company in Red Wing, circa 1910. E. S. Hoyt was president of the company for more than forty years.

house before arriving at the front door, which is plain except for a sheltering canopy adorned with two fret-sawn panels.

Inside, the house offers a superb array of rooms that have come down through the years largely intact. Wright's Prairie houses generally have open plans, with partitions rather than full walls separating downstairs rooms so as to provide strong visual connections. The Hoyt House is more restrained in this regard. Only the living and dining rooms flow directly into each other, but numerous art-glass doors, sidelights, and interior windows combine to create a sense of interpenetrating space.

The downstairs is organized around an entry hall that shimmers with a symphony of art glass. On the left, a glass door with sidelights leads to a small library. To the right, a pair of sliding doors opens into the living room,

Two pairs of art-glass windows are set at one corner of the house amid walls of colorful tapestry brick. Recessed mortar between the brick courses helps to emphasize the house's horizontal lines.

The living room, trimmed in oak, includes a beautiful glass mosaic above the fireplace designed by Elmslie and executed by Minneapolis artisan Edward L. Sharretts.

Elmslie designed nearly a hundred art-glass windows for the house, among them a row of seven that brings in rich, warm light to the living room.

which, along with the dining room and an enclosed porch, forms the front of the house. At the end of the hall is the main staircase, which features a wood screen on one side and a window on the other, allowing views into the living room. There's also a door to the kitchen across from the stairs.

The living room, spacious but not huge, and all trimmed in oak, is the heart of the house. One corner is taken up by a brick wall with a built-in fireplace and a lovely ultramarine, black, and gold glass mosaic depicting a moonlit scene with trees. The mosaic was designed by Elmslie and executed by his frequent collaborator, Edward L. Sharretts of Mosaic Arts Shops in Minneapolis. Elmslie also designed two built-in lamps, set next to the wall of windows, that illuminate the room.

Glass doors on the east side of the living room provide access to an enclosed porch. This room was originally an open, screened sleeping porch. Purcell

Minnesota's Greatest Corner

The E. S. Hoyt House, at the southwest corner of Hill and Third Streets in Red Wing, forms part of what is perhaps the most stunning residential ensemble in Minnesota. The other three homes around the corner include the state's finest surviving octagon house, a towered French Second Empire mansion, and a more modest bungalow that occupies the site of a vanished estate built by a pioneering doctor whose son became one of Minneapolis's most prominent architects.

The corner's oldest architectural citizen is the James Lawther House, a two-story brick octagon outfitted with a wraparound porch, elaborate cresting, and a cupola. The Irish-born Lawther, a real estate developer and early Red Wing civic leader, built his home in 1857, at a time when octagon houses had become something of a fad. The man who popularized octagons was an eccentric New Yorker named Orson Squire Fowler. A phrenologist by trade, Fowler took time out from measuring heads in 1848 to produce a book titled *The Octagon House: A Home for All*. In it he argued, with perhaps more enthusiasm than common sense, that an octagon was the most efficient shape for a house, never mind all of those inconvenient triangular rooms that resulted from his designs.

While the nation wasn't exactly swept by octamania, several thousand homes were ultimately built to Fowler's plans. Most were constructed in the 1850s, although a few appeared as late as the 1880s. Lawther's octagon, which received a large addition in 1872, is one of only a handful remaining in Minnesota, and it's now listed on the National Register of Historic Places.

Standing catty-corner from Lawther's angular wonder is the French Second Empire–style Philander Sprague House of 1868. Tall and somewhat gawky, it features a three-story corner tower wearing the usual mansard hat, paired and triple-arched windows crowned by terra-cotta hoods, and an L-shaped entry porch. Sprague, who hailed from New York state, opened the first terra-cotta factory in Red Wing, and his house remains one of the city's most impressive Victorians.

The 1915-vintage bungalow at the northeast corner of the intersection doesn't quite pack the architectural punch of its neighbors, but it's a good example of the Arts and Crafts style. The bungalow replaced a Victorian-era mansion owned by Dr. Charles Hewitt, who arrived in Red Wing in 1867. Local legend holds that the remains of a horse he brought back from the Civil War are buried on the property. Hewitt was instrumental in creating the Minnesota Board of Health in 1872, and he later established a laboratory in Red Wing for producing smallpox vaccine. The laboratory, at 216 Dakota Street, was added to the National Register in 1979.

Hewitt's only son, Edwin, born in 1874, spent four years studying architecture at the prestigious École des Beaux-Arts in Paris before setting up his own office in Minneapolis in 1904. Six years later, he joined Edwin Brown in a partnership, and the firm went on to design such downtown Minneapolis monuments as the Cathedral Church of St. Mark (1908–1911), Hennepin Avenue Methodist Church (1916), and what is now the CenturyLink Building (1932), a twenty-six-story Art Deco skyscraper.

The James Lawther House, a brick octagon built in 1857 and enlarged in 1872, stands directly across Hill Street from the Hoyt House. Two other historically significant homes can also be found at the intersection of Third and Hill Streets.

The dining room, with its precise oak woodwork, conveys a sense of Shaker simplicity and also reflects the Arts and Crafts style so popular in the early 1900s.

and Elmslie included such porches in many of their homes, in part because sleeping outdoors was thought at the time to be particularly healthy.

The home's oak-trimmed dining room, reached via a wide opening next to the fireplace wall, is close to Prairie perfection. Crisp and inviting, it features a pair of built-in sideboards and a small bay fitted with art-glass windows to either side of a clear glass pane. The room weds Shaker simplicity to the Prairie aesthetic, and it conveys a quiet sense of harmony that will never go out of style. The dining room connects through a butler's pantry to the remodeled kitchen, where there's also a back stairway.

Upstairs, there are four bedrooms, two bathrooms, a maid's room, and a sewing room, all arranged along a narrow hall with a tent ceiling.

A plain oak railing, its posts very closely spaced, extends along one side of the hall as it doubles back past the open staircase. Many of the upstairs rooms have corner windows, which help create a sense of openness and bring in additional light. The master bedroom suite also comes with a delightful little sitting porch.

William Purcell, who could be critical of his firm's work, pronounced the Hoyt House "a successful dwelling in every way," and his pride seems entirely justified. In an unfinished "parabiography" Purcell had a good deal to say about the house, which seems to have been as close to an ideal commission as the firm of Purcell and Elmslie ever enjoyed. The Hoyts were wonderful clients—knowledgeable but not overbearing, easy to work with, and willing to pay what was required to obtain the first-class house they wanted. Purcell described Hoyt as a man of "genial and kindly disposition" who "laid down sufficient funds to build and finish this house very beautifully."

When the Hoyts moved into the house in 1914, they appear to have found it satisfactory in every way. Purcell noted, "The Hoyts rather enjoyed the new excitement of being pioneers in art, and were delighted with the practical arrangements and conveniences of their home." Their satisfaction did not diminish. One day in 1925, Purcell reported, Florence Hoyt chanced by his office in Minneapolis and told him, "I had to come in and tell you what joy our home has given us these dozen years we've lived in it."

By the time Florence Hoyt made her comments, the Prairie school was all but defunct. After a stint in Japan, where he designed the now-lost Imperial Hotel (1922) in Tokyo, Wright explored new styles in California before making another breakthrough with his Usonian houses of the 1930s, beginning with the Willey House in Minneapolis. The firm of Purcell and Elmslie wasn't able to adapt as readily, and the partnership was dissolved in 1921. Purcell then remained in Minneapolis for a time, while Elmslie returned to Chicago. Neither architect enjoyed great professional success in his later years. Elmslie died a poor man in Chicago in 1952. Purcell fared better, eventually retiring to California, where he died in 1965.

The Hoyts, meanwhile, were content to remain in Red Wing, where they lived in the house for the rest of their lives, E. S. dying in 1947 and Florence in 1960. Their daughter, Hazel, who had moved in earlier to help care for her ailing mother, then became the sole occupant of the home. A year before her death in 1976, the house was added to the National Register of Historic Places. The next owners, Frank and Jean Chesley, were also deeply rooted in Red Wing. Jean Chesley was a daughter of Alexander Anderson, whose Tower View estate just outside of town had begun taking shape only two years after the Hoyts moved into their house.

Frank Chesley died in 1997, and Jean, in 2010. The house was then

An interior art-glass window provides views into the living room from the main staircase, which features simple, closely spaced oak balusters.

A tent ceiling adds a dynamic note to the upstairs hall, where oak trim ties all of the doors together.

purchased by Adam and Allison Gettings. Like the Chesleys and the Hoyts before them, Allison has strong connections to Red Wing. Her great-grandfather J. R. Sweasy bought the Red Wing Shoe Company in the early 1900s, and members of her family have run the business ever since. Allison, who now has her own small shoe company, says she and her husband, Adam, who works in robotics and consumer technology, fell in love with the house the first time they saw it. "From the minute you walk in the front door," she says, "the house feels very comfortable. It just has great character."

The Gettingses hope to modernize the kitchen one day but otherwise plan few major changes to the house, which with its sparkling light and graceful sequence of rooms seems to have enchanted everyone who's had the good fortune to call it home. ❧

Architects William Purcell and George Elmslie were influenced by Frank Lloyd Wright, but the Hoyt House is more compact and practical than many of Wright's designs.

Glass doors in the living room lead to what was originally an open sleeping porch (now enclosed). Such porches were common features in Prairie-style homes.

David Park House
Bemidji, 1937

David Park in the yard of his house, circa 1930s. He moved to Bemidji in the 1920s and soon became one of the city's leading businessmen.

Opposite: The David Park House is an outstanding example of the sleek Moderne style that enjoyed a brief period of popularity in the 1930s. It was built for the owner of a large dairy in Bemidji.

N THE MID-1920S, AN AMBITIOUS YOUNG MAN NAMED DAVID PARK moved to Bemidji, a town of about seven thousand people that had been carved out of the north woods less than forty years earlier as a logging outpost. In the town's rough-and-tumble pioneer days, four thousand or more men labored every winter in the surrounding woods, cutting down vast stands of prized red and white pine. All of that sawing, felling, and hauling made for thirsty lumberjacks, and as late as 1913 Bemidji was said to have three times as many saloons as churches, a proportion not generally considered to be ideal.

By the time of Park's arrival, however, the mother lode of high-grade timber around Bemidji had been exhausted, and the town entered a period of transition. Tourism became an important business—one especially florid advertisement proclaimed that Bemidji was "set like a jewel in the billowy folds of nature's green, luxurious drapery"—and the town's first resort hotel opened in 1915. It wasn't until the 1930s, however, that the now-iconic statues of Paul Bunyan and Babe the Blue Ox debuted in all their glory along the shores of Lake Bemidji. In the meantime, logging had given way to dairy farming on much of the cutover land. As it so happened, this new economic order perfectly suited Park, who was intent on starting his own dairy business.

One of ten children born to an Irish farm family in Michigan, Park was the kind of man Sinclair Lewis might have described in his 1920 novel *Main Street* as a "live wire." Despite his modest beginnings, Park graduated from the University of Michigan (his nine siblings also obtained college degrees) and then headed west to Worthington, Minnesota, to work in a creamery. Within a year, he was offered a partnership but decided instead that he wanted to go out on his own. His search for a place to begin his own business took him to Bemidji, where a creamery had recently closed. He bought the building and in 1926, at the age of only twenty-four, opened the David Park Company.

The new company proved to be a resounding success. Park not only produced milk, ice cream, and butter at his dairy but also opened a chain

Park's dairy in Bemidji sold ice cream under the Luxury label in Minnesota and four other states.

of ice cream shops, under the Luxury label, which eventually expanded to more than thirty outlets in five states. The business was sufficiently sound to weather the Great Depression, and by the mid-1930s Park and his wife, Edna, decided to build a new home for their family, which by then included three children.

Bemidji in the 1930s was hardly a hotbed of avant-garde architecture, and the usual course for a man such as Park would have been to build a home in one of the then-fashionable period revival styles. These styles, which came in flavors ranging from Tudor to Norman to Spanish Colonial, had become especially popular in the 1920s, not only for mansions but also for everyday tract houses. Yet even though Park seems to have been a conservative man in most respects—he was a churchgoing Presbyterian, a devoted husband and father, a civic booster who served for two years as Bemidji's mayor, and a stout Republican—his taste in architecture turned out to be anything but conventional. Instead of settling for a standard home of the era, he chose to build a startling white house that remains one of Minnesota's chief domestic monuments in the Moderne style.

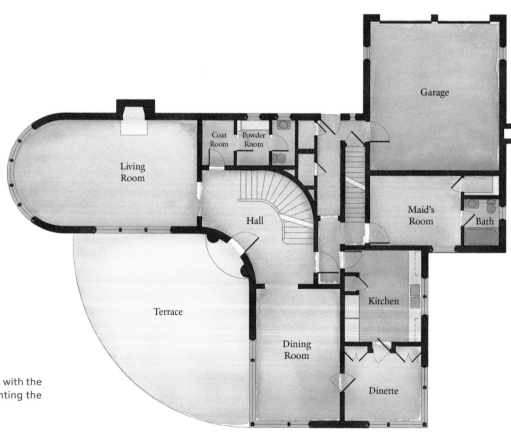

Graceful curves dominate the Park House's floor plan, with the terrace functioning as an outdoor "room," complementing the architecture of Edward K. Mahlum.

This front elevation shows the front door at the very center of the house, at the intersection of its L-shaped wings. The photograph below shows the home from the right side, and again the front door is at the center.

The house's horizontal banding, corner windows, and rounded edges are all common elements of the Moderne style, which sought to convey a sense of movement and sleek sophistication. This is a side view of the house.

With its smooth walls, blocky profile, flat roof, well-placed curves, and lack of traditional ornamental flourishes, the 5,300-square-foot house offered a sophisticated vision of modernism at a time when home building in Minnesota, and the nation as a whole, had just begun to climb out from the deep pit of the Great Depression. The house also served, in its own small way, as a statement of hope that a bright, clean new world was ready to emerge from the ruins of the most soul-crushing economic collapse in the nation's history.

Exactly why Park decided to build such a novel house remains something of a mystery, since he left behind no letters or other documents that might explain his surprising choice. There is, however, at least one tantalizing clue in the historic record. It's known that Park, like many other well-off midwesterners of the time, visited the Century of Progress International Exposition held in Chicago in 1933–1934. Commonly known as the Chicago World's Fair, the event drew as many as 125,000 people a day and was also widely publicized in magazines and newspapers. Among the fair's most popular exhibits were thirteen demonstration homes, including the spectacular glass and steel House of Tomorrow, which gave visitors a chance to see the latest in materials and building techniques. Virtually all of Minnesota's Moderne-style houses were built between 1935 and 1940, within a few years of the fair, and it's certainly possible that Park was influenced by what he saw in Chicago.

Once Park was ready to build a new house, he didn't have far to go to find an architect who was capable of delivering his dream, Edward K. Mahlum. Only twenty-six years old, Mahlum was working at the time for Foss and Company, a small architectural firm based in Fergus Falls, about a hundred miles southwest of Bemidji. Raised in Norway (where as a U.S. Army officer he would later work as an undercover agent with the resistance during World War II), Mahlum had returned to the United States in the late 1920s and then gone on to earn an architecture degree at what is now North Dakota State University in 1934. He was just a year out of school when he designed Park's house. It must have been an exciting commission for the young architect, giving him a chance to design a large home in the most modern style of the time.

The house stands at 1501 Birchmont Drive in what is today a well-developed residential neighborhood directly across the street from Bemidji State University. When Park built the house, however, it was, as one of his daughters described it, "out in the woods," on a swampy tract of land at the edge of town. The university, known as Bemidji State Normal School when it opened in 1919, was in the 1930s still a very small institution, with a campus that consisted of only three buildings near Lake Bemidji. Park bought an entire square block of land for his house but didn't use it

The living room extends past the main body of the house to form a curving wall of windows. The smooth, white walls are built of poured concrete.

Opposite: The front door, sheltered by a small balcony, is at the center of the L-shaped house between its two wings. Fluted side piers, decorative railings, and wavy molding at the base of the balcony are among the home's few exterior ornamental touches.

all. Instead, he sold off extra lots to friends, thereby allowing him to select his immediate neighbors.

Park's L-shaped, two-story house is unusual not only for its style but also for its structure. The home is built of poured, reinforced concrete, a material introduced in Minnesota in the early years of the twentieth century and at first used mainly for heavy warehouse and commercial construction. A few homes, mostly very large and costly ones, were also built of poured concrete, beginning around 1910, but Park's house was almost certainly the first of its kind in Bemidji. It took about a year to complete the house, as workers using wooden forms meticulously constructed the walls layer by layer. The concrete construction ensured a very sturdy, if not especially well-insulated house, and a powerful heating system was needed to keep everyone warm. The builder, Robert Nasvik, was so struck by the project that he had Mahlum design a similar, but smaller, Moderne house next door for his own family.

The Park House has an especially fine front entrance. Set at a forty-five-degree angle between the two wings, the entrance offers a lively tour de force in the geometry of curves. A granite-paved entry terrace guarded by outward-curving metal rails leads to the front door, which is flanked by fluted piers that bend inward, while overhead a small curved balcony provides shelter from the elements. The effect of this curvaceous entry sequence is both elegant and pleasing and provides a strong focal point for Mahlum's design.

Inside, fun with geometry continues in what is the house's most dazzling feature—a sweeping curved staircase that extends from the basement to the second floor. Positioned directly inside the front-door entry hall, the staircase serves as the home's literal centerpiece, conveying a sense of dynamic movement that is one of the defining elements of Moderne design.

A curved balcony hovers over the back door. The attached two-car garage at left was an unusual feature at the time.

Minnesota Moderne

The Park House is one of a relatively small number of homes in Minnesota—probably no more than a hundred or so—built in a distinctive 1930s style that goes by a number of names, among them Moderne, Streamline Moderne, Art Moderne, and Depression Modern. All refer to a style whose key features include rounded corners, continuous corner windows with horizontal mullions, flat wall surfaces (usually of white stucco), and grooved lines (typically arranged in groups of three or more) to provide added horizontal emphasis. Architect Edward Mahlum incorporated all of these stylistic elements into his design of the Park House.

Although Moderne is sometimes viewed as an outgrowth of the Art Deco style of the 1920s, it was in many ways a reaction against the sumptuous excesses of the Jazz Age. Art Deco (a term that didn't come into widespread use until the 1960s) was inspired by a 1925 exposition of industrial and decorative arts in Paris. Designers in the United States quickly adopted the style, which led to the design of everything from clothing and furniture to skyscrapers (including the Rand and Foshay Towers in Minneapolis). Rarely used for houses because of its expense, Art Deco was a style that evoked a world of privilege and luxury.

That world came crashing to an end in 1929, and as the Great Depression deepened, the opulence of Art Deco seemed increasingly out of place. Designers began looking for a leaner, tauter style that would better reflect the times yet would also be recognizably modern. By the mid-1930s industrial designers such as Raymond Loewy, Walter Dorwin Teague, Norman Bel Geddes, and Minnesota-born Donald Deskey began creating everyday objects, especially furniture and appliances, with a rounded look. Loewy's Cold Spot refrigerator of 1938 (manufactured for Sears, Roebuck by the Seeger Refrigerator Company in St. Paul) was among the most famous of these Moderne designs. Automobiles, locomotive engines, steamships, and airplanes also took on a streamlined look, and architects soon followed suit. World fairs in Chicago (1933–1934) and New York (1939) also helped popularize the Moderne style.

In Minnesota, one of the first businesses to embrace the new look was the Greyhound Bus Company (founded in Hibbing), which commissioned a series of Moderne-style depots. The largest, in Minneapolis, was completed in 1936 (it's now the First Avenue night club). Numerous industrial buildings of the time also display Moderne lines. Perhaps the state's premier Moderne monument is the Minneapolis Armory, also completed in 1936. Notable Moderne-style homes in Minnesota, in addition to the Park House, include the V. Mel and Henet Kaufman House (1936) in Minneapolis, the Frederick V. Nash House (1937) on Lake Minnetonka, and the Abe and Mary Engelson House (1939) in St. Paul.

The outbreak of World War II brought vast changes to the construction industry, and when the war finally ended a new style of architecture now called Midcentury Modern quickly became dominant. Although a few Moderne-style buildings appeared in the late 1940s (including several at the Minnesota State Fairgrounds), the style had pretty well run its course by 1950.

The Abe Engelson House in St. Paul, built in 1939, is among Minnesota's major monuments in the short-lived Moderne style.

A dramatic curved staircase in the front entry hall forms the visual heart of the house and extends from the basement to the second floor.

The staircase's magnificent railing heightens this effect. Consisting of three parallel bronze rails, the uppermost of which is capped with brass, the railing has no visible joints or seams along its entire length, and it twists its way up from one level to the next like a switchback highway. Where it was fabricated is unknown, but the work wasn't done locally, since the railing is said to have been shipped to Bemidji in one piece on a flatbed truck.

Off to one side of the stair hall is the home's spacious living room, which culminates in a curving wall of windows. Unlike period revival rooms with their busy detailing, many-paned windows, and sense of dark intimacy, the living room in the Park House conveys a feeling of openness, clarity, and light. Park is said to have particularly enjoyed sitting by the big windows, which face south, thereby bringing in plenty of welcome sunlight during Bemidji's long winters. Among the room's few ornamental touches is a fireplace grille sporting an Art Deco–style zigzag motif. The room is trimmed in Philippine mahogany, which is treated quite simply except for distinctive scrolls over the main doorway.

The stair hall also opens into a light-filled dining room that features a dramatic coved ceiling. Much of the light pours in through huge corner windows—a hallmark of the Moderne style. These windows are so large that unlike virtually all of the others in the house, they cannot be opened. The dining room's hardwood floor is the only one original to the house. All of the other rooms, as built, had concrete floors.

Connecting to the dining room through a small paneled dinette is the kitchen, which has survived through the years with remarkably few changes to its original design. In keeping with the house's Moderne theme, the kitchen cabinets are rounded near the windows, and there's also a curving, built-in side table propped up by a single leg. As built, the house fea-

Opposite: A view from the second floor highlights the staircase's elegant geometry. The railings are made of bronze and capped with brass handrails.

Paul Bunyan in Bemidji

Although the David Park House is a superb design, it's not Bemidji's most revered icon. That honor undoubtedly goes to an outsized lumberjack and his bovine pal, whose statues adorn a park near the center of town. Many states along the U.S.–Canadian border have claimed folk hero Paul Bunyan and his legendary sidekick, Babe the Blue Ox, as their own, but most people now acknowledge Bemidji as the official home of the monumental duo. Their statues by Lake Bemidji were proclaimed cultural resources worthy of preservation by the National Park Service and named to the National Register of Historic Places in 1988.

The legend of Paul and Babe grew out of the experiences of lumberjacks who felled primeval pine forests in the early years of North American settlement. The increasingly outrageous tales of Bunyan's size ("eight feet tall and three hundred pounds") and strength spread among the lumberjack camps all along the Canadian border.

There is much debate about the origins of the legend, but some trace Paul's roots to the Papineau Rebellion of 1837, in which a man called Paul Bonyenne fought against England for the French Canadians. Others claim the stories are based on actual French Canadian lumber-

Revelers celebrate with the newly created statues of Paul Bunyan and Babe the Blue Ox during the 1937 Bemidji Winter Carnival.

men such as "Big Joe" Mufferaw and Fabian "Saginaw Joe" Fournier. In any case, the stories did not see print until journalist James MacGillivray published a series in a Michigan newspaper in 1906. An advertising executive named William Laughead seized upon the stories in 1914 to promote the Red River Lumber Company in Minneapolis. Because many of the Paul Bunyan tales emerged after this ad campaign, they have been called "fakelore," not true traditional folklore. But it tickled Minnesota hearts to believe that, as reported, Babe and Paul's heavy footprints created the state's ten thousand lakes.

Bemidji's statues were created for a Paul Bunyan Carnival in the fall of 1937. Promoters commissioned builder Cyril Dickinson to create an enormous statue of Paul in the image of the city's mayor, Earl Bucklen. The eighteen-foot-tall statue, built that winter, was three times the height of the mayor. Concrete footings were topped with a wood framework, reinforced with steel bars and laths, and covered with cement stucco, giving the statue the weight of two-and-a-half tons. Paul's huge wooden shotgun (now gone) stood at his side.

James Payton was asked to create a statue of Babe in the same proportions as Paul. He began with a truck, which would make the statue portable, and used a skeleton of wooden ribs, covered with wire lath, topped with wool padding, and covered with canvas. Babe's nostrils spewed pipe smoke, and his eyes, made of battery-operated car taillights, glowed red beneath his fourteen-foot span of tin horns. But after being used in parades nationwide to promote the city, Babe became somewhat dilapidated. He was taken off the truck and permanently installed next to Paul, where he was reworked in concrete. Both statues receive annual paint touch-ups. Hidden tour guides with microphones give a voice to Paul, who delights children with his personal greetings.

tured a top-loading dishwasher that would have been a rare amenity in the 1930s. A maid's room, powder room, and attached two-car garage are also located on the main floor.

The basement originally contained a large recreation room, warmed by a fireplace. It was a favorite gathering place for the family and was also used for dances. Upstairs, the family enjoyed four spacious bedrooms, all with corner windows. The master bedroom suite included a curving wall of windows, a small terrace, a bath, and a handsome little dressing room equipped with a built-in mirrored vanity. All told, the house as built had six bathrooms—an unusually large number for the time.

Park and his family moved into their new home in late 1937 or early 1938. Park had every right to be proud of his dream house, and by all accounts he was, protecting its every feature. His youngest daughter, Mary Morton, remembers that he insisted the children keep their hands off the brass stairway rail so as not to mar its shiny surface. Violators of this rule could be sentenced to polishing the rail, no small task. The house also attracted curious passersby on a regular basis, and Morton recalls her father would gladly give tours to anyone who showed up at the door. "He just loved the house," she says.

Edna Park, unfortunately, did not enjoy the house for long, dying of cancer in 1941. Three years later, David Park married Wanda Hartman, and the couple had one child, Mary. Perhaps the most memorable event in the history of the house—a visit from Eleanor Roosevelt—occurred in the early 1950s, when Mary was a small child. The former first lady and longtime social activist was on a nationwide speaking tour that included a stop in Bemidji. On the day she arrived, it was discovered that no one

The kitchen retains its original cabinetry as well as a small built-in side table supported by a single leg.

Portions of the Bemidji State University campus are visible through the living-room windows. The university's foundation acquired the house in 1991 for use as offices.

had thought to plan a reception for her. David Park then stepped in and quickly arranged an event at the house, much to his wife's surprise. She was out with friends, and family lore holds that Park called her and said, "You'd better come home. We're having the whole town over." The reception went off without a hitch, and Morton, who was only about four at the time, says she was fast asleep in her room when, she learned later, Roosevelt came in and kissed her on the forehead.

David Park closed his dairy business in 1960 but never left Bemidji or moved out of his beloved house. He died, at age seventy-five, on New Year's Eve of 1977. Wanda Park stayed on in the house, and in 1988 it was listed on the National Register of Historic Places. After her death in 1991, the Bemidji State University Foundation, a nonprofit organization that helps raise funds for the university, bought the house for use as its offices. The Bemidji State Alumni Association, which also has offices in the house, became co-owners the next year.

Once the foundation acquired the house, it raised funds to undertake a variety of improvements, including new windows, a new roof, and upgraded heating, wiring, and plumbing. More than a hundred volunteers also helped with sanding, priming, and painting walls. As part of the renovation, some rooms were modified to accommodate the home's new institutional use. The bedrooms, for example, now serve as offices, while the old basement recreation room is a meeting space.

Despite these changes, the house—which is open for tours on a regular basis—retains many of its original features, including some light fixtures, fireplaces, and of course the magnificent staircase. Visitors will discover that a sense of sleek modernity still infuses the house. So too does the spirit of David Park, a small-town businessman who dreamed big and left behind a remarkable monument in an unlikely place.

The dining room, just off the entry hall, includes a coved ceiling with recessed lighting.

Harry A. Blackmun House

Golden Valley, 1950

Harry Blackmun, who went on to become an associate justice of the U.S. Supreme Court, was working for a large Minneapolis law firm when he built his new home in Golden Valley in 1950.

Opposite: Harry and Dorothy Blackmun chose the Minneapolis architectural firm of Thorshov and Cerny to design their L-shaped Midcentury Modern–style home in Golden Valley, a Minneapolis suburb whose population exploded after World War II.

Harry Blackmun, who was raised in St. Paul, is best remembered today as the author of the majority opinion in *Roe v. Wade*, a landmark abortion case decided by the U.S. Supreme Court in 1973. But long before he became a justice on the nation's highest court, Blackmun was among millions of Americans who, in the years immediately after World War II, built new houses in the suburbs. The housing boom in which Blackmun participated came at a time when the public, more so than perhaps any other time in history, eagerly embraced new approaches to architecture and design. Blackmun's Golden Valley home—impeccably restored and renovated by its current owner, Bill Lyons—is an exceptionally well-preserved example of the style now called Midcentury Modern, which transformed the look of much of America in the two decades following the war.

When the fighting ended, Blackmun and his fellow Americans were ready for a clean, fresh start in almost every aspect of their lives, including where and how they lived. The war had brought nonmilitary construction across the country to a virtual standstill, and as millions of servicemembers returned home to start families, an acute housing shortage developed. In the Twin Cities, the housing supply was so tight that thousands of veterans and their families moved into temporary Quonset hut villages, which were hastily assembled in parks and other open areas. Other families lived with relatives crowded into tiny apartments, all the while dreaming of new houses of their own.

Blackmun's situation wasn't quite so dire. In 1949, when he began planning for a new home, the forty-year-old Blackmun was a respected junior partner at the Dorsey law firm in Minneapolis. His wife, Dorothy, had just given birth to their third daughter, and the newly enlarged family needed more room than their South Minneapolis apartment could provide. With little desirable land left for development in the city proper, Blackmun bought a homesite at 4435 Tyrol Crest in suburban Golden Valley, not far from downtown. At the time, Golden Valley was still quite small, with just over five thousand people, but its population would triple by 1960 as part

A 1947 "idea house" built by the Walker Art Center in Minneapolis offered a vision of modernism at a time when many young families were looking for new homes.

of a powerful postwar surge that brought tremendous growth to suburbs across the United States.

It was no surprise that Blackmun chose a modern look for his new house, since the decorated period revival styles popular in Minnesota and elsewhere in the 1920s and 1930s had quickly fallen out of favor after the war. In part this happened because the need to build millions of new homes as quickly as possible favored a simpler approach to design. But modernism was also the dominant design philosophy of the era, to the exclusion of almost everything else. Gripped by a deep sense of social purpose, architects were especially interested in remaking the traditional American home. Their goal was to create a new kind of house that was free from the weight of the past, and they embraced the latest in building technologies, materials, and furnishings.

High-style Midcentury Modern houses, especially in the first decade after the war, emphasized efficiency, rationality, and in many cases, a kind of monastic simplicity that eschewed the accoutrements of luxury. The result was a brief period when even so-called executive houses often didn't exceed five thousand square feet and could be surprisingly chaste. This devotion to compact living didn't last long, however, and by the mid-1950s houses began to grow larger, although they were still modest compared with today's outsized McMansions.

Midcentury Modernism drew its inspiration from at least three sources. One was the work of European modernists, from Le Corbusier in France to Ludwig Mies van der Rohe in Germany, who in the 1920s radically departed from architectural tradition by designing taut white houses that featured large expanses of glass, open asymmetrical plans, and absolutely no ornament. Le Corbusier's Villa Savoye (1931), just outside Paris, was perhaps the most famous of these houses. In the United States, Austrian-born architect Rudolph Schindler's Lovell House (1926), near Los Angeles, offered a similar vision of chaste modernity. A book titled *The International Style*, published in 1932 as part of an exhibition at the Museum of Modern Art in New York City, gave this new work a name, and it would soon be widely publicized in both the popular and architectural press.

Another important influence came not from overseas but from Wisconsin, where Frank Lloyd Wright in the 1930s began designing relatively small, one-story houses he called Usonians, after his name for the United States. The Nancy and Malcolm Willey House (1934) in Minneapolis was the first of Wright's designs to incorporate many Usonian features, such as a dramatic glass-walled living room, which would reappear in various forms in many high-style homes built after the war.

The casual, free-flowing ranch houses that first appeared in California in the 1930s also had a significant impact on midcentury design across the United States. With their long, spreading wings and openness to the outdoors, ranch houses were a modern response to California's warm, sunny climate. In chilly Minnesota, however, ranch houses tended to be more conservative, shrinking into the rectilinear ramblers that became a staple of suburban tract developments in the 1950s.

As they considered their own house, Blackmun and his wife could hardly have been unaware of these design trends. Newspapers and periodicals of the time were filled with articles touting the latest housing innovations. The Blackmuns may also have toured demonstration homes such as the Walker Art Center's Idea House II. Built in Minneapolis in 1947, the house displayed modern-style living at its best, complete with architect-designed furniture and the latest appliances.

Early in 1949 the Blackmuns chose the Minneapolis architectural firm of Thorshov and Cerny to design their home. Roy Thorshov, the senior partner, was the son of longtime Minneapolis architect Olaf Thorshov and had deep roots in the city. Robert Cerny, born in Wisconsin, held a master's degree from Harvard, had traveled extensively in Europe, and was well acquainted with the most up-to-date trends in architecture. He'd designed his first modernist house in St. Paul in 1940 and tended to favor strong, simple forms. At the time Thorshov and Cerny took on the Blackmun commission, they were among the busiest architects in Minnesota, with schools, churches, and a variety of commercial and industrial buildings in the works. Their most novel project was the state's first nuclear power plant (gone), completed just north of the Twin Cities in Elk River in 1950.

The Blackmun House was designed for a choice hilltop site in the Tyrol Hills neighborhood, one of the best-planned and most attractive suburban communities in the Twin Cities. Located just three miles west of downtown Minneapolis in a landscape of low, wooded hills and small ponds, Tyrol Hills—divided into north and south sections—was laid out

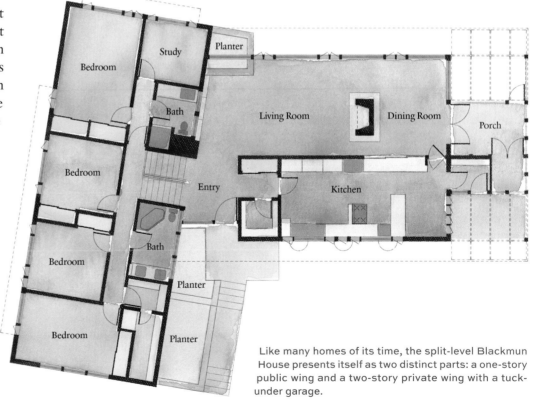

Like many homes of its time, the split-level Blackmun House presents itself as two distinct parts: a one-story public wing and a two-story private wing with a tuck-under garage.

Midcentury Modernism in Minnesota

Midcentury Modernism is today most commonly associated with glassy, open-plan houses of the kind built for Harry Blackmun. But during its period of peak popularity between 1945 and the early 1960s, the style was universal. Commercial buildings, factories, schools, and churches all took on a modern look as architects strove to discard old forms in favor of design solutions untethered from the demands of tradition. In Minnesota, Midcentury Modernism was so pervasive in the 1950s that it is hard to find significant buildings from that period in any other style.

Large corporations were among the first to embrace the new style. Less than a mile from the Blackmun House, the Prudential Insurance Company constructed a new regional office (1954) on a park-like thirty-acre site overlooking Brownie Lake. The Prudential Building (now home to Target Financial Services) signaled the start in the Twin Cities of a corporate movement to the suburbs that would continue for decades to come. In 1958, General Mills took an even bigger step by completing Minnesota's earliest example of a suburban corporate campus accommodating a group of linked buildings. A few years later, the 3M Corporation followed suit with a complex of its own in Maplewood, just east of St. Paul. The ultimate statement of modernist corporate cool, however,

appeared in Rochester in 1958 when IBM opened a new office and manufacturing facility designed by Eero Saarinen, perhaps the greatest of all midcentury architects. Clad in two-tone blue glass, the IBM complex conveys a sense of both hyperrationality and sleek glamour—two attributes of some of the best midcentury architecture.

Church congregations were also drawn to the Midcentury Modern style, for both aesthetic and practical reasons. Traditional churches—with their carved stonework, vaulted interiors, and intricate stained-glass windows—were expensive to build, whereas modernist churches often carried lower price tags. Minnesota's first great Midcentury Modern church—Christ Lutheran (1949) in Minneapolis—was built in part because it cost less to construct than a Gothic Revival design of the same size. Christ Lutheran, as it turned out, was a brilliant work of architecture. Now a national historic landmark, the church was designed by Eliel Saarinen (Eero's father), and it became a template for numerous brick churches built in the 1950s. A far different church designed by Marcel Breuer is equally famous. His St. John's Abbey Church (1956) is a soaring sculpture in poured concrete that showcases the expressionistic side of Midcentury Modernism, which wasn't always as buttoned-down as it may seem.

For many people, schools may well be the most familiar legacy of Midcentury Modernism. Before World War II, schools were usually multi-story red-brick buildings finished in a style called Collegiate Gothic. Schools built after the war in the suburbs were far different. Long and low and almost always built of brick, they typically spread out in a series of wings featuring walls of windows in every classroom. For millions of baby boomers, these modernist schools—thousands of which still stand across the United States—remain a rich source of childhood memory.

The new Prudential Building in Minneapolis, 1955. Straightforward, functional design was a hallmark of the Midcentury Modern style that dominated architecture in Minnesota and across the nation in the 1950s.

in the mid-1930s with narrow, winding roads and irregularly shaped lots. World War II had brought development of the neighborhood to a halt, but once the fighting was over, building quickly resumed. Today, Tyrol Hills forms one of Minnesota's major outposts of high-style midcentury housing.

The 3,800-square-foot Blackmun House is not the largest or most luxurious home in Tyrol Hills, but with its understated design and clear expression of function, it serves as an exemplar of Midcentury Modernism. Despite its modest demeanor, the house was by no means inexpensive. Featuring high-quality materials, including white Frontenac limestone from Wisconsin, the house cost $40,000, four times the price of a standard suburban home in 1950.

Like many homes of its time, the split-level Blackmun House presents itself as two distinct parts: a one-story wing joined at a slightly skewed angle to an oblong, two-story section with a tuck-under, two-car garage. The front door, reached by a set of stone steps that climb up along the side of the garage, is located at the inner corner where the two sections of the house meet. This L-shaped arrangement is similar to that of Wright's Usonians, although they usually were limited to a single level. The house is entirely clad in vertical redwood siding, except for a stone base around the garage. Flaring eaves and trellises help control sunlight in the one-story wing, which includes a wall of south-facing windows and a screened porch at one end. Built-in sunshades—a device popularized by Le Corbusier—protect the smaller bedroom windows on the uppermost floor.

Befitting its minimalist aesthetic, the home offers very little in the way of showy exterior architecture, except perhaps for two wood trellises that extend past either side of the screened porch. The trellises are formed by standard two-by-ten-inch boards that taper at one end to suggest a dynamic sense of movement.

The front door, reached by a set of stone steps along the side of the garage, is located at the inner corner where the two sections of the Blackmun House meet.

At dusk, the house glows dramatically and the wood trellises seem to soar. The home has been impeccably restored by its current owner, architect Bill Lyons.

The living room combines the clean lines of the International style with natural vistas to create a sense of peace and harmony. Lyons has selected both restored and replica period furnishings to complement the architecture.

Opposite, top: Walls of south-facing windows at the rear of the Blackmun House offer a great hilltop view of the Tyrol Hills neighborhood and welcome warm sunlight into every room.

Opposite, bottom: During the day, the glass walls of the Blackmun House reflect trees throughout the well-planned grounds. From this angle the house conveys a sense of transparency and unhindered freedom.

A view from the stairwell shows the junction between the private and public sides of the house. High-grade redwood paneling and a limestone wall mark the point of transition.

As prescribed by modernist doctrine, the house has no ornament. Even the front door is treated plainly, with a plate-glass window to one side providing the only architectural accent.

The home's rather stark exterior yields to a gracious, light-filled interior that embodies the best qualities of midcentury design, beginning at the front door, where there's no entry hall of the kind found in more traditional homes. Instead, a small foyer without doors serves to introduce the house's layout. On the left, stairs bordered by a handsome stone wall lead up to four bedrooms and down to a lower level that includes the garage and a family room. Straight ahead, at the back of the house, is the combined living-dining room. To the right is a long kitchen that looks out from the front. The house's straightforward plan does not seem unusual today, but the placement of the kitchen at the front and living room at the rear, common in midcentury design, represented a sharp departure from time-honored practice.

The living and dining rooms, separated only by a stone fireplace with a cantilevered concrete bench, form a classic midcentury space. Both rooms enjoy copious natural light from the home's south-facing wall of floor-to-ceiling windows, which are subdivided vertically and horizontally to create a pleasing architectural rhythm. Three sets of casement windows set within the fixed panes of glass provide natural ventilation in warm weather. Overhead, a redwood-clad ceiling rises at a shallow angle toward the window wall, and this upward movement energizes the entire space. Here, the midcentury dream of openness and light is fully realized in rooms that offer a beautiful release from the confinements of the past.

The "private" part of the house, in the two-story section, is very straightforward, in keeping with the design principles of the time. The four upstairs bedrooms are arranged in a row along one side of a narrow hall, with two bathrooms, a storage room, and a study on the other side. The study, next to the master bedroom at the northeast corner of the house, was expressly designed for Blackmun, who often took work home.

The lower level originally included a maid's room in addition to the garage and family room, but it does not appear the Blackmuns or later owners ever employed a live-in maid. On the architects' original drawings, the family room, as it would be called today, was labeled a "play room." This type of room was another midcentury innovation, and the family room soon took on an added role as the preferred place for the television set, still a novelty in 1950 but soon to find its way into virtually every American household.

As built, the house featured one other conspicuously modern feature: an in-floor radiant heating system. Architects liked such systems in part because they eliminated the "clutter" of radiators or vents. Wright in partic-

"Minnesota Twins"

In the early part of the twentieth century, two bright young boys lived just a few blocks from each other in St. Paul's working-class neighborhood of Dayton's Bluff. Born just a year apart, they attended the same grade school and became fast friends. They also, by remarkable coincidence, both became U.S. Supreme Court justices, serving together on the bench for sixteen years, from 1970 through 1986.

Harold Andrew Blackmun (1908–1999) and Warren Earl Burger (1907–1995), young men of very modest means, encouraged each other to excel academically. Bookish and somewhat insecure, the slightly built Harry began keeping an elaborate diary when he was eleven years old, writing continuously in it for twenty years. The more robust and athletic Warren played sports and also excelled in academics. When it came time for college, the two were expected to attend the University of Minnesota. Warren did; Harry received a last-minute scholarship to Harvard. After graduation, they encouraged each other to go to law school, Warren to William Mitchell College of Law (then called the St. Paul College of Law) and Harry to Harvard Law School.

Both became adjunct professors of law, practiced in private firms, and were eventually appointed judges. As conservative Republicans, both men attracted the attention of President Richard M. Nixon when the time came to fill vacancies on the nation's high court. Nixon nominated Burger to be chief justice in 1969, and Blackmun came on board a year later as an associate justice. Colleagues on the court nicknamed the two the "Minnesota Twins" after the state's beloved baseball team.

During their time together on the Supreme Court, Burger became more conservative as Blackmun became more liberal, and they grew apart. This became clear in the landmark abortion case of *Roe v. Wade*, for which Blackmun wrote the court's decision.

Blackmun, who had preserved his diaries and meticulously ordered his letters and extensive legal and personal writings, died in 1999, leaving his full complement of papers to the Library of Congress. As prescribed in his will, the papers were opened five years later, in 2004, resulting in two excellent biographies, one by historian Tinsley Yarbrough and the other by *New York Times* reporter Linda Greenhouse.

Burger, who died in 1995, drafted a one-page will, leaving all of his papers to the College of William and Mary. He specified they be opened in 2026. It will be interesting to hear his take on the parallel lives of the "Minnesota Twins."

Harry Blackmun (*left*) was best man at Warren Burger's wedding in 1933. The two future justices of the U.S. Supreme Court were longtime friends who both grew up in St. Paul.

Placing the kitchen in the front of the house was a new concept in 1949. Past the doorway, stairs lead to a two-story wing that consists of a garage and recreation room below and four bedrooms above.

ular used in-floor heating for many of his Usonians. Early systems did not always prove durable, however, and repairs were costly. The system in the Blackmun House eventually failed, and electric heat was used for many years thereafter by the second owners.

The Blackmuns and their three daughters, who ranged in age from one to seven, moved into the house in the spring of 1950 but did not stay for long. Even as the house was under construction, Blackmun was being wooed by the Mayo Clinic in Rochester to become its resident counsel, a prestigious position. He took the job that October, but he didn't change houses. Blackmun apparently liked his Golden Valley house so much that he had a duplicate built in Rochester, and it's still there today.

After the Blackmuns left, another family purchased the house and remained in it for more than fifty years. The second owners made a few changes, such as enclosing the screened porch for year-round use, but did not alter the home's basic layout. By the time the house came up for sale in 2003, however, it was badly cluttered and in need of extensive repairs. Lyons, who had long admired midcentury design, first saw the property at an open house. He recalls that another prospective buyer who was leaving the open house told him, "Don't even look at it. It's a teardown."

But with his architect's eye, Lyons could see through all the clutter to the underlying beauty of the home's design. It took several months, but he was finally able to purchase the house, after which he took on the task of restoring its lost elegance. Guided by the original architects' drawings, and doing much of the work himself, Lyons over a period of four years transformed the house from its run-down condition into an exquisite midcentury showpiece.

His projects included returning the screened porch to its original appearance, refinishing all of the interior birch woodwork, rebuilding sunscreens, repairing damaged windows, restoring the bathrooms, and repainting walls. He also removed a small storage room near the front entrance so he could

The bright, updated kitchen includes its original row of eye-level windows above the countertops.

The dining area is separated from the living room by a fireplace built of Frontenac limestone. Both rooms now have terrazzo floors, replacing wood floors that were removed along with a nonfunctioning in-floor heating system.

renovate and enlarge the kitchen, which now features sleek birch cabinetry. Some original features, such as wood flooring in the living-dining room and the in-floor heating system, could not be salvaged. Lyons replaced the wood flooring with terrazzo, which suits the house perfectly. The cost of repairing the in-floor heating system, which hadn't functioned for years, was prohibitive, so Lyons installed a standard forced-air system and added air-conditioning. He also took great care in furnishing the house, selecting sofas, chairs, tables, and other items designed by midcentury icons such as Charles Eames, George Nelson, Eero Saarinen, and Isamu Noguchi.

The Blackmun House represents the early and purest phase of Mid-

A porch and patio extend past the dining room. The porch had been enclosed by a former owner, but Lyons opened it back up and restored it to its original seasonal use.

century Modernism in Minnesota, which retained its popularity through the 1950s, even as the high idealism behind it gradually faded. Today, Midcentury Modernism is back in fashion, although teardowns of architect-designed midcentury houses still occur with distressing regularity. The wonderfully inventive furniture of the period, much of it designed by architects, is especially prized. Among young buyers, midcentury homes are also earning renewed appreciation for their virtues of openness, simplicity, and modernity, the very qualities Harry Blackmun and his family were seeking more than sixty years ago when they moved to Golden Valley in pursuit of a better life. ⚬

Nancy and Malcolm Willey House
Minneapolis, 1934

Nancy and Malcolm Willey in front of their new house, circa 1930s. Nancy Willey persuaded Frank Lloyd Wright to design a house that she and her husband could afford.

Opposite: Small but elegant, the Nancy and Malcolm Willey House in Minneapolis is one of Frank Lloyd Wright's seminal designs, the first in a series of compact homes he called Usonians.

THE SIZE OF A HOUSE IS NOT ALWAYS A MEASURE OF ITS ARCHITEC-tural importance or its ability to bring joy to its owners. No one understood this better than Frank Lloyd Wright, who in the 1930s, as the nation sagged under the weight of the worst depression in its history, began to experiment with a new kind of house—compact, low-slung, built from a handful of basic materials, relatively inexpensive, and yet radiant with beauty and elegance. He called these houses Usonians, after a name he used for the United States, and the first one to incorporate most elements of the style was built in Minneapolis in 1934 for Nancy and Malcolm Willey. Although the house is no bigger than a typical rambler, it qualifies as one of the seminal designs of Wright's career.

Now impeccably restored after a long period of neglect and decay, the house was built for a client, Nancy Willey, who was every bit as strong willed as the famous architect she hired. Willey and her husband, Malcolm, commissioned the house in 1932, at a time when Wright, like virtually all members of his profession, was desperate for work. The early years of the Great Depression brought private building to a standstill, and many architects had to find other ways to make a living. A few big public projects—the St. Paul City Hall–Ramsey County Court House (1931) was a prominent Minnesota example—provided what little employment there was for the architectural profession and the building trades.

Wright, however, had made his mark primarily as a domestic architect. In the late 1890s he'd pioneered the Prairie style, creating revolutionary houses that broke the traditional bounds of architectural space. But the style had largely run its course by 1914, when Wright produced one of the last of his great Prairie houses, for Francis Little on Lake Minnetonka in Deephaven. Wright had managed to stay busy in the 1920s by designing a series of houses in California and the Imperial Hotel in Tokyo.

Wright's brilliance as an architect, however, was not the sole source of his notoriety. His disordered personal life, a grand opera full of tempests and tragedies, had more than once made front-page news. In 1914 a grisly mass murder at his Taliesin estate in Wisconsin claimed the lives of his mistress and her children. There was another well-publicized episode in 1926 when he spent a night in jail in Minneapolis on trumped-up charges brought by his second (and soon to be divorced) wife, Miriam Noel.

By the late 1920s, Wright's indiscretions and his ever more-strident criticisms of American society had made him something of an outlaw architect. He had little work and few prospects, and once the Great Depression hit, his job file dwindled to nothing. Wright retreated to Taliesin, where he began an apprenticeship program known as the Taliesin Fellowship and kept busy with writing projects while waiting for the economy to improve.

Then, in June of 1932, a welcome letter arrived from Nancy Willey in Minneapolis. She began the letter by praising Wright's recently published autobiography, a tendentious accumulation of visionary ideas, personal history, and self-justification, all delivered with Wright's characteristic mix of eloquence and bombast. "It is one of those books that makes ideas," Willey wrote, adding that she had an idea of her own to propose. "I want to build a house in Minneapolis for about eight thousand dollars. What do you think are the chances of my being able to have a 'creation of art'?"

She went on to describe the hilltop lot she and her husband owned at 255 Bedford Street Southeast in the Prospect Park neighborhood, not far from the University of Minnesota campus, where Malcolm Willey served as an assistant to the president. It was a beautiful lot with panoramic views of the Mississippi River and Minneapolis skyline—just the kind of property that Wright, who always took great pains in siting his houses, was sure to find intriguing. Even so, the $8,000 budget Willey had in mind was hardly enough to generate a substantial fee for Wright or any other architect. "I have little hope you would take on anything so trivial, that was also not near you," Willey concluded, but said she would be grateful if Wright could recommend "an architect you respect."

The letter was a canny piece of work in which Willey managed to stroke Wright's outsized ego—he would never have recommended an archi-

From the street the house conveys an aura of mystery and anticipation, with a narrowing flight of steps leading past the garage to a recessed front door.

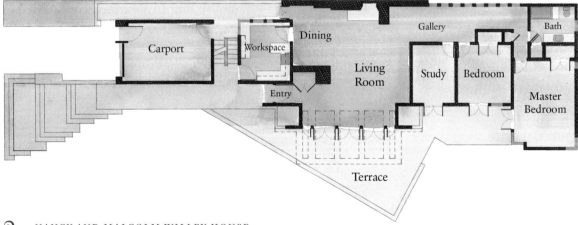

At only 1,350 square feet, Frank Lloyd Wright's Usonian home design for Nancy and Malcolm Willey is packed with drama and elegance.

The Usonian House

The Nancy and Malcolm Willey House is the first of about sixty relatively modest homes designed by Frank Lloyd Wright between 1934 and the late 1950s that are today known as Usonians. Although the houses share certain features, they are far from identical in appearance and vary in size, ranging from about 1,300 to 4,000 square feet. Most Usonians are, however, under 2,000 square feet and were intended to offer high-style design at a reasonable cost.

Before designing his first Usonians, Wright had created mostly large homes, including a few opulent mansions, for affluent clients. This was true of many of the Prairie houses he designed in the early 1900s. Even so, he experimented with less costly housing options for the middle class. One of his best-known proposals, published in the April 1907 edition of *Ladies' Home Journal*, was a foursquare, all-concrete house that in theory could be built for $5,000. As it turned out, only a few versions of the house were ever constructed. The Usonians, by contrast, were quite successful, even if they did not always prove as affordable as Wright had hoped.

Despite its many Usonian characteristics, the Willey House doesn't quite follow the standard pattern that Wright later developed for homes of its type. As a result, most historians regard another house—built in Madison, Wisconsin, in 1936 for Herbert and Katherine Jacobs—as Wright's first fully realized Usonian. Built for just $5,500, it's a small one-story home that has no basement and features an L-shaped plan with bedrooms in one wing and a large living room in the other. It also incorporates such standard Usonian features as in-floor radiant heating, built-in shelves and furniture, a terrace off the living room, and a carport (Wright didn't like garages).

There is, however, one key difference between the Willey and Jacobs houses, and it has to do with their floor plans. The Willey House is laid out so that the living room separates the bedrooms from the kitchen, whereas in the Jacobs House Wright placed the kitchen in a central core at the crook of the L. He would follow this basic layout, with some exceptions, in most of his later Usonians. As time went on, Wright produced many varieties of Usonians, including some with angled plans, raised living rooms, second floors, and other features not found in either the Willey or Jacobs house.

Most of Wright's Usonians were built in the fifteen years after World War II, a period in which one-story homes of all kinds, including ranch houses and ramblers, attained great popularity in Minnesota and elsewhere across the United States. All told, there are ten existing Wright-designed homes in Minnesota in addition to the Willey House. Among them are the Henry and Frieda Neils House (1951) on Cedar Lake in Minneapolis, the Donald and Virginia Lovness House (1955) near Stillwater, and the Elam-Plunkett House (1950) in Austin, which is one of the largest of all Usonians.

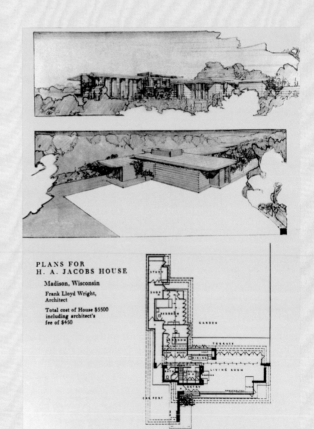

A house built in Madison, Wisconsin, in 1936 for Herbert Jacobs is generally regarded as Frank Lloyd Wright's first complete Usonian design. It shares many features with the Willey House.

All of the home's major rooms face south and open out to an angular brick terrace. The cantilevered trellis over the living-room doors is an especially dramatic feature of Wright's design.

tect other than himself—while also laying down clear financial boundaries regarding the cost of the house project. Wright wrote back a week later: "Nothing is trivial because it is not 'big.' And if I can be of any service to you neither the distance nor the 'smallness' of the proposed home would prevent me from giving you what help an architect could give you." After another exchange of letters, Willey went to Taliesin to visit with Wright, who agreed to design the house.

Nancy Willey would in the end prove to be one of Wright's most formidable clients. Born in Brooklyn and educated at Barnard College in sociology and economics, she clearly admired Wright's singular genius but never let that admiration cloud her practical judgment. She was in every respect the force behind the house, handling virtually all of the correspondence

Before Interstate 94 was constructed directly in front of the Willey House in 1968, the living room offered a panoramic view of the Mississippi River Valley and beyond.

with Wright and also acting as de facto construction superintendent. Her husband, Malcolm, played a lesser role. A well-regarded academic, he was hired as a sociology professor at the university in 1927 and became an assistant to the president in 1932 and a dean two years later.

Once they hired Wright, the Willeys quickly discovered that working with the great architect was an adventure at once glorious and maddening. The glory lay in the brilliance of Wright's designs. His houses have an intensified presence, a kind of glow their owners often describe in almost religious terms, and the Willeys found just such a quality in their own home when it was finally completed. "We are terribly happy in it," Nancy Willey wrote to Wright in November of 1934. "It is more thrilling than we ever imagined it could be, even in our most exalted moments!"

But the road to Wrightian nirvana did not prove easy, and the Willeys had to cope with one crisis after another—some induced by Wright, some by contractors—as they struggled to get their distinctive home built. The couple's biggest challenge was sticking to their modest budget. Wright's original design called for a blocky two-story brick house with banded windows, a flat roof, and a long, cantilevered front balcony. But when the Willeys found a contractor willing to build it, the bid came in at $17,400, twice what the couple wanted to spend. Wright suggested a number of schemes, all impractical, to get around the high price tag, but gave no indication he was willing to alter his design.

Nancy Willey finally confronted Wright head on in a letter written in November 1933. "I do not want a seventeen thousand dollar house even at ten or twelve thousand dollars," she wrote. "I want an eight to ten thousand dollar house at eight to ten thousand dollars. Can I have it?" She went on to say that she and her husband "place such a high value on having a Frank Lloyd Wright house that we are unwilling to poison our joy in it by having too large a debt on it, and we always feel that way." The next step, she said, would have to be "drastic simplifications to the design" or the house couldn't be built.

The ultimatum worked. Wright agreed to simplify his plans, producing a one-story house that the Willeys were able to afford, although just barely. "Have redesigned the Willey House and they will now get poetry instead of drama," Wright wrote to one of his apprentices. "Drama always comes high, I guess." Construction began early in 1934, and when the Willeys moved in late that year, the house still lacked its front steps, its terrace, and the long brick wall on the east side from which it takes its name, Gardenwall.

But the result was, as Wright had promised, "poetry." Long and low, the L-shaped house, which gracefully nestles into its site, features a simple but beautiful material palette. The walls are built of alternating bands of sand-mold and paver bricks, while red tidewater cypress—Wright's favorite wood—is used for all of the doors, window sash, and trim. Within this basic format, Wright was able to create a house that was the most radical of its day in Minnesota, anticipating the Midcentury Modern style that became dominant after World War II.

The house also represented a major new design direction for the sixty-six-year-old Wright. His Prairie-style houses and his California homes had typically been two stories high and at least three thousand square feet (the largest of his Prairie houses, built for Darwin Martin in Buffalo, New

Wright strove to dissolve traditional barriers between inside and outside. When all the doors are open, the terrace and living room flow into each other to form a unified space.

York, is fifteen thousand square feet). Even so, Wright had long been interested in creating compact, affordable homes for the middle class, and the 1,350-square-foot Willey House demonstrated that his Usonian ideals could be realized. Although the Willey House isn't quite the complete Usonian package, it represents a prototype of what was to come.

Despite the house's small size, Wright was able to achieve all manner of architectural effects in its design. The house begins with a classic Wrightian entry sequence up a narrowing flight of brick steps to a walkway that runs beneath the wide eaves of the house's semiattached garage before reaching the front door. There's also a parallel passageway on the north side of the garage that serves as a more private entrance. The two passageways connect via another set of steps in a small breezeway between the house and garage. Wright loved to make the act of entering an exercise in anticipation, and one of the marvels of the Willey House is how he was able to create so much entry drama for such a small home.

Even so, the house—largely hidden from view—remains a mystery in waiting at the front door. Wright's manipulations continue once a visitor steps inside, where a low entry ceiling with bands of wood trim suddenly swoops up at two distinct angles above the home's large "living area," as it's described on Wright's plans. Finished with the same brick used for the outside of the house, the room is the home's functional and visual heart. On its south side, past three skylights, a wall of glass formed by French doors opens out to a brick terrace sheltered by a cantilevered trellis. Once, this glass wall offered a magnificent vista that Nancy Willey described in her first letter to Wright as "seventy five per cent of the horizon." The construction of Interstate 94 directly to the south in 1968 ruined the view, and the house now overlooks nothing except an unsightly noise barrier built in 1974.

A massive brick fireplace with Wright-designed iron utensils anchors the north wall of the living area. Kite-shaped clerestory windows to either side of the fireplace bring in natural light. Next to the fireplace, a built-in table forms the dining area. Wright designed furniture for the house, but the Willeys' limited budget meant some pieces were never built. The dining-room table, for example, had only two chairs initially, with most guests seated on stools when the Willeys had company. The kitchen, or "workspace," as Wright called it, features a Dutch door and is visible from the dining area through open shelves. Small by modern standards but not unusual for its time, the kitchen incorporates one Wrightian touch in the form of corner casement windows—a feature also found in the master bedroom.

The modest elevation of the Willey House belies the poetry within.

The home's most Usonian feature is the in-line plan for its private wing, which includes two bedrooms, a study, and a bathroom. Except for the bath, the rooms are arranged in single file along the south side of a window- and bookcase-lined gallery that extends east from the living-dining area. The gallery's nine small casement windows are protected by a screen with strategically omitted bricks so as to allow views to the outside. Because the north side of the house is almost on the lot line, the brick screen also provides an added layer of privacy. The master bedroom, which juts out to create the house's L shape, is at the end of the gallery. It's a lovely, light-filled room with a tent ceiling, built-ins, and a pair of west-facing doors that open onto the terrace.

Finishing throughout the house is simple but elegant, in accord with Wright's philosophy of design. Walls are either brick or plaster; the floors are brick or wood (except for linoleum in the kitchen). Wright used cypress wood for built-in shelves and cabinets, furniture, trim, and bedroom flooring.

The experience of being in the house—its distinctive Wrightian feel—is hard to describe. It stems in part from Wright's handling of light, his way of at once defining and expanding space, and his careful selection of materials. But the real secret may well be his mastery of scale—the hardest element in architecture to bring under complete control. In the Willey House, everything seems to be exactly the right size, from the smallest detail to the largest spaces. This underlying harmony gives the house a quality of deep-breathing calm.

For Wright, the house was in many ways the beginning of a new life that would by the 1950s make

The kitchen is visible from the living and dining areas through open shelves. Wright used the same materials—brick, cypress wood, and glass—for both the inside and outside of the house.

Prospect Park

Prospect Park is a little rhombus of land sandwiched between the University of Minnesota's East Bank, the Mississippi River, and St. Paul. It's a crossroads for much activity in both Twin Cities. One of Prospect Park's gems is the Willey House, which was an important player in the 1950s when Interstate 94 was coming through. The home was slated for demoli-

The Prospect Park Water Tower, circa 1915, about two years after it was built. The neighborhood landmark occupies one of the highest points in Minneapolis.

tion, but the fiercely loyal Prospect Park residents saved it, along with a hundred other homes.

Prospect Park residents have banded together for the good of their neighborhood since its founding in 1884 by real estate developer Louis Menage. The picturesque neighborhood, with its winding streets, quickly began to attract upper-middle-class homeowners. The first version of the Prospect Park East River Road Improvement Association was formed in 1901, and the group has shaped its own destiny for more than a hundred years. Its "Squabbles, Skirmishes, and Sieges," according to a neighborhood history published in 2003, included petitioning the Minneapolis Park Board to purchase its tallest hill for the construction of a water tower in 1906; arguments over zoning, traffic, and pollution; a controversial low-income housing project; and the struggle over I-94, which produced a remarkable compromise that rerouted the interstate.

Prospect Park's signature water tower (nicknamed the "Witch's Hat" for its distinctive roof) was designed by Frederick William Cappelen and built in 1913, functioning as such until it was decommissioned in 1952. In 1955, the picturesque old water tower was struck by lightning, and the city deemed it unsalvageable. Again, the neighborhood association stepped in, and the tower was repaired and preserved, eventually being named to the National Register of Historic Places in 1997.

There is a pride of community and a sense of place in Prospect Park, home to many university professors and administrators, as well as students and residents of modest means. The preserved 1898 Pratt School hosts an ice cream social every year on the first Friday after Memorial Day and opens the water tower to the neighborhood for that one day. Its panoramic view includes both Minneapolis and St. Paul, physically as well as psychologically linking the Twin Cities.

A gallery off the living room provides access to two bedrooms, a study, and a bathroom. Small windows above the gallery's built-in bookshelves bring in light.

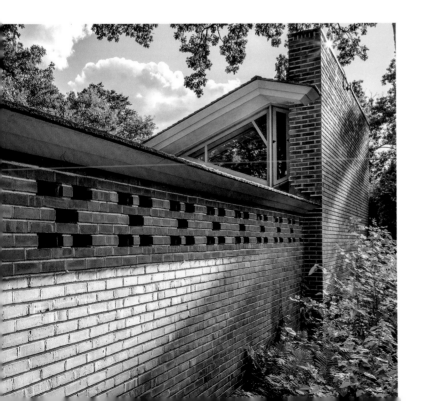

him the beloved, if cantankerous, grand old man of American architecture. The first big step toward the fame and fortune that would crown his golden years came right after completion of the Willey House, when he designed a little place in the Pennsylvania woods called Fallingwater.

The Willeys, meanwhile, remained in the house through the 1950s but were eventually divorced. They sold the house in 1963 to another University of Minnesota professor, who lived there with his family until 1972, when Harvey Glanzer—a Wright aficionado from Wisconsin—purchased the property. Glanzer hired architect John Howe, who had worked on the house as one of Wright's draftsmen in the 1930s, to remodel the kitchen in 1974 but otherwise made few alterations. Although the house was added to the National Register of Historic Places in 1981, it was only sporadically occu-

The gallery windows are set behind punched-out brick openings that act as a privacy screen along the home's north side, which is close to the lot line.

The master bedroom is a bright, comfortable space that features a tent ceiling, small corner windows, and wood flooring instead of the brick found elsewhere in the house.

pied during Glanzer's long tenure as owner. By 1995 the house was vacant, and its condition grew ever more dilapidated until it was finally acquired by new owners, Steve Sikora and Lynette Erickson-Sikora, in 2002.

Owners of a Minneapolis graphic design firm, the couple had long admired the house, and their goal was to restore it to its original appearance down to the last detail. Although Wright once wrote that the house was "well-constructed for a life of several centuries if the shingles are renewed in twenty-five years," it required much more than a new roof to bring the home back to pristine condition. It also took time—nearly six years—to complete the work. Lynette's son, Stafford Norris III, supervised the project with assistance from his brother, Joshua.

A restoration journal at the home's beautiful website, thewilleyhouse .com, provides a step-by-step, year-by-year account of the painstaking project, which began with the exterior. This work included repairing damaged brickwork (a task that sent Steve to Menomonie, Wisconsin, to find just the right replacement brick), inserting new steel beams to prop up the sagging cantilevered trellis above the front terrace, refinishing all of the wood trim, and installing new skylights as well as a new cedar-shake roof.

The home's interior was also completely restored. A key part of this work entailed constructing Wright-designed shelves, cabinets, and furniture that had never been built, because of the Willeys' limited budget. In addition, new rugs were woven to Wright's designs. The kitchen proved to be a particular challenge because of the 1970s remodeling. As it turned

The entire house, including its only bathroom, has been impeccably restored by the current owners, Steve Sikora and Lynette Erickson-Sikora.

The desk, chairs, and shelves in the study were designed by Wright. Many of the home's furnishings were built to Wright's plans by the current owners as part of their six-year restoration project.

out, some of the kitchen's original cypress cabinetry and shelving was still stored in the house, and it was reinstalled during the restoration. Kitchens in historic homes are typically updated with all of the latest appliances and gizmos, but Sikora and Erickson-Sikora opted for total authenticity by finding a 1932 General Electric refrigerator and stove just like those the Willeys owned when they moved into the house.

Today, the house is once again used as a residence, but it's also open on occasion for tours and special events. Visitors will find that for all of its quirks the house remains a place of glorious architectural magic, conjured up by the old wizard of Taliesin, and it would be hard to find a better use of 1,350 square feet in another house in Minnesota. ❧

✒ GREAT ESTATES

❧ Southways
Orono, 1919

John and Eleanor Pillsbury, 1944. John's father, Charles, was cofounder of the family milling company; Eleanor, born in South Dakota, was the granddaughter of a U.S. Army general.

Opposite: The front (west) entrance to Southways is set back from Smiths Bay and approached gradually by a long, winding drive. Its facade is a Tudor Revival fantasy of brick, stucco, and half-timbered walls beneath a steep, multihued slate roof, a trademark of architect Harrie T. Lindeberg.

"Soon after our marriage in 1911, John and I began thinking about building a summer home at Minnetonka." So begins Eleanor Pillsbury's decisive and at times delightfully tart account of how she and her husband, John S. Pillsbury, came to build the mansion known as Southways. Still *the* great house on Lake Minnetonka, it occupies a spectacular site of nearly thirteen acres at 1400 Bracketts Point Road in the middle of a prominent peninsula. The mansion is the only Minnesota work of a New York architect who specialized in country homes for some of the nation's wealthiest families, and it speaks to a lost age of elegance. What makes Southways even more remarkable, given its size and the quality of its detailing, is that it was indeed used for many years only as a summer residence.

John S. Pillsbury was a member of Minnesota's business aristocracy. His father, Charles A. Pillsbury (1842–1899), who hailed from New Hampshire, had arrived in Minneapolis in 1869 and almost immediately purchased an interest in a small flour mill at St. Anthony Falls. John's father, George, and his uncle and namesake, John Sargent Pillsbury, also took a stake in the business. Under Charles's leadership, the enterprise flourished, and in 1881 the company built what was said to be the world's largest flour mill, the Pillsbury A, on the east side of the falls. Although the flour business itself did not always prosper, the Pillsburys hedged their bets by acquiring thousands of acres of timberland in northeastern Minnesota that later proved to be rich with iron ore. These investments added enormously to the family's fortune.

John and his twin brother, Charles, were born in 1878 and grew up in the heady early days of the milling industry in Minneapolis. Talkative and likeable, John knew virtually all of the businessmen, engineers, and other pioneer figures who built an empire of flour at St. Anthony Falls, and his late-life reminiscences became a prized source of information to historians. After graduating in 1900 from the University of Minnesota (where he served as student manager of the football team), he traveled widely before settling down to work for the family company as vice president for sales.

He also became the company's most visible face in the business community through his membership in numerous clubs and civic organizations.

In 1907 he met twenty-year-old Eleanor Jerusha Lawler (usually called "Juty") at a theater party in Minneapolis. Smart and beautiful, she did not have a typical debutante's background. Her maternal grandfather, General Samuel Davis Sturgis, was a Civil War veteran and frontier cavalry officer after whom the town of Sturgis, South Dakota, is named, and one of her uncles, Jack Sturgis, died with General George Armstrong Custer at Little Big Horn. Born in Mitchell, South Dakota, Eleanor spent part of her youth in St. Paul after her father's death, but later traveled widely in Europe and even attended school in Rome for a year. When John Pillsbury met her, she had just moved back to Minneapolis following her mother's second marriage, to Edmund Pennington, president of the Soo Line Railroad.

John and Eleanor were married on December 5, 1911, in Pennington's Lowry Hill mansion, with no less a figure than Archbishop John Ireland presiding. After their marriage, it was hardly a surprise that the couple began looking at the idea of building a summer home at Lake Minnetonka. Members of the Pillsbury clan had begun summering on the lake in the 1880s, establishing a colony of sorts in the Ferndale area of Wayzata. John and Eleanor, however, decided to build their home just to the west of Ferndale, on a narrow finger of land known as Bracketts Point. The couple bought the land from the estate of William Dunwoody, another prominent miller from Minneapolis, who had died in 1914, and tore down his lake house to make way for their own.

The Pillsburys' choice of an architect for their summer home was intriguing. Instead of hiring local talent, as most of their family had in the past, the

Custom wrought ironwork by Polish-born master craftsman Samuel Yellin and his colleague, Oscar Bach, decorates the home's superb front entrance. When current owners James and Joann Jundt renovated the estate, they called on Yellin's granddaughter, Clare, to create additional metalwork.

Southways, at 32,000 square feet, displays architect Harrie T. Lindeberg's skill at blending historical styles to create an aura of permanence.

When it opened in 1881 on the east side of St. Anthony Falls in Minneapolis, the Pillsbury A Mill, now a National Historic Landmark, was said to be the world's largest flour mill.

Samuel Yellin eschewed manufactured cast iron in favor of the medieval-style hand-wrought iron employed in old English manor homes. A detail of the front gate at Southways reveals Yellin's hammered and forged technique.

The home's rear facade, which directly overlooks Browns Bay from the east side of Bracketts Point, is a classic red-brick version of a Georgian Revival manor house. Lindeberg sited the house at an angle, providing a view of the widest part of Lake Minnetonka.

couple turned to Harrie T. Lindeberg of New York. Today, Lindeberg is an obscure figure, but he was well known in the early decades of the twentieth century as a designer of country estates for such prominent families as the Armours, DuPonts, Morgans, and Vanderbilts. His homes typically employ a mix of familiar historical styles that are combined in distinctive ways, all with meticulous attention to detail. His aim was always to create a livable house, as opposed to a bloated showpiece. "The well-designed house," he once wrote, "should be significant of, and adapted to the habits and life of its occupants."

How Lindeberg rose to his choice position in the world of architecture is a story in itself. Born to poor Swedish immigrants in what is now Hoboken, New Jersey, in 1879, he managed as a teenager to gain admission to the

Samuel Yellin in Minnesota

The iron peacocks, herons, and other ornamental motifs that grace so much of Southways showcase the talent of master ironworker Samuel Yellin and his crew of craftspeople in Philadelphia. While the Pillsbury home was Yellin's first commission in Minnesota, he went on to design ironwork for many other Minnesota projects, both residential and commercial.

Yellin was born in Galicia, Poland, in 1885, where he showed precocious artistic talent. He was apprenticed to a local ironworker at a tender age and soon dazzled his mentors with his blacksmithing abilities. His colleagues called the youthful phenom a "devil born with a hammer in his hand." The nickname stayed with Yellin during his long career.

After traveling and studying throughout Europe, Yellin immigrated in 1906 to the United States. He soon began teaching at the Philadelphia Museum School of Industrial Art, just as the Arts and Crafts movement was coming to full flower. Predicting a new American taste for handcrafted art objects, he fashioned medieval-style hand-wrought iron (which had been replaced for years by manufactured cast iron). He started Samuel Yellin Metalworkers as a small shop but quickly expanded his firm as his popularity spread. At the company's peak in 1928, Yellin employed 268 meticulously selected and trained metalsmiths. Americans embraced Yellin and his old-world charm, and he eventually won residential commissions for families with such storied names as Morgan, Mellon, Rockefeller, and Vanderbilt.

Yellin Metalworks crafted ornamental iron fencing, gates, railings, balconies, fireplace grates, and tools for numerous educational institutions, including Yale, Harvard, Princeton, and Swarthmore. Many of the firm's other notable clients were in New York City, where Yellin's work can be found in the Federal Reserve Bank, St. Patrick's Cathedral, and The Cloisters at the Metropolitan Museum of Art.

After the Pillsbury project in 1919, Yellin received many commissions in Minnesota, including Cass Gilbert's state capitol in St. Paul (1893–1905), the same architect's Federal Reserve Bank in Minneapolis (1922), the Mayo Clinic's Plummer Building in Rochester (Ellerbe Architects, 1928), and the home of Paul Watkins (1927), who headed the Watkins Product Company in Winona.

Upon Yellin's death in 1940, the firm was passed down to "the devil's" son, Harvey, and then to Harvey's daughter, Clare—who acted as a consultant to James and Joann Jundt as they restored the Pillsbury home. An exhibition of Yellin's work presented by the National Building Museum in Washington, D.C., traveled to the Minnesota Historical Society in 1986.

Samuel Yellin with striker, circa 1920s. Yellin's exquisite wrought ironwork for Southways was his first commission in Minnesota.

A boat docked at Bracketts Point on Lake Minnetonka, circa 1900. The Pillsburys built Southways on a portion of Bracketts Point once owned by Minneapolis milling titan William Dunwoody.

prestigious National Academy of Design in New York City, where he studied for three years. By age twenty-two he was working as a draftsman for the nation's architectural royalty, the huge and highly influential New York firm of McKim, Mead and White. His talents were such that he soon became an assistant to Stanford White, the firm's famed designer and also one of the great playboys of his era. White's dalliances, mostly with teenage girls, ended in 1906, when he was shot dead on the rooftop of Madison Square Garden by the husband of his latest conquest, Evelyn Nesbit. That same year, Lindeberg struck out on his own and eventually built a highly successful national practice that included projects in at least twenty-six states.

The Pillsburys, who would have known about Lindeberg from magazine articles or possibly friends, hired him in 1916, and the design he produced was characteristic of his work. Lindeberg preached a gospel of simplicity (though of a kind only the very rich could afford), and this accounts for the somewhat austere, understated feel of Southways. More so than many other costly homes of its time, the mansion demonstrates that the Pillsburys spent their money well, eschewing showy luxuries in favor of high-quality materials and exquisite ornament. By the time Southways was ready for occupancy in May of 1919, the Pillsburys had four children—three sons and a daughter—the oldest of whom was seven. Another daughter was born in 1920 and a son in 1921 to complete the family.

Eleanor Pillsbury and Lindeberg, two people who knew exactly what they wanted, frequently clashed during construction of the house, which was slowed by World War I. One big point of contention

The estate's pool house complex and tennis courts were restored and renovated in 1996 by the Jundts, working with Beyer Blinder Belle Architects and landscape architect David Varnell. Bluestone paths unite the grounds overlooking Browns Bay.

Clare Yellin designed the bronze fireplace door in the living room, incorporating her grandfather's peacock theme. The peacock is considered a symbol of everlasting beauty.

centered on the walls in the home's living room. Lindeberg wanted the walls finished with butternut paneling, but Mrs. Pillsbury had other ideas. She thought the paneling would be too dark and insisted on green paint. After much back-and-forth, she won the battle. Despite her many disagreements with Lindeberg, she wasn't angry enough to dismiss him and admitted that "he was right many times" in his design decisions.

The finished house, which encompasses about 32,000 square feet, displays Lindeberg's full range of skills. Blending historical styles with practiced ease, it has the feel of something old and comfortable planted in the earth, an effect Lindeberg achieved in part by using bricks recycled from demolished buildings. The house's exceptional craftsmanship, reflecting a way of building that all but ended with the ascendancy of modernism after World War II, reinforces its aura of age and permanence.

Because of its site on a narrow peninsula, the house in effect has two fronts overlooking the lake—a fact that Lindeberg clearly recognized by designing two very different facades. The east side, which directly overlooks Browns Bay and is very visible from the lake, offers a classic red-brick version of Georgian Revival, with a symmetrical center section flanked by projecting wings that once included second-floor sleeping porches. This facade is strikingly similar, except for the porches, to that of another Georgian home Lindeberg designed in 1914 on New York's Long Island. Lindeberg didn't want the porches, but the Pillsburys, who knew the glories of summer nights in Minnesota, insisted on them.

It may be that Lindeberg decided to endow this side of the house with a monumental character precisely because it's so visible. He also took great care in siting the house. Instead of paralleling the shoreline in typical fashion, the house is placed at an angle so that it looks directly across the lake at its widest point.

The front entrance is on the home's west side, which stands well back from Smiths Bay behind a broad lawn. Here, the house sheds the formality of the east side in favor of a picturesque Tudor Revival spectacle of brick, stucco, and half-timbered walls beneath a steep slate roof that unfolds like a richly textured tapestry. An angled, half-timbered wing to the north provides room for service quarters. Lindeberg designed the approach to the house—a long driveway from Bracketts Point Road that ends in a graceful oval at the front door—to create a sense of expectation.

The home's nearly all-glass front door offers a gorgeous introduction to the work of master ironworker Samuel Yellin in the form of a magnificent peacock—symbol of everlasting beauty. Perched on the door's highest crossbar, the peacock strikes quite a pose, its tail spreading out into delicate lines of wrought iron that spool out into graceful curls. Other examples of Yellin's work can be found throughout the house. When current owners

Lake Minnetonka's Great Estates

In the late 1870s Charles Gibson, a prominent St. Louis lawyer who'd long sought emancipation from that city's sultry summers by heading north to Minnesota, purchased a quarter section of land near Carsons Bay and built the first true estate on Lake Minnetonka. It wasn't long before other wealthy families, most from Minneapolis, began building summer homes, usually called "cottages," along the sprawling lake's wooded shoreline. Some of these cottages were close to palatial in size, but they were nonetheless true summer places, without the kind of heating systems that would allow them to be used year-round.

Initially, reaching the lake from the Twin Cities required quite a trip, by either stagecoach or private carriage, but rail lines soon cut down the travel time substantially. Although the St. Paul and Pacific Railroad (later to become the Great Northern) reached Wayzata on the north side of the lake in 1867, it wasn't until the early 1880s that lines extended to Excelsior and other points along the south shore, setting off a construction boom. Streetcars reached Excelsior in 1905, by which time many of the lake's wealthy summer residents were already traveling by automobile.

Frank Peavey's summer home in Wayzata, circa 1900. Once part of a 111-acre estate on Lake Minnetonka known as Highcroft, the home was demolished in 1953.

The Pillsburys were among the families who established an early presence on the lake, in what is now the Ferndale area of Wayzata. John Sargent Pillsbury and his nephew, Charles, founders of the family's milling fortune, both had summer homes in Ferndale. So did Charles's brother, Frederick, who in 1886 built a fanciful Queen Anne cottage that stood for just eleven years before burning down.

The lake's greatest age of estate building occurred between 1890 and 1910, when many notable Minneapolis businessmen—including Frank Peavey, John Wilcox, Frederick Noerenberg, and Albert Loring—established large properties centered around summer homes. In most cases, these estates were working farms (Loring's was one thousand acres in size). Peavey, who made his money in the grain business, built perhaps the most lavish estate of all in Wayzata in 1895. Known as Highcroft, the estate encompassed well over a hundred acres and included an impressive Georgian Revival mansion (razed in 1953), magnificent gardens, plus an array of barns and outbuildings for Peavey's prized herd of Guernsey cows.

Frederick Noerenberg, a founder of the Grain Belt Brewery in Minneapolis, built another of the lake's most splendid estates in 1893 in what is now the community of Mound. Although the property included an eighteen-bedroom Queen Anne–style mansion (razed in 1972), it was especially renowned for its gardens, which have been preserved as part of a public park.

Today, a dwindling number of the lake's historic mansions—Southways among them—remain intact, while virtually all of the old estate grounds have been subdivided into much smaller lots. New mansions, many of which seem to value size over architectural merit, now ring the lake. Most of these big houses, however, occupy relatively small lots, and it seems safe to say Lake Minnetonka's estate era is gone for good.

Extending from the glass-walled orchid room (originally a screened porch) on the south side of the house is the Vista, a beautiful garden John and Eleanor Pillsbury added to the property in 1921.

James and Joann Jundt renovated the house in the early 1990s, they engaged Yellin's granddaughter, Clare Yellin, to add new metalwork in keeping with the spirit of the original.

The front door opens into an entry hall with an oak-paneled staircase to the left and a long gallery to the right that extends along the west side of the house. Large and small rooms alternate along the gallery as part of Lindeberg's straightforward but subtle floor plan. The gallery, which is lit by large west-facing windows, features an arched ceiling with bands of plaster ornament, and is perhaps most notable for its colorful floor made by the American Encaustic Tiling Company. Based in Zanesville, Ohio, the company, which operated from 1875 to 1935, was a leading producer of encaustic tiles, a type of inlaid tile in which clays of different colors are used to create distinctive patterns. The gallery's tiles are reddish brown with gold-colored ornamental inlays.

Only one major room—a library with walls paneled in Italian walnut—is located on the west side of the gallery. Eleanor Pillsbury had a bit of a quarrel with Lindeberg over this room. "When it was first built," she wrote, "he had a high ceiling in that small room. I said I didn't like the high ceiling, so he put in a false ceiling. He gave in to me on that point and I think he thought I was right." The false ceiling was removed when the Jundts renovated the house.

The gallery ends in a glass-walled orchid room (originally a screened porch) on the south side of the house. Windows here overlook the Vista, a beautiful garden the Pillsburys added to the property in 1921. A pathway in the garden continues the line of the gallery, thereby linking outdoors to indoors in a very direct way.

The home's focal point, on the east side of the gallery, is a fifty-five-by-twenty-four-foot living room with refinished butternut paneling, a fireplace set

Doors leading from the long gallery to the orchid room provide views out to the Vista, linking inside and outside. The gallery's colorful tile floor was made by the American Encaustic Tiling Company of Zanesville, Ohio.

beneath a curved split pediment, and French doors leading out to a terrace overlooking the lake. Lindeberg and Eleanor Pillsbury seem to have argued about this room from the very beginning, and not just over the color and composition of its walls. Size was also an issue. Mrs. Pillsbury wanted a small living room—thereby leaving space for a large family room—but Lindeberg wouldn't hear of it, and he won this struggle of wills. Today, however, Southways has a spacious family room, which the Jundts created by filling in what was once a porch on the south end of the house. The living room includes a large new fireplace screen designed by Clare Yellin. The room originally had an unusual curly-pine floor, but it became so deteriorated that it had to be replaced with oak parquet.

A lovely tiled conservatory with a basin and fountain separates the living room from the formal dining room, which offers a view of the lake through three French doors. Just off the dining room is an octagonal breakfast room with a stunning blue-tile floor and more French doors. The kitchen and other work spaces are in the service wing to the north.

The main staircase—which features turned-oak balusters, bands of hand-carved wood ornament, and a carved owl roosting atop the newel post—proved to be another source of contention between architect and client. "Lindeberg wanted to bring in carvers from New York," Mrs. Pillsbury recalled. "John wouldn't hear of that. He said we had marvelous carvers in Minnesota, so we had local men do the carving. Finally, Lindeberg came out one day to see it and he looked at it and said, 'Oh, it's too perfect—I don't want it so perfect. What you should do is to get those men drunk.'" Sobriety prevailed, however, and Lindeberg eventually approved of the carvers' work.

Upstairs, the home originally had eight second-floor bedrooms, many of which have been reconfigured by the Jundts to create a series of suites. The most charming of the original bedrooms is the barrel-vaulted Princess Suite, named in honor of Princess Louise of Sweden, who with her husband, Crown Prince Gustaf Adolf, and his son, Bertil, stayed at

Yellin's graceful wrought iron peacock provides an elegant entry into the home, announcing at once a respect for the handmade artisanship favored by the Arts and Crafts movement. Yellin also designed the chandelier.

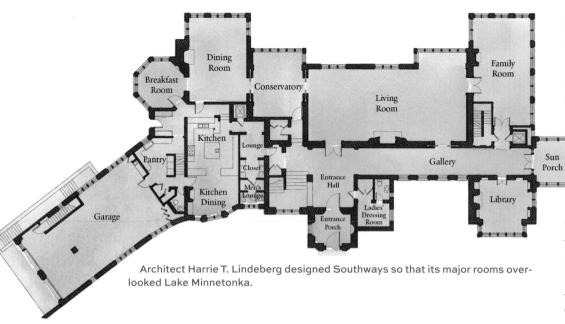

Architect Harrie T. Lindeberg designed Southways so that its major rooms overlooked Lake Minnetonka.

Southways in 1938 during an American tour that included a stop in Minneapolis.

The house also has a large attic, which came as quite a surprise to Mrs. Pillsbury. "I had no idea that Lindeberg was building us a third floor," she wrote, "and when the house was practically finished, he informed us about this additional space." The third floor now contains an adult game room, a children's playroom, and two bedrooms.

It's likely, given all of their disputes over the design, that both Lindeberg and the Pillsburys were happy to see the house finally completed in 1920. Lindeberg, who does not appear to have suffered from any deficiency of ego, was well satisfied with his achievement. According to Mrs. Pillsbury, "When Southways was finished, I asked him exactly what style the architecture was, and he answered, 'It's a Lindeberg house!'" The home's name, however, came from Mrs. Pillsbury: "I thought—you have to go south a ways from the county road [now called Shoreline Drive] to approach the house—so we named it Southways."

The house remained a cherished part of the Pillsbury family's life for more than seventy years. It was the scene of dinner parties, picnics, scavenger hunts, weddings, Fourth of July celebrations, and family get-togethers of all kinds. It also served as headquarters and eponym for an annual boat race that drew as many as four hundred sailors and their families.

After John Pillsbury died at age eighty-nine in 1968, Eleanor wasn't sure she needed a house as large as Southways and asked a contractor to advise her on the possibility of demolition. The contractor, it turned out, was a wise man. He told her, as she later recalled, "He had never destroyed anything that could not be replaced, and that my house could not be replaced." Taking the contractor's advice to keep the house "as long as possible," Mrs. Pillsbury made

© KAREN MELVIN PHOTOGRAPHY

The formal dining room at Southways offers views of the lake through three sets of French doors.

changes, including the installation of a garage in the service wing, but otherwise continued to use Southways as her summer residence until her death, at age 104, in 1991.

The Jundts became Southways' second owner in March of 1992 after purchasing the home from Mrs. Pillsbury's estate. They spent several months acquainting themselves with the house's history, which included talks with members of the Pillsbury family, before beginning the complex task of restoring and renewing Lindeberg's masterpiece and converting it to year-round use. James Jundt, who owns an investment firm, and his wife, Joann, selected Beyer Blinder Belle of New York, along with Minneapolis-based MacDonald and Mack Architects, to undertake the three-year project. New York landscape architect David Varnell was also part of the design team.

The scope of the work was such that virtually every feature of the house inside and out, as well as the grounds, received attention. Workers refurbished the main downstairs rooms, installed new energy-efficient doors and windows, upgraded or replaced all of the wiring and plumbing, and added air-conditioning and a new heating system. A spa and a wine cellar were also built in the basement. The Jundts, always mindful of the home's exceptional quality, went a step further by hiring craftspeople such as Clare Yellin to add many new ornamental touches to the house. Improvements to the grounds included a new swimming pool and pool house, the addition of a historic fountain in the Vista garden, and an enlarged terrace off the living room.

As of 2014, the Jundts, who have reached retirement age, were looking for a new owner for their beloved home. Their hope is to find a buyer who will view Southways as they do, as an irreplaceable piece of Lake Minnetonka's much frayed architectural fabric, as well as one of Minnesota's grandest country estates. "We could have torn the house down and were advised by some people to do so," James Jundt notes. "But you truly don't own this property. You're a guardian." ⚬

An open side window in the front entrance porch offers a view of the north side of the home, where the kitchen and servants quarters are located. Oscar Bach designed the window's exquisite ironwork.

Worsted Skeynes
Gem Lake, 1930 and later

Thomas Daniels and his son, John, at a horse show, 1934. Thomas Daniels was an avid horseman who entered many shows and even held occasional fox hunts at his estate.

Opposite: Thomas and Frances Daniels chose St. Paul architect Edwin Lundie to build their Gem Lake estate, commonly known as The Daniels Farm. The couple, however, dubbed it Worsted Skeynes, after the name of a fictional estate in a 1907 novel by English author John Galsworthy.

THE COMMUNITY OF GEM LAKE, WHICH ENCOMPASSES LITTLE MORE than a square mile and wasn't incorporated as a city until 1959, has long been an unusual place. Only seven miles northeast of St. Paul, it has a population of fewer than four hundred even though it's surrounded by densely built-up suburbs. What spared Gem Lake from the usual suburban development is that much of its land once consisted of large country estates owned by some of the Twin Cities' wealthiest families. The biggest estate of all, which includes a superb house designed by Edwin Lundie, was built more than eighty years ago for Thomas and Frances Daniels. Today, the estate—owned by Michael P. Garrett and Anthony Scornavacco—is much smaller than it once was. Fortunately, the house itself, at 7 Daniels Farm Road, has come down through the years largely intact and retains all the charm and elegance of Lundie's original design.

The Danielses began work on the estate as soon as they returned home to Minnesota in 1930 after a decade abroad, during which Thomas had served as a U.S. diplomat in Brussels, Rome, and Rio de Janeiro. They settled with their three young sons into a home in St. Paul but also wanted a more rural place nearby where they would have room for their seven horses (Thomas was an avid polo player) and "loads of dogs," as Frances put it. A year earlier, the couple had purchased 160 acres just south of the small body of water after which the community of Gem Lake was named. The Daniels Farm, as it came to be called, eventually grew to include not only the main house, barn, and garage but also a guest house and two small servants' homes.

Thomas Daniels's diplomatic service was not the source of his fortune. He was the only son of John W. Daniels, a founder of the Archer-Daniels-Midland Company (ADM), which began as a producer of linseed oil and later branched out to become a corporate giant across a wide spectrum of food-related businesses and services. Educated at Yale, Thomas Daniels served as a bookkeeper at his father's company after graduating and before embarking on his diplomatic career. He would in time become ADM's president and, later, chairman of its board of directors.

St. Paul architect Edwin Lundie's plan for Worsted Skeynes is highly irregular, with a large living room at the center of the house. Lundie added the dining room four years later.

Frances Daniels was an equally formidable figure. After moving to St. Paul with her family, she plunged into civic and business affairs. In 1939 she became the first president of the St. Paul Women's Institute and staged a huge fashion show. Designed in part to attract more shoppers to downtown stores, it turned into a popular annual event. The inaugural show attracted a special guest—First Lady Eleanor Roosevelt—who was eager to revive the nation's sagging garment industry.

As built, Worsted Skeynes was a working farm. The Danielses, who adopted a girl in 1936 to complete their family, maintained a large vegetable garden on the property and raised alfalfa to feed their horses. There was for many years an annual horse show at the estate, and it also became the scene of occasional fox hunts, a quaint if not universally admired custom rarely practiced in Minnesota. Despite its proximity to Gem Lake, the estate did not actually extend as far north as the shoreline. Although the children sometimes boated or swam in the lake, they also had use of a swimming pool on the east side of the house. Built primarily as a summer residence, the main house nonetheless had a full heating system, as well as a large basement, much of which was taken up by a recreation room. Parts of the house were also cooled by an early version of air-conditioning.

The Danielses dubbed their property Worsted Skeynes, after the name of a fictional estate in a 1907 novel by the popular English author John Galsworthy. As it turned out, Worsted Skeynes had more than a nominal connection to England. In September of 1941 the Danielses hosted a much-publicized dinner at the house for the Duke of Windsor, formerly King Edward VIII of England, and the American woman he married after abdicating the throne, Wallace Simpson, thereafter known as the Duchess of Windsor.

Given her interest in design, it's likely Frances

Current owners Michael P. Garrett and Anthony Scornavacco completely rebuilt the original garage, which had been damaged by fire.

Daniels had a big say in selecting St. Paul–based Edwin Lundie as the architect of Worsted Skeynes. It was an inspired choice. Although he is justly regarded as one of Minnesota's finest architects, Lundie was for much of his career well outside the mainstream, a traditionalist in a modern world. By 1930, when the Danielses began their project, visions of modernism—clean, straightforward, free of ornament or any references to the past—had already begun to entrance many architects. But Lundie, who practiced until his death in 1972, never found much of interest in modernism. Instead, he designed meticulously crafted buildings and homes that employ familiar historic styles—Gothic, American Colonial, and Cotswold Cottage, among others—in a highly personal way. Like Harrie T. Lindeberg, architect of the John and Eleanor Pillsbury House, Lundie saw historic forms not as a straightjacket but as a discipline in which original design could flourish.

How the Danielses came to select Lundie as the architect for their estate isn't known. By 1930, however, he had already designed one notable home nearby—a Colonial Revival summer house for Frederick E. Weyerhaeuser on Manitou Island at White Bear Lake. It's possible the Danielses saw that home, or one of Lundie's St. Paul houses from the 1920s, and decided he was their man.

The Daniels project displays Lundie's ability to create a warm, intimate living environment even in a very sizeable home. In fact, what may be most striking about Worsted Skeynes, aside from its gorgeous detailing, is its sheer coziness, the way it seems to envelop its occupants as com-

Edwin Lundie's pencil drawing of the 1934 dining room addition to Worsted Skeynes displays his delicate artistry. Lundie learned his profession from the ground up and had no formal academic training as an architect.

Most of the house's long front facade is clad in brown shingles, but walls of gray and buff rough-faced limestone surround the understated front entrance.

Lundie's attention to detail and his dedication to the best materials are evident in this electrical switch plate that like all of the home's hardware was custom crafted of wrought iron.

fortably as a well-worn sweater. Like Frank Lloyd Wright, Lundie was a master of scale who knew how to manipulate form and volume to give his houses that "just right" feel lesser designers often fail to achieve.

Approached by a long driveway that takes a sweeping curve before reaching its destination, the house at first glance resembles a colony of cottages strung together beneath a steeply pitched roof. Lundie reinforced this sense of the house as a casual assembly of parts by offsetting the walls from one section to another. A prominent central gable rises above the off-center front door, which makes no attempt at pomp or grandeur. Most of the house's long front facade is clad in weathered brown shingles, but walls of gray and buff rough-faced limestone, laid up in random ashlar, surround the front entrance. Lundie used the same stone for a massive chimney with a patterned brick crown at the east end of the house. Four other ornate chimneys rise elsewhere above the roof.

The west side of the house, where the original servants' wing is located, includes a flower garden behind a limestone wall. Here, Lundie designed an utterly charming cylinder of stone and brick that serves as a birdhouse, complete with tiny ledges for its avian visitors. At the rear of the house, overlooking the lake, is its only major addition—a dining room (with a bedroom above) designed by Lundie in 1934. Clad in brick, it forms a wing of its own set at a ninety-degree angle to the rest of the house. Lundie's beautiful pencil drawing of the addition demonstrates the artistry he brought to all of his work.

Inside, the house is something of a maze, revealing one of Lundie's prime tricks, which was to intersperse constricted spaces and narrow halls amid one or two very large rooms. The front entry—through a wide, arched Dutch door with superb wrought iron bracing and hardware—leads into a deliberately underwhelming hall. The main staircase, also far

At first approach Worsted Skeynes resembles a colony of cottages, each with distinct materials and chimneys, all strung together beneath a steeply pitched roof.

"Supermarket to the World"

Corn and soybeans have become the lifeblood of agriculture in the American Midwest. In addition to human and animal foods, these precious crops can be made into engine fuel, inks, plastics, and hundreds of other products. Many of these products originated through the early scientific research and development efforts of the Archer-Daniels-Midland Company (ADM).

John W. Daniels first began pressing linseed oil from flaxseed in 1878 in Ohio. The oil was used in the production of paints and varnishes, and the leftover "cake" was exported to Europe for use as a high-protein livestock feed. After serving with several linseed companies, Daniels moved to Minneapolis to establish Daniels Linseed Company in 1902. Eventually his Ohio colleague, George A. Archer, also in the linseed business, joined Daniels in Minneapolis. In 1905 they established Archer-Daniels Linseed, which became a great success. It was later joined by Midland Linseed Products Company and incorporated in 1923 as Archer-Daniels-Midland Company.

Fascinated by biology, the leaders of ADM enlisted the aid of Professor H. L. Bolley of North Dakota Agricultural College to find the solution to a parasitic fungus that was known to produce wilt in flax plants, eventually destroying them. Their efforts were successful and they revolutionized the industry with a wilt-resistant flax seed. Later, the company added storage and transportation divisions and began acquiring or partnering with companies worldwide to provide the firm with opportunities in corn, soybeans, wheat, oats, barley, peanuts, cocoa, and other commodities.

Since its inception and into the 1990s, ADM has retained members of the Daniels and Archer families (including Thomas L. Daniels, who served as president from 1947 to 1958) at or near the firm's helm. The original founders died a little over a year apart—John W. Daniels in 1931, at age seventy-four, and George A. Archer in 1932, at age eighty-two.

Another family dynasty—that of Dwayne O. Andreas ("The Soybean King")—came aboard in 1966. Under the Andreases, ADM flourished and became one of the world's largest food companies. But ADM suffered a big black eye in the 1990s when the FBI uncovered a price-fixing scheme at the company involving lysine, high-fructose corn syrup, and citric acid. An ADM executive named Mark Whitacre acted as a whistleblower. Several ADM executives were prosecuted and three served terms in federal prison. ADM was forced to pay millions in a class-action antitrust suit. As it turned out, Whitacre also ended up in prison after it was discovered that he had embezzled money from ADM. In 2009 Warner Bros. released a feature film titled *The Informant!* based on the case, starring Matt Damon as Whitacre.

ADM eventually recovered from this public-relations blow and has redoubled efforts to reduce its carbon footprint through air-quality initiatives. ADM was named the world's most admired food production company by *Fortune* magazine in 2009, 2010, and 2011. The firm now boasts 30,000 employees, 265 processing plants, and more than 460 sourcing facilities in more than 140 countries on six continents.

A laboratory at the Archer-Daniels-Midland Company in Minneapolis, 1937. Thomas Daniels's father, John W. Daniels, was one of the founders of the firm, now a global giant in agribusiness.

Attention to detail was a hallmark of Lundie's practice. Even the estate's avian residents received their due in the form of a cylindrical, shingle-topped bird-house (visible to the right of the second-floor flower boxes), complete with tiny brick ledges for its occupants.

from grand, is straight ahead, and the kitchen is to the left. But take just a few steps to the right and the house suddenly opens out into a great hall with crossbeams and a cathedral ceiling. The eighteen-by-thirty-foot hall, which originally served as both the home's living and dining rooms, feels especially big because the spaces around it are so tight.

Fireplaces at both ends add a warm glow to the hall, which is illuminated by bands of leaded-glass windows on its two long sides. A small gallery above the east fireplace provides a spot where musicians sometimes played during parties and other events. Two sets of doors on the north side of the hall lead out to a patio with views of the lake. Lundie's legendary attention to detail is visible throughout the hall—in the fir woodwork fumed with an acetylene torch to give it the exact look he wanted, in the gracefully curved queens-post ceiling trusses, and in the custom-made wrought iron door and window hardware. Similar details enliven the rest of the house, which was designed to have a rustic, settled-in atmosphere even when it was brand new.

On the east side of the living room, down a few steps, a narrow hallway provides access to a paneled library that features a fireplace, corner casement windows with leaded-glass bookshelves, and a beamed ceiling. It's a room made for nestling in with a good book and letting the hours fly by. A staircase in the hallway goes up to a pair of bedrooms and a shared bath. These high-ceilinged rooms were used by the Danielses; the children's bedrooms were at the other end of the house. This split arrangement of the bedrooms, now common in newer homes, was unusual at the time.

The Georgian-style dining room, where the duke and duchess were feted in 1941, is the home's most formal space. Located at the rear of the front entry hall, it includes a bay window that looks out over the lake. The bedroom above is linked to the main part of the house by a beautiful gallery lined with leaded-glass windows on one side and closets on the other.

The Duke and Duchess of Windsor's brief visit was a huge event, not only for the Danielses but also for all of St. Paul. Coming at a time when England was already at war and the United States soon would be, the couple's visit was nonetheless treated by the local press purely as a celebrity event, with much ink devoted to what the duchess wore and how friendly she was with the commoners. The forty-seven-year-old duke, a handsome man reputed to be something of a rake in his youth, was also quite an attraction, especially to the women of St. Paul, or so press accounts claimed.

A crowd estimated at anywhere from ten to twenty thousand people greeted the couple at the Union Depot in St. Paul when they arrived on the night of September 27, 1941, in a private rail car. The duke was at the time a controversial figure, and not just because of his abdication. In 1937 he and the duchess had traveled to Germany, where they met with Adolf Hitler on

Back stairs lead to the tiny musicians' gallery at the east end of the great hall. Barn-like doors and many portraits of the Daniels family's horses proclaim their love for the steeds they raised on the property.

A charming series of three rounded doors gives a distinctive look to the master bedroom upstairs. All of the home's bedrooms are nestled quaintly into the roofline, giving shape and individuality to each.

very friendly terms. Suspected thereafter of being Nazi sympathizers, the couple lived in France until the outbreak of World War II in September 1939. Unhappy with the duke's "defeatist" attitude, the British government in 1940 assigned him the no-doubt arduous task of governing the Bahamas, where he could have no impact on the war effort. He was on his way from the Bahamas to a huge farm he owned in Alberta, Canada, when he and the duchess made their stopover in St. Paul.

It appears the Danielses were chosen as dinner hosts in part because of Thomas's diplomatic connections but also because their relatively isolated home provided a secure environment. A motorcade took the duke and duchess past the state capitol and then out to the farm. News reporters went along for the ride and later stationed themselves in the guest house, along with city, state, and federal security forces. The reporters didn't have much of substance to write about because the royal duo had already announced they would "give no interviews" and "make no statements." They did pose for photographs, however, and Speed Graphic cameras flashed away in the night.

The dinner went off without a major hitch, although an ophthalmologist from St. Paul had to be called in briefly to treat an eye infection that had been bothering the duchess throughout the trip. Six crisply uniformed maids served the dinner, which offered such Minnesota fare as fresh trout, prairie chicken, and wild rice. Among the eighteen guests were various political dignitaries, as well as John and Eleanor Pillsbury. Guests later reported that they were charmed by the duke and duchess but that "the European war was avoided as a topic of conversation"—probably a wise idea in view of the duke's apparent regard for Hitler and the Nazis. The dinner was over in less than two hours, and the royal couple returned to the Union Depot to continue their journey.

Nothing quite as exciting ever happened again at the house, which remained in the Daniels family for many years. Lundie's last project on the estate came in 1945, when he designed additions to the guest house. By then, he'd also designed one other home overlooking Gem Lake—a rambling wood-frame and log cottage built in 1934 for lawyer Francis Butler.

Thomas Daniels became president of ADM in 1947. A year later, he and Frances bought 7 Heather Place in St. Paul (one half of the Goodkind Double House) as their in-city residence but continued to spend time at the farm property. Frances Daniels died in 1969. Thomas, who later remarried, died in 1977. Well before then, one of the couple's sons, John H. Daniels (who like his father became president of ADM) and his wife, Martha, had

The eighteen-by-thirty-foot great hall, which originally served as the home's living and dining rooms, soars up into a cathedral ceiling. A small gallery above one of the fireplaces provided a place for musicians to play during gatherings.

On the east side of the living room, down a few steps, is a paneled library that features a fireplace, corner casement windows, leaded-glass bookshelves, and a beamed ceiling. It's one of the coziest, most inviting rooms in the house.

Handmade iron sconces, lamps, and chandeliers, as well as door hardware, can be found throughout the house.

Edwin Lundie

Edwin Lundie was one of the last great Minnesota architects who learned his profession from the ground up, rather than through formal academic training. Born in Cedar Rapids, Iowa, in 1886, Lundie never attended college, but he had a gift for drawing—his pencil renderings in particular are extraordinary—and at age eighteen he began work as an unpaid apprentice in the St. Paul offices of Cass Gilbert. In 1908 he went to work for Thomas Holyoke, who had once been Gilbert's chief draftsman. Lundie then moved on to the offices of Emmanuel Masqueray, the French-born architect of the St. Paul Cathedral (1915).

After Masqueray's death in 1917, Lundie formed a partnership with two other members of the office to complete projects already in hand. He went out on his own two years later, specializing in residential design. Over the next fifty years, he produced designs for more than three hundred projects from his office in downtown St. Paul. Many of his commissions, usually for homes or lake cottages, came from wealthy St. Paul families such as the Ordways, Shepards, and Weyerhaeusers. He also designed more than a half-dozen Scandinavian-tinged cabins on the north shore of Lake Superior that are cherished today for their beauty and craftsmanship. Among them is a cabin built for the Danielses in 1941.

Some of Lundie's finest work dates to the late 1920s and early 1930s, when various period revival styles were much in vogue. The Edwin S. Binswanger House (1926) and the David Aberle House (1927), both in St. Paul, display Lundie's deft handling of the Tudor Revival style, as well as his unstinting devotion to fine craftsmanship. For smaller homes, Lundie often favored the Colonial Revival style, which can be deadly dull in the wrong hands but which he brought to life by means of meticulous detailing.

One of Lundie's largest commissions came in the 1950s, when he designed a Norman Revival–style home and other buildings for a 180-acre estate in Owatonna owned by Daniel C. Gainey, then president of Josten's. The property is now owned by the University of St. Thomas, which operates it as the Gainey Conference Center, and it's the only Lundie-designed home open for public tours. Although residential design accounts for the bulk of Lundie's work, he also took on some larger projects, including the Lutsen Resort (1949 and later) on the North Shore and the Minnesota Landscape Arboretum (1966–1972) in Chanhassen.

Because he never embraced architectural modernism, Lundie in the latter part of his career was viewed as a quaint, old-fashioned architect who had failed to keep up with the times. But with the rise in the 1980s of the postmodern movement, which revived interest in traditional styles of architecture, Lundie's star once again began to shine, as it should have all along. Good design, no matter how it's wrapped, is a gift, and Lundie's exquisite houses will never go out of style.

Edwin Lundie (*left*) looking over a project with two men. Lundie's career was remarkable. He began work in 1904 as an apprentice in the St. Paul offices of Cass Gilbert and continued to practice architecture until his death in 1972.

The surprising Georgian-style dining room—an addition designed by Lundie in 1934—is the most formal space in the house. It was the setting for a much-publicized dinner for the Duke and Duchess of Windsor in 1941.

begun living at the farm. When ADM moved its headquarters from Minneapolis to Decatur, Illinois, in 1968, John and Martha Daniels left Minnesota. Afterward, much of the farm property—including the guest house and the former employees' houses, as well as agricultural land—was sold to different owners. The main house was owned by ADM for a time and, later, by another corporation.

Garrett and Scornavacco, a St. Paul antiques dealer, purchased the house and barn, and fifteen surrounding acres, in 2001. The house was in good condition, and other than upgrading three bathrooms, they've made

The bedroom above the formal dining room addition is linked to the main part of the house by a beautiful gallery lined with leaded-glass windows on one side and closets on the other.

few changes. They did move the barn, which includes eight horse stalls as well as quarters for a groomsman once employed by the Danielses, a bit closer to the house. After a fire, they also rebuilt the garage.

Today, a visit to the house still feels a little like a trip out into the country, even though traffic on Interstate 35E now buzzes along less than a mile away and huge auto dealerships cluster along nearby Highway 61. But the world the Danielses knew—of horses and fox hunts and starry night skies unmolested by city lights—now belongs to another time. ◈

Tower View
Red Wing, 1921

Alexander and Lydia Anderson and their four children at Tower View, 1917. The estate was both home and workplace for Anderson.

Opposite: The Tower View estate is anchored by Alexander Anderson's unpretentious two-story brick family home (*left*) and one of two original laboratories (*right*), now used as the offices of the Anderson Center for Interdisciplinary Studies.

LATE IN HIS LONG AND THOROUGHLY REMARKABLE LIFE, ALEXANDER P. Anderson—farmer, teacher, botanist, inventor, businessman, and occasional poet—wrote: "I like dreamers, people who wonder why the bird sings so sweetly there beside its little nest. It must be the sunshine and the rain drops that sparkle, and the hope that all will be well. If nature is kind to the little birds, it must be kind to us." Anderson was an optimistic spirit who believed in those words, and his own dreams ultimately led him to build, on the outskirts of Red Wing, an estate like none other in Minnesota.

Known as Tower View, the estate at its peak spread out over nine hundred acres above and along the Cannon River. It included large expanses of farmland, laboratories where Anderson pursued his varied scientific interests, and a handsome residence that was home to Anderson and his close-knit family for many years. Now listed on the National Register of Historic Places, the estate at 163 Tower View Drive was also a celebration of Anderson's triumphant return home after a life of study and unceasing work that took him to Europe, South Carolina, New York, and Chicago.

Anderson lived a life that seems too improbable to be true. His parents, John and Britta Maria Anderson, were Swedish immigrants of very limited means who arrived in Minnesota in 1855 and claimed, at a cost of fourteen dollars, a 160-acre homestead along the banks of Spring Creek, not far from Red Wing. Their first home was a rude dugout clawed out of a hillside, but they later built a small log cabin, where Anderson (one of eight children) was born in 1862. He spent his youth on the farm while attending that icon of rural life, a one-room schoolhouse. Gifted with intelligence, drive, and boundless curiosity about the natural world, he began teaching school when he was only nineteen, even as he continued working on the family farm. In 1890, after both of his parents died, the farm fell into foreclosure. It was both a terrible loss and a great opportunity for Anderson. Free of his responsibilities on the farm, he was finally able to pursue the advanced education that had long been his dream.

At age twenty-eight, with money he'd saved from working odd jobs, Anderson enrolled at the University of Minnesota. A brilliant student, he

Anderson in his laboratory, 1933. He developed puffed cereal by heating grain in a tube and then cracking it open so that water inside the kernels flashed into steam.

obtained a bachelor's degree in botany in 1894 and a master's degree in 1895. The next year found him studying under some of the leading botanists in the world at the University of Munich in Germany, where he earned a PhD. His thesis, written in German, dealt with resin in diseased trees—not a topic to stir the soul, but the experimental work he poured into it was a harbinger of things to come.

By fall of 1896, Anderson was back in the United States, where he found a position teaching botany at the newly formed Clemson Agricultural College in South Carolina. He also became South Carolina's state botanist. It was at Clemson, a year later, that he met Lydia McDougall Johnson, a native of Scotland who had been serving as a nanny for a military family. They were married in 1898. He was thirty-six by then, she just twenty-two. Anderson called her his "sweetheart of the valley," and when they were apart—as they sometimes were for long periods because of Anderson's work—they wrote to each other twice a day. They ultimately had five children, four of whom survived to adulthood.

Although botany was Anderson's chief field of study, he was something of a mad scientist at heart, a restless tinkerer who loved experimenting with new ideas. While in Germany, Anderson had become interested in the idea that grain kernels might hold small amounts of water. The idea proved to be correct, and when Anderson, in 1901, found a way to flash that water into steam and explode it, he invented what would one day become puffed breakfast cereal. It was a discovery that changed his life. Within a year, he went to work for the Quaker Oats Company in Chicago, and in a laboratory there he perfected his puffing process. The first fruit of his labor was puffed rice, which Quaker introduced to the breakfast cereal market in 1905.

Anderson's invention made him one of the most famous scientists in America as well as an advertising icon—the man who "shot food from guns." It also brought him wealth for the first time in his life and thereby set the stage for his return home to the wooded hills and deep valleys of Goodhue County that he had always loved. By 1907 his finances were such that he was able to embark on a land-buying spree that continued for more than ten years. He began by repurchasing much of his parents' old farm. He soon built a new house on the property, for use by the tenants, and made other improvements. Anderson also acquired land in North Carolina, where he built another house. But his biggest plans centered on the estate that would become Tower View, located along Highway 61 at the western edge of Red Wing. Anderson bought his first acreage there in 1910 and continued to add to it over the next decade.

Alexander Anderson's spacious new home was completed in 1917 to the designs of Chicago architect Carl Westerlind. Unlike most Georgian Revival–style homes of its day, the front door is situated on the narrow side of the house.

Anderson's five-thousand-square-foot house included two main-floor bedrooms, identified as "chambers" on the plan. There were five more bedrooms and a library upstairs.

When Anderson began planning Tower View, he did not have in mind the usual kind of rural estate. Most estate properties of the time, such as those found around Lake Minnetonka just west of Minneapolis, consisted of a grand manor house surrounded by a collection of farm buildings. The business tycoons who owned them were, with a few exceptions, gentlemen farmers who liked to maintain fine horses and prized cattle but rarely dirtied their fingers by tilling the soil.

Anderson, by contrast, was a farmer to the core who loved nothing better than getting out on a tractor, or behind a team of horses, to work the land. Tower View, as he planned it, was to be a real farm. But it was also to have another, more unusual function. Weary of Chicago, Anderson decided to equip the estate with modern laboratories where he could continue his work for Quaker Oats. His stature was such that the company agreed to his plan and even sent workers to Red Wing to install the machinery he needed.

After what must have been a long period of planning, Tower View began to take shape in 1915 with construction of the distinctive brick-clad water tower from which the estate derives its name. Like all of the estate's major buildings, the tower, which culminates in a picturesque witch's-hat roof, is constructed of reinforced concrete. It was designed to hold 25,000 gallons of water pumped up from a deep well below. The water was then distributed by gravity to other buildings on the estate. Anderson also provided his own electricity by installing a direct-current, gasoline-driven generator and a bank of storage batteries.

In addition to the tower, a granary, barn, chicken coop, and silo were completed in 1915. A greenhouse, icehouse, and two concrete tunnels were added in 1916. Tunnels eventually connected all of the estate's main buildings. Other buildings, among them the main house and two laboratories, went up over the next few years. The estate was virtually complete by 1921, when a long brick wall was constructed along Highway 61.

The estate's centerpiece—a spacious new home for Anderson, his wife, and their four children—was completed in 1917 to the designs of Chicago architect Carl Westerlind. Virtually unknown today, Westerlind was, like Anderson, of Swedish descent, and it's likely that the two men had met at some point in Chicago during Anderson's long tenure there working for Quaker Oats. Anderson and his family watched the home being built during the summer of 1916, when they all lived in a big tent on the grounds.

The two-story house, clad in red brick with white stone trim beneath a tile roof, is a rather burly example of the Georgian Revival style. Very popular in the early twentieth century, the style drew its inspiration from

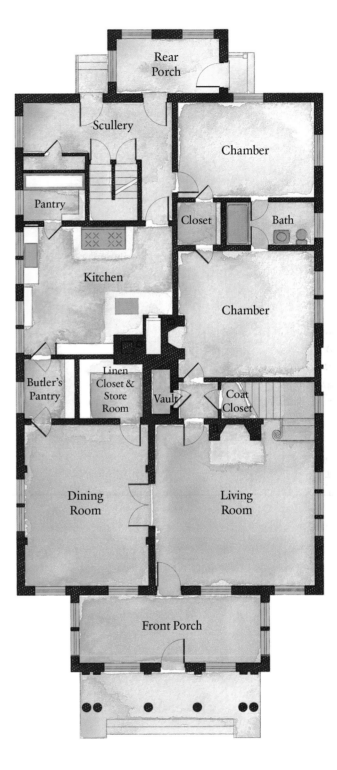

Breakfast Revolution

For much of the nineteenth century, the standard American breakfast—a scrum of sausage, bacon, bread, and gravy, with a shot of whiskey sometimes thrown in for good measure—was a high-calorie regimen that frequently ended in a bout of indigestion. Reformers, many of them basing their theories more on religion than food science, eventually sought to end this day-opening exercise in gluttony, and out of their efforts the American cereal industry took root. Granola (originally dubbed "granula") appeared in 1863, while the first toasted-wheat cereal—Wheatena—was introduced in 1879. But it wasn't until the 1890s, not long before Alexander Anderson invented his process for puffing grain, that such staples as Kellogg's Corn Flakes and Post Grape-Nuts (actually made of wheat and barley) found their way to the breakfast table.

Anderson's invention produced a new kind of cereal—light and tasty and able to float with ease in a bowl of milk, sometimes even snapping, crackling, and popping as it did so. The inspiration for Anderson's breakthrough came in the 1890s during his studies in Germany at the University of Munich, where he learned of a theory that grain kernels might contain tiny amounts of water. In 1901, while conducting research at the New York Botanical Garden, he set out to test the theory with a series of ingenious experiments designed to turn this trapped water to steam. He filled long tubes with kernels, heated them to five hundred degrees in an oven, removed the tubes, and then immediately cracked them open with a hammer. The result was an explosion as the water within the kernels flashed into steam. Puffed cereal had been born.

Anderson the scientist also turned out to be a canny businessman who was well aware of his discovery's profit potential. Early in 1902, with the help of his cousin, John Lind (a New Ulm lawyer who had recently served two years as governor of Minnesota), Anderson demonstrated his work to a group of prominent Minneapolis businessmen, who were sufficiently impressed to invest in a new cereal company to be headed by the inventor. A few months later, however, the fledging firm was acquired, as a wholly owned subsidiary, by Chicago-based Quaker Oats Company. In late 1902 Anderson moved to Chicago to work in Quaker's laboratories, where over the next nineteen years he oversaw thousands of experiments that ultimately led to numerous refinements in the puffing process.

Anderson introduced the first fruit of his work, puffed rice, at the St. Louis World's Fair in 1904. He set up eight cannon-like cylinders loaded with rice, heated them, and then shot out the puffed product into a two-story-high, forty-foot-wide cage. It was quite a spectacle, and the crowds loved it. Anderson ended up selling a quarter million bags of his novelty, at a nickel each, to hungry fairgoers. A year later, Quaker Puffed Rice went on the market, bolstered by an advertising campaign that showed rice being exploded from cannons and proclaimed Anderson's invention, with perhaps a wee bit of hyperbole, as "The Eighth Wonder of the World."

Wonder or not, breakfast would never be the same again.

Alexander Anderson, standing in the background third from right, unveiled puffed rice at the St. Louis World's Fair in 1904, selling a quarter million bags of the new wonder food for a nickel apiece.

colonial-era American homes, which in turn reflected English architecture as filtered through sources going all the way back to the Renaissance. Symmetry, simplicity of form, multilight windows, corner quoins, a columned front portico, sparse classical detailing, and an overall sense of repose are among hallmarks of the style evident in Anderson's house.

Georgian Revival houses were usually built with their broad side facing to the front, an arrangement that lent itself to a central-hall plan with flanking rooms. The Anderson House, however, follows a different format. Its front entrance is on the short side, much like homes built on narrow city lots, and as a result it doesn't have a standard Georgian hall plan. The house has other quirks, including a pair of all-brick front dormers that look as though someone forgot to install the usual windows. The entry sequence—a columned porch extending across a one-story entry hall that projects from the main body of the house—is also atypical of Georgian design.

Overall, the house has a rather mechanical feel, suggesting it was more the work of an engineer (which Anderson in many ways was) than an architect. Even so, it's worth noting that the house, as designed, was to have included a number of grace notes, such as ornate terra-cotta finials and chimney caps, that would have softened its appearance. These features were probably left out to save cost. There was also an elaborate landscape plan that was never fully implemented.

Inside, the five-thousand-square-foot house (not counting basement and attic) was never intended to be highly luxurious. Too much fanciness would have offended Anderson, who was never given to the sort of conspicuous consumption famously pilloried by his fellow Scandinavian and Minnesotan Thorstein Veblen (who grew up on a farm about forty miles from Anderson's birthplace). Although it lacked the trappings of baronial splendor, the house offered a solid and comfortable place to live for the Andersons and their children, who ranged in age from one to thirteen when the family moved in.

An aerial view of the Tower View estate, which originally included a large working farm with fields spreading into the Cannon River Valley.

The first floor consists of an entry porch and hall, living and dining rooms, a large kitchen and pantry, and two bedrooms, one of which was for Anderson and his wife. There were five more bedrooms and a library upstairs. Downstairs bedrooms were not a typical feature of two-story homes at the time, but the arrangement gave the Andersons some extra nighttime privacy and quiet in a household full of active children. The upstairs library is also unusual, but was probably necessitated by the decision to place bedrooms on the main floor. Finished with oak floors and birch woodwork, the house's main rooms are quite understated by the often lush, decorative standards of the era.

Almost all of the rooms feature distinctive ornament in the form of colorful geometric patterns painted on the upper walls and ceilings. Completed in the early 1920s, these were all the work of a German-born church painter named Joseph Kiemen, whose life and career are obscure. It's not known how Anderson came to hire Kiemen, but it proved to be a wise decision, since the painter's work adds a unique touch to the house.

Connected to the house via a tunnel are two laboratories where Anderson conducted scientific experiments. Anderson eventually developed a "continuous puffing process" that allowed a special mix of dough to be expanded in the same manner as grains. A cereal called Crackels resulted from this technique but did not thrive on the market (much later, Cheerios—made in a similar way by General Mills—became the most popular of all breakfast cereals). Anderson kept notes for all of his experiments, and these were eventually collected in forty volumes consisting of twelve thousand handwritten pages.

Anderson and his wife supported many charitable ventures, but the one closest to their hearts was the Vasa Children's Home. Founded in 1865 in the small town of Vasa near Red Wing, it served as a home for the orphaned children of Swedish immigrants. In 1924 the Andersons donated four hundred acres of land across Highway 61 from Tower View as the site of a new building for the home, which was completed two years later. Crown Prince Gustaf Adolf of Sweden laid the cornerstone for the building, and the Andersons established a trust fund to help maintain it.

In the years that followed, Anderson continued to conduct numerous experiments at Tower View. He was particularly fascinated by tornadoes, at least two of which ripped through Goodhue County in his lifetime. He wrote a chapter about tornadoes in *The Seventh Reader*, a collection of stories, memoirs, poetry, and country wisdom published near the end of his life. The chapter is illustrated with charts, possibly the first of their kind, showing the paths of two tornadoes, in 1865 and 1879, that just missed his old family farm. Anderson also maintained a "farm museum," as he called it, and among the objects he preserved were a brick and other pieces of a farmhouse destroyed by the 1865 tornado.

The distinctive brick-clad water tower that inspired Tower View's name was designed to hold 25,000 gallons of water pumped from a deep well. It provided water to all of the buildings on the estate.

The Anderson family house falls loosely into the category of Georgian Revival, a variant of the Colonial Revival style popular in the early 1900s. The two windowless front dormers constitute a quirky departure from the norm.

Chicago architect Carl Westerlind, like Anderson of Swedish descent, designed a simple, sturdy family home for his client. It features abundant woodwork, seen here in the passage between the dining and living rooms.

The Colonial Revival Style

Alexander Anderson's solid but unpretentious brick house is an example of one of the most popular of all American housing styles—Colonial Revival. The style first appeared in Minnesota in the late 1880s and reached its peak during the first two decades of the 1900s. Colonial Revival is actually an umbrella term that takes in a cluster of related styles to which architectural historians have assigned an array of names. The Anderson House fits loosely into a subtype usually called Georgian Revival.

As its name indicates, the Colonial Revival style is based on the English-inspired architecture of the American colonies before the Revolutionary War. That architecture came in several varieties, the most common of which is Georgian (named after the kings who ruled England for most of the eighteenth century). American Georgian houses are typically oblong, two-story boxes with central entrances, symmetrical multipane windows aligned vertically and horizontally, and modest amounts of classically derived ornament. The best examples convey a sense of simplicity, dignity, and repose.

The Georgian style fell out of favor after the Revolutionary War, but only gradually. The Greek Revival style, another classical variant, became dominant in the 1820s. After that, romantic Victorian styles such as Gothic Revival and Italianate enjoyed a long run. In 1876, however, a huge Centennial Exposition that drew nearly ten million visitors to Philadelphia helped revive interest in all aspects of American colonial life, including its architecture. A few years later, homes in the Colonial Revival style began to appear on the East Coast, many designed by the prominent New York architectural firm of McKim, Mead and White. The style then spread rapidly to the Midwest and beyond.

St. Paul architect Cass Gilbert—who had worked for McKim, Mead and White—produced one of the earliest Minnesota examples of the style in 1887 for Charles and Emily Noyes. The Noyes House still stands at 89 Virginia Street in St. Paul's Historic Hill District. Another pioneering Colonial Revival home, now known as the Hinkle-Murphy House, is at 619 Tenth Street South in downtown Minneapolis. Designed by William Channing Whitney, it also dates to 1887. Architects like Gilbert and Whitney saw Colonial Revival as an antidote to the wild excesses of the Queen Anne style that had peaked in the mid-1880s. The Chicago World's Fair of 1893, with its gleaming assemblage of white buildings in classical styles, gave further impetus to the Colonial Revival movement.

Colonial Revival houses in Minnesota rarely, if ever, offer a precise re-creation of their eighteenth-century models, and that is certainly true of the Anderson House. Its paired and tripled windows, for example, are features never found on eighteenth-century colonial homes, and its floor plan also departs in many ways from tradition. Although Colonial Revival achieved its greatest level of popularity in the early twentieth century, it's never really gone out of style. St. Paul architect Edwin Lundie continued designing exquisite Colonial Revival homes well into the 1950s, and houses large and small bearing at least some features of the style are still being built today.

The Charles P. Noyes House at 89 Virginia Street in St. Paul is one of Minnesota's earliest examples of the Colonial Revival style. Designed by Cass Gilbert, it was built in 1887.

The colorful geometric patterns painted on the upper walls and ceilings throughout the Anderson House were the work of German-born church painter Joseph Kiemen.

Stairs lead from the living room to five bedrooms and a library on the second floor. The master bedroom is on the first floor, an unusual arrangement for the time.

The great experimenter stayed on at Tower View until his death, at age eighty, in 1943. Lydia had died nine years earlier, at age fifty-eight, of cancer. Over the next half century, the estate's well-preserved buildings were used as research laboratories, a rehabilitation center, and a secondary campus for what is now the Red Wing Technical College, which added a glassy addition to one of the laboratory buildings in 1980. The house itself became, for more than thirty years, the residence of one of Anderson's daughters, Jean Chesney, and her family. Chesney and her husband, Frank, later became owners of one of Red Wing's other famous homes, the E. S. Hoyt House.

Today, Tower View is home to the Anderson Center for Interdisciplinary Studies, established in 1993 under the direction of Anderson's grandson, Robert Hedin, and his wife, Carolyn. Hedin—a former college teacher who is also a poet, a translator, and the editor of numerous books—has presided over $2 million of improvements to the estate, which now includes several small schools, an environmental center, a foundry, and a literary press on its grounds.

Finished with oak floors and stained birch woodwork, the living room is elegant, yet understated, providing a comfortable and practical space for the large Anderson family.

A small room atop the tower is painted with decorative motifs similar to those found throughout the house.

The center is perhaps best known for its summer residency program for artists, writers, and scholars, who in turn share their knowledge by making presentations throughout the community. In addition, the center offers classes in everything from fiction writing to glassblowing, hosts many events year-round, and features an excellent permanent art collection and a fifteen-acre outdoor sculpture garden.

There can be little doubt that Anderson, who so successfully combined a life of the mind with a tangible appreciation of nature, would have approved of the use of his estate as a place for study, contemplation, and the

The upper level of the barn at Tower View is now a finished space for performing and visual arts. Anderson Center hosts a summer residency program for artists, writers, and scholars.

flowering of art and literature. He was a believer in hard work, the virtue of love, and the beauty of the natural world, and he had a poet's knowing heart. In *The Seventh Reader*, he wrote: "This business of going through life is a sort of big one, after all. One has to watch one's steps daily in order to come out even with the big universe in which we live and do our work." It is fair to say, on the basis of his life and legacy, Anderson came out more than even. ❧

🪶 Quarry Hill
Rochester, 1924

Henry and Daisy Plummer with their two children, Robert and Gertrude, circa 1916.

Opposite: Dr. Henry Plummer's Tudor Revival house, now owned by the City of Rochester, is one of three great estate properties built by founding doctors of the Mayo Clinic.

O N DECEMBER 30, 1936, AFTER ATTENDING A MEDICAL MEETING IN Rochester, Dr. Henry S. Plummer—a founding partner of the Mayo Clinic—began the short drive home to his forty-nine-room hilltop mansion. Along the way, Plummer began experiencing the symptoms of what he realized must be a terrible stroke. By the time the sixty-two-year-old doctor reached home, he was barely able to walk. His wife, Daisy, and the family chauffeur helped him up to his bedroom. There, he coolly informed them that he would become unconscious within an hour, that death would inevitably follow, and that family and friends should gather at his bedside. Plummer's self-diagnosis proved perfectly correct, and with his death eighteen hours later on New Year's Eve, the Mayo Clinic lost perhaps the most brilliant of all the doctors who had helped create a medical colossus in a most unlikely place.

Today, Plummer's vast Tudor Revival mansion is, along with the elegant 1928 clinic building that bears his name, one of two prominent landmarks in Rochester that commemorate his life and career. Located at 1091 Plummer Lane, the mansion and its wooded grounds have the feel of a sanctuary, a calm and orderly place where the great doctor found relief from the demands of his all-too-busy life. Hardly known today outside medical circles, Plummer was in every way an astonishing character, eccentric and driven, whose medical skills were matched only by his talents as a seat-of-the-pants engineer. He played such a crucial role in developing the clinic that Dr. William Mayo is said to have remarked, "Hiring Henry was the best day's work I ever did."

Plummer was a homegrown genius. The son of a country doctor, he was born in 1874 near the small town of Racine, just south of Rochester. Although he had a deep interest in mechanical engineering, he ultimately decided on a career in medicine. After graduating from Northwest Medical College in Chicago, he returned to Racine in 1898 to help with his father's practice. It was while on a call to see a patient one day in 1901 that he met William Mayo, who along with his brother, Charles, headed a successful but still quite small medical practice in Rochester.

Quarry Hill took its name from a limestone quarry that once occupied the site.

William Mayo—who was blunt, square-faced, and muscular, a surgeon to the core—took an immediate liking to Plummer as the gangly young doctor explained, in great detail, techniques he had developed for analyzing diseases of the blood. Mayo was so impressed that he asked Plummer to join the practice in Rochester, and before long Plummer became the Mayo Clinic's indispensable man, not only a superb physician but also a great organizer, inventor, and visionary.

The Mayo Clinic was the nation's first private group medical practice, and it was Plummer, as much an anyone else, who created the functional foundations for this unprecedented approach to delivering health care. He invented a new dossier-style method of keeping patient records, organized the clinic's medical laboratories, helped develop a standardized examination room, pioneered the use of X-ray equipment, built numerous medical tools, and devised an elaborate system of pneumatic tubes and conveyors to deliver information to doctors. The first building in Rochester expressly designed for the clinic, completed in 1914, was packed with Plummer's innovations, as was the much larger 1928 building later named in his honor.

Tall, stooped over, and perpetually lost in thought, Plummer also found time to tend to patients. Thorough but kind (he was known to pay

The 1928 Plummer Building at the Mayo Clinic incorporated many of its namesake's innovations, including an elaborate system for conveying patient records to doctors.

poor patients' fees out of his own pocket), he specialized in the treatment of goiter and disorders of the esophagus. One of his most notable achievements was to identify a specific type of hyperthyroidism now known as Plummer's Disease. He was a renowned diagnostician as well, with an ability to reason his way quickly through a problem that might have impressed even Sherlock Holmes (who was, in fact, modeled on a Scottish physician).

Plummer was also, by all accounts, a very odd duck, and anecdotal tales of his unusual behavior abound. In one instance, or so the story goes, he sent a male patient into an examining room, only to discover that another doctor's patient, a woman, was already there. Ignoring the woman, Plummer told his patient to completely undress, which the man—no doubt reluctantly—did. Plummer then asked the naked man if he had lost any weight, but he was apparently too embarrassed to answer, so Plummer turned to the woman and asked her what she thought about the man's condition. The woman, who seems to have gotten into the spirit of the moment, supposedly replied, "I never saw him before, but he looks awfully skinny to me."

Other stories tell of Plummer ignoring someone's question and then suddenly answering it a day later or of disappearing from his office only to be found sitting in a dusty corner of the clinic's basement, thinking. It must have been both exhilarating and a bit disconcerting to be around him. Yet his colleagues recognized that his seeming absentmindedness served its own deep purpose, since he possessed such extraordinary powers of concentration that once an idea seized his attention it blotted out the rest of the world. Or, as a biographer put it, "When engaged in deep thought, he possessed the remarkable ability to even exclude environment from his consciousness."

Plummer's entire adult life centered around the Mayo, and it was there in 1903 that he met Daisy Berkman, who worked in the clinic's laboratory and who was also a member of the Mayo family. Her mother, Gertrude, was the sister of William and Charles

The mansion is a fairly conventional exercise in the fashionable Tudor Revival style of the era. The exterior is quite picturesque, with random courses of stone erupting from stucco walls.

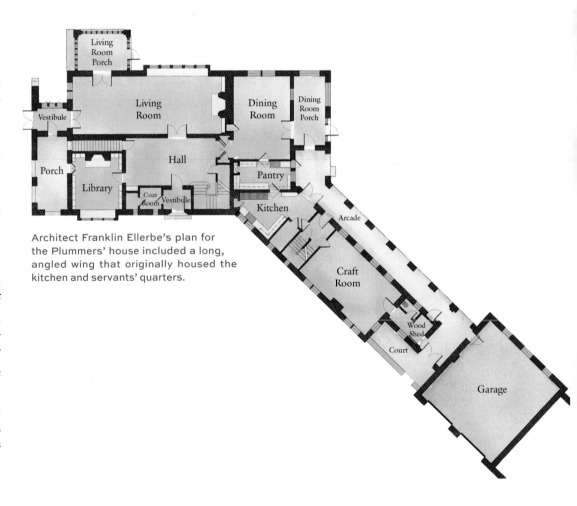

Architect Franklin Ellerbe's plan for the Plummers' house included a long, angled wing that originally housed the kitchen and servants' quarters.

Set on a high hill amid lush plantings, Plummer's home served as a place of refuge for the busy physician, who was responsible for numerous medical innovations at the Mayo Clinic.

Mayo Estates

The doctors who established the Mayo Clinic, led by brothers Charles H. and William J. Mayo, not only created a world-renowned medical center but also became very wealthy men in the process. Like their colleague Henry Plummer, the brothers built enormous mansions that are among Rochester's most historically significant works of architecture. The mansions are quite different—Charles's was built as a country estate, William's as an in-city residence within blocks of the clinic—but both demonstrate how the brothers prospered as their clinic blossomed into a huge institution. Before building their mansions, the brothers had lived in neighboring Queen Anne–style houses (gone) on what is now Fourth Street Southwest in Rochester. Winona architect Charles Maybury designed the houses, which were spacious but not especially grand.

Around 1910 Charles Mayo, usually called "Dr. Charlie," began building a vast estate, known as Mayowood, on three thousand acres of wooded land a few miles southwest of Rochester along a branch of the Zumbro River. The estate included a thirty-eight-room mansion set behind a series of terraces, elaborate English and Japanese gardens, and an artificial lake created by a dam that was also used to generate electric power. Dr. Charlie did much of the design work himself, and while he was perhaps a better surgeon than architect, the Renaissance Revival–style house—built of concrete, stone, and stucco—remains impressive by virtue of its size and its beautiful grounds. Dr. Charlie and his wife, Edith, who had eight children, lived in the house until their deaths (his in 1939 and hers in 1943), after which descendants occupied the home for many more years.

Members of the family donated the home, its furnishings, and ten surrounding acres to the Olmsted County Historical Society in 1965. Mayowood has functioned as a museum house since then and is open for regularly scheduled tours. In 2013, the Mayo Clinic assumed ownership of the house and began a multimillion-dollar restoration and renovation, which is expected to take several years.

Less than a decade after his brother's estate was completed, William Mayo—known as "Dr. Will"—built an equally magnificent home for himself and his wife, Hattie, at 701 Fourth Street Southwest in Rochester's old College Hill neighborhood. Like so many other early Mayo buildings and homes, it was designed by architect Franklin Ellerbe. Built with walls of Kasota stone quarried eighty miles to the west near Mankato, the 24,000-square-foot Tudor Revival–style mansion features a monumental five-story front tower that Dr. Will, an amateur astronomer, insisted upon as a place for stargazing. Two smaller homes for servants, a car-

riage house, and a greenhouse were also built on the mansion's grounds, which occupy an entire square block.

Dr. Will and Hattie, whose children were grown by the time they moved into the mansion, stayed in the home until 1938, when they donated it to the clinic as a place where doctors and others could gather to discuss medicine. Today, the mansion is known as the Mayo Foundation House and continues to host medical gatherings and events. After leaving the mansion, the couple moved into a house they had built on the southwest corner of the property. A year later, in July of 1939, Dr. Will died at age seventy-eight, outliving his younger brother by only two months. Hattie remained in her house on the property until her death in 1952.

A Country Home, Rochester, Minn.

Dr. Charles Mayo's mansion, known as Mayowood, was built beginning in 1910 on a three-thousand-acre estate just outside Rochester. This postcard view was published in the early 1900s.

A small pond is one of the estate's many beautiful features. Both Plummer and his wife, Daisy, were deeply interested in horticulture, and Plummer himself laid out the grounds, which originally encompassed sixty-five acres.

Mayo. Her father, David Berkman, was—naturally enough—a doctor. She and Plummer married in 1904 and then moved into a new house built for them on Second Street Southwest in Rochester. The house, a standard Arts and Crafts foursquare, was to be the couple's residence for the next twenty years, until the completion of their enormous second home about a mile away on an elevation known as Quarry Hill.

There have been at least three sites called Quarry Hill in and around Rochester, all named because they were once mined for the buff-colored limestone used for many of the city's early buildings. In about 1912 Plummer bought sixty-five acres atop one of these hills on the southwestern side of Rochester. The site Plummer chose was, at the time, just outside the city limits but not far from Rochester's finest residential neighborhood, originally called College Hill but later dubbed "Pill Hill" because of the many doctors who lived there.

Plummer began laying plans for his mansion, which itself acquired the name Quarry Hill, just as Charles Mayo was completing his huge county estate, Mayowood (1911), a few miles outside Rochester. William Mayo would follow his brother's lead in 1917 by building a massive, towered stone mansion (now the Mayo Foundation House) on Fourth Street Southwest in Rochester, a few blocks from Plummer's far-more-modest home. Whether Plummer was motivated by edifice envy isn't known, but with his two most famous colleagues occupying monumental new dwellings, he must have felt his unremarkable four-square was decidedly inadequate.

At some point after acquiring the Quarry Hill property, Plummer hired Franklin Ellerbe as his architect. Ellerbe—who also designed William Mayo's mansion—was personally known to Plummer, having worked with him on the first Mayo Clinic building. Born in Mississippi in 1870 but raised in St. Paul, where he gained experience as a building inspector, Ellerbe established his own firm in 1911. Two years later, he secured his first commission in Rochester, for a hotel, and later opened an office in the city.

It's likely Ellerbe and his draftsmen began working on Plummer's new home sometime in 1915 or 1916. Ellerbe, however, wouldn't live to see the mansion completed. He became very ill in the summer of 1921 and was hospitalized in St. Paul. Waiving rules that normally prohibited Mayo doctors from seeing patients outside Rochester, Plummer went to St. Paul to examine Ellerbe. The diagnosis was grim—pancreatic cancer. Ellerbe was rushed to Rochester for emergency surgery but died two days later. His son, Thomas Farr Ellerbe, then took over the business. Under his direction the firm of Ellerbe Architects would go on to design many buildings for the Mayo Clinic (including the 1928 Plummer Building) as well as numerous homes on Pill Hill.

Plummer's estate—which as built included a water tower, a greenhouse, garages, formal gardens,

The estate's picturesque water tower, which includes a delightful little balcony, was built in part from limestone quarried on the property.

The Mayo Clinic

Doctors and medical students look on as Dr. Charles Mayo operates on a patient at the Mayo Clinic, 1913.

When Dr. Henry Plummer in 1901 joined the staff of what would soon be called the Mayo Clinic, he became part of a young but remarkable organization that was transforming the practice of medicine in the United States. Today, Mayo has grown to become the largest nonprofit medical practice and research center in the world, and its story is one that could only have happened in America.

The Mayo Clinic's roots, however, reach back to Great Britain, where William Worrall Mayo was born, raised, and educated in medicine and science. A true adventurer, he boarded a ship bound for America in 1845 and became a pharmacist at Bellevue Hospital in New York City. He eventually moved west to Lafayette, Indiana, and earned his medical degree at Indiana Medical College in 1850. The following year he married Louise Abigail Wright, herself of Scottish origins. She stood slightly taller than her husband, nicknamed "The Little Doctor," who stood all of five feet four inches. After a stint at the University of Missouri's medical department, Dr. Mayo contracted malaria and decided to move to the supposedly healthier, fresher air of Minnesota. There, the family settled in Le Sueur.

With a front-row seat to American history, Dr. Mayo practiced military medicine during the U.S.–Dakota War of 1862 and again as military surgeon for the draft board in Rochester during the Civil War. He liked Rochester and brought his growing family to live there, eventually sending his sons William and Charles to medical school. Both became exceptional surgeons often called "Dr. Will" and "Dr. Charlie."

In 1883 Rochester fell prey to a devastating tornado. Dr. Mayo organized treatment for the dozens of people injured in the storm, assisted by his two sons and the nuns of St. Francis. That collaboration became St. Mary's Hospital, and the basis for the Mayo Clinic. Other partner physicians were called in, and by 1889 a new model for American medicine—the private, integrated group practice—was born.

William Worrall Mayo, who had been active in city and state politics, retired from the medical practice in 1892, at age seventy-three. Both of his sons served as colonels in the U.S. Army during World War I and were later promoted to brigadiers general in the Army Reserve. Dr. Charlie retired in 1930, and his own two sons and a grandson succeeded him at Mayo.

The practice expanded throughout the twentieth century to a huge complex of medical buildings offering an increasingly wide range of patient services, research, and education. In addition to Rochester, the Mayo Clinic now has a presence in both Jacksonville, Florida, and Phoenix, Arizona. Mayo is also planning a $5 billion economic development initiative in Rochester designed to ensure that the clinic will remain a worldwide destination for medical care.

and a gazebo—was under construction from 1917 to 1924, an unusually long time. It's not clear why construction dragged on for so many years. One possibility is that Plummer, who was intimately involved in every aspect of the design, made numerous changes to the plans, thereby causing delays.

To be certain they liked the property, Plummer and his wife spent part of a summer there camping in a tent. Later, Plummer had a temporary house built on the site so that he could be close to the work. By the time construction of the estate began in 1917, Plummer's family had expanded to include two adopted children. He and Daisy, who had no children of their own, adopted an infant son, Robert, in 1912 and a daughter, Gertrude, two years later.

The estate's fanciful water tower, constructed of random ashlar limestone and half-timbered stucco, was built before the mansion. It was used to store water pumped from a well on the property. A stone staircase rising above an arch leads up to the tower's entry, which is sheltered by a porch. The observatory atop the tower features a charming balcony set beneath a tiny, pent roof. Some of the stone used to build the water tower and mansion was mined on the property, with the rest coming from other quarries around Rochester.

An oil portrait of Plummer overlooks the front staircase. The diamond-paned windows that illuminate the landing are often found in Tudor Revival homes.

The mansion's tiled foyer is elegant without being ostentatious. Double glass doors open directly to the living room, with the dining room at right.

Banks of windows provide a fine view from the living room. Floor grates next to the fireplace allowed music to be heard from a pipe organ in the basement.

The mansion, which extends for three hundred feet along its front elevation, is a fairly conventional exercise in the fashionable Tudor Revival style of the era. Its exterior is quite picturesque, with random courses of stone erupting from the stucco walls. This kind of calculated irregularity was often used to give a rustic, handmade look to Tudor homes in the 1920s. The mansion's other stylistic hallmarks include a pointed-arch entry, a stepped-up stair window with diamond-shaped panes, an open side arch, a steep slate roof, and patterned brick chimneys. A half-timbered service wing, set at an angle to the main body of the mansion, adds a note of dynamism to the long front facade.

The home's understated front entrance, reached from a circular driveway, opens into a broad, tiled foyer with a beamed ceiling and a staircase to the right. Straight in from the foyer is a forty-by-twenty-foot oak-paneled living room situated along the south side of the house overlooking the crest of the hill. A bank of bay windows above a built-in bench extends nearly the full length of the room, offering views out to a rear patio and sun porch. When the house was built, the patio and porch overlooked open countryside to the south, but today the vista is marred by extensive commercial development along Highway 14.

The living room also features a molded-plaster ceiling, an arched stone fireplace incised with delicate ornamental motifs, and built-in bookshelves. Daisy was a talented pianist, and one of her grand pianos—a rare Mason and Hamlin model—was refurbished and is now used at the Mayo Civic Center in Rochester. A pipe organ in the basement provided another source of music, which could be heard in the living room through floor grates next to the fireplace. French doors on the east end of the living room lead to the mansion's greenhouse.

Two other major rooms are located off the foyer—a study to the east and a large formal dining room to the west that like the living room provides views to the south. A butler's pantry off the dining room connects to the kitchen, located in the service wing. The book-lined study must have been Plummer's favorite room, as he was a great reader. Here, too, he could access a panel that controlled the home's utility systems. Plummer was fond of gadgets and mechanical contrivances of all kinds, and the mansion came equipped with central communications, security, and vacuum systems as advanced as any of their time.

The second floor consists of five large bedrooms with interconnecting baths, along with two sun porches and maids' quarters in the service wing. The master bedroom, at the southeast corner of the mansion, contains some of the Plummers' original furniture. One of the two guest bedrooms was dedicated to Thomas Ellerbe, who became a close friend of the Plummers after working with them on the design of the mansion. Much of the home's third floor is taken up by a ballroom.

The home's cozy library is where Plummer spent much of his time. He was an avid reader and an intuitive engineer who invented many devices used at the clinic.

The dining room, at the west end of the house, opens out into a screened porch and patio beyond.

Both Plummer and his wife were passionate horticulturists. Plummer himself planned the estate's gardens, pools, rock walls, and winding pathways. Two full-time gardeners worked to maintain Plummer's handiwork. He also designed and installed an underground sprinkling system, possibly one of the first in Minnesota. A heated outdoor swimming pool, located next to dressing rooms reached through a tunnel from the mansion, was also one of the first of its kind in the state. Although the estate offered all the pleasures of life in the country, the Plummers often decamped in the summer to a lake cabin they owned just north of Rochester. They also had a small cabin cruiser and made frequent trips on the Mississippi River.

Plummer's sudden death in 1936 became front-page news in the *Rochester Post-Bulletin*, which included the story of how the "scientist to the last" had diagnosed his own fatal stroke. Flags at the clinic flew at half staff on the day of his funeral, and some stores in Rochester were closed during the services at Calvary Episcopal Church. William and Charles Mayo were among those who paid tribute to Plummer. The brothers were by then growing old, and they died within two months of each other in 1939.

Daisy stayed on at Quarry Hill for more than thirty years after her husband's death, living alone in the mansion except for a housekeeper and a chauffeur. With no need of such large grounds, she sold fifty-four acres from the estate. The land was then subdivided into residential lots, and about thirty homes were ultimately built on the former estate acreage.

In 1969, Daisy—who in addition to being an accomplished pianist was a longtime patron of the arts—donated the mansion and its eleven remaining acres of ground to an arts organization in Rochester. The property then became known as the Plummer House of the Arts. It was added to the National Register of Historic Places in 1975, a year before Daisy died at age ninety-eight.

In 1972 the City of Rochester acquired the property, which proved too costly to maintain as an arts center. Now managed by the Rochester Park and Recreation Department, the Plummer House is open for tours, weddings, and other events. Although it was among Minnesota's largest estate properties when built, the mansion—especially compared with the homes built at about the same time by the Mayo brothers—doesn't have an overwhelming presence. The same was true of its builder—a quirky, caring genius who left behind a legacy of service to his patients and to the world of medicine that still resonates today. ❧

❧ Glensheen
Duluth, 1908

Chester Congdon (*center*) and Clara Congdon (*second from left*) with family members, on the west porch at Glensheen.

Opposite: Set above a two-level terrace overlooking Lake Superior to the rear, Glensheen (viewed here from the back) may well be Minnesota's greatest estate, its architectural splendor matched by the rugged beauty of its grounds.

O F ALL THE MANSIONS IN MINNESOTA, NONE IS MORE ELEGANTLY appointed, more beautifully sited, nor more deeply connected to its place than Glensheen, the magnificent home on the shores of Lake Superior built by Chester Adgate Congdon, a quiet striver who rose from unexceptional circumstances to become one of the state's richest men. When Congdon and his family moved into their new home in 1908, it wasn't the largest mansion in Minnesota (the James J. Hill House in St. Paul held that honor), but it was in many ways the finest, a bravura architectural performance at once grand in scale and intimate in its details. The estate's grounds—a North Shore wonderland of creeks, canyons, gardens, trails, and forests—are every bit as impressive as the mansion.

Home for nearly seventy years to members of the Congdon family, Glensheen in 1977 became the scene of a riveting murder mystery when Elisabeth Congdon—the last surviving child of Chester Congdon and his wife, Clara—and her night nurse were slain inside the mansion. Some of the 65,000 visitors a year who tour the home and grounds, now owned by the University of Minnesota Duluth, undoubtedly come to see where the crime occurred. Yet even visitors with a taste for sensational mayhem soon realize that the real story of Glensheen is the estate itself and the remarkable man who built it.

The oldest son of a Methodist minister, Chester Congdon was born in 1853 in Rochester, New York. He barely survived into adulthood after scarlet fever swept through his family in 1868, claiming the lives of three younger siblings. Intelligent and industrious, he graduated in 1875 with the first class of Syracuse University, where he met his future wife, Clara Bannister. In 1877, he passed the bar examination in New York and for a time considered working in the town of Clifton Springs, where George Draper Dayton had been born twenty years earlier.

Finding it difficult to establish a legal practice in New York, Congdon accepted a teaching position in Chippewa Falls, Wisconsin, primarily because he wanted to spend some time looking at career opportunities in

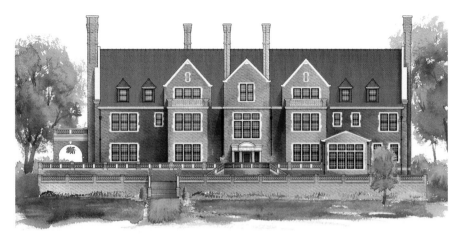

Three prominent gables dominate Glensheen's lakeside elevation. A two-level terrace steps down to Lake Superior.

A pool and fountain occupy the lower level of the terrace. Lake Superior lies just beyond.

the Midwest. He toured cities in Iowa, Illinois, Missouri, Nebraska, and Kansas but found none to his liking. Early in 1879 he paid a visit to St. Paul, then a rapidly growing city of more than forty thousand people, and quickly decided it was a place where he could build a legal career. He quit his teaching job and, with a grand total of thirty-one dollars in his pocket, moved to St. Paul and joined a small law firm.

By 1881 Congdon was serving as an assistant U.S. attorney and felt financially secure enough to marry Clara. After their wedding in Syracuse, the couple returned to St. Paul, where they lived in a home on Wilkin Street near Irvine Park, just a few blocks from Alexander Ramsey's mansion. The couple's first child, a son, was born in the Wilkin Street house in 1882. The Congdons would go on to have six more children—three boys and three girls, all but one of whom survived to adulthood. Their last child was born in 1898, when they also added to the family by adopting one of Clara's nephews.

In 1883 Congdon quit his position in the U.S. Attorney's Office to start his own practice, which proved to be successful. St. Paul and much of Minnesota was then expanding at a dizzying pace as farmers spread out across the prairies, lumberjacks stalked the north woods, and railroad lines forged new links to markets all across the country. In this fast-developing world there was plenty of work for a good lawyer, and Congdon by all accounts possessed a superb legal intellect. In time he became the consummate corporate lawyer, master of the ironclad contract, who let nothing escape his sharp eye. Congdon's personality perfectly suited his line of work. He was reserved almost to the point of being shy—a Duluth newspaper once described him as "a man of stern and even rather grim exterior, of distance and aloofness"—but he was also a strategic thinker, and very shrewd. Just as important, he knew how to make the right kinds of friends.

Although Congdon did extremely well as a lawyer, it was his skill as an investor that ultimately made him a multimillionaire. His first big investment, however, did not pan out. In 1887 he and a group of

New Yorkers formed a company to develop Grays Harbor, Washington (then a U.S. territory) as a major new port city. The project failed to thrive, encountering one setback after another, and in the end soaked up more money than it made. Congdon's biographer describes it as "undoubtedly the least lucrative investment" of his career.

In 1892 Congdon made a momentous decision when he and his family moved to Duluth so that he could establish a law firm with William Billson. The two men had known each other since Billson's days as the U.S. attorney in St. Paul, and Billson believed—correctly—that Duluth was an incipient boomtown where talented lawyers could prosper. The city was in fact on the cusp of a stunning growth surge tied to the discovery of gigantic iron ore deposits on the nearby Mesabi Range.

The turning point in Congdon's life came one summer day in 1892 when he met Henry W. Oliver, an Irish-born steelmaker from Pittsburgh. Oliver was among the first to recognize the Mesabi's vast potential, leasing land from the Merritt family, led by brothers Leonidas and Alfred, who had discovered the rich lode of ore. After concluding his deal with the Merritts, Oliver realized that he needed top-notch legal representation in Duluth. Congdon became Oliver's trusted lawyer and lifelong friend.

By the mid-1890s mining on the Mesabi had also attracted industrial titans such as Andrew Carnegie (who became Oliver's partner) and John D. Rockefeller. Congdon proved to be indispensable when it came to nego-tiating the legal thickets of land leases and partnerships. Later, Congdon also invested in land on the western part of the Mesabi and formed his own mining companies. By the time of his death, Congdon was reputed to be the second-richest man in Minnesota, behind only James J. Hill.

As Congdon's wealth grew, he and his family in 1895 moved into a house at 1509 East Superior Street, originally designed by and built for Duluth architect Oliver Traphagen. Chester and Clara had always dreamed of building a home of their own, however, and began to make plans for a large estate as early as 1901. Two years later, Congdon purchased twenty-two acres of mostly wooded land that extended from Lake Superior north along Tischer Creek, in a largely undeveloped area about three miles east of downtown Duluth. By July 1903 the Congdons had looked over their new property, at 3300 London Road, and found a perfect site for their mansion, on high ground just off the lake between the creek and a smaller stream called Bent Brook. From the start the Congdons envisioned their new home as part of a self-sufficient estate, which as built would include four green-houses, a carriage house, a gardener's cottage, a boathouse, vegetable gar-dens, an orchard, and its own water reservoir.

To design the mansion and other buildings on the property, the Cong-dons in 1904 hired Clarence Johnston of St. Paul, then the best-known and most prolific architect in Minnesota. Johnston had ample experi-

A footbridge over Tischer Creek, viewed from the mansion's west porch. A smaller creek called Bent Brook also courses through the estate.

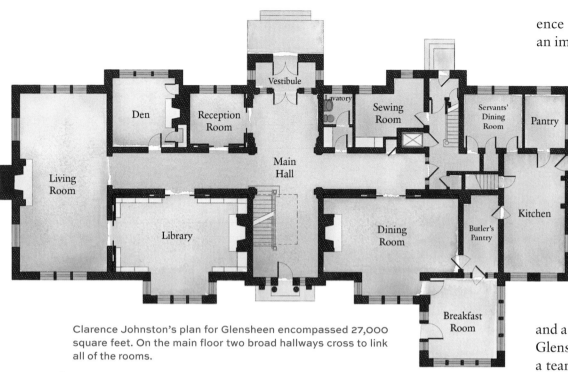

Clarence Johnston's plan for Glensheen encompassed 27,000 square feet. On the main floor two broad hallways cross to link all of the rooms.

ence designing big houses. His résumé contained an impressive list of homes in St. Paul, among them the magnificent Amherst Wilder House (razed in 1959) on Summit Avenue next door to James J. Hill's mansion. All told, Johnston would end up designing nearly forty houses on Summit Avenue alone, far more than any other architect. In 1901 Johnston added to his luster when he was named the State of Minnesota's architect, a position that brought responsibility for the design of numerous institutional buildings.

There's little in the record to indicate how the Congdons came to select Johnston, who had designed only two other buildings in Duluth—a church and a hospital—before receiving the commission for Glensheen. From the start, however, Glensheen was a team project. Charles W. Leavitt Jr., a prominent landscape architect from New York, was hired to lay out the estate's grounds. The Congdons also brought in the firm of William A. French and Company to design the mansion's interiors. Founded in St. Paul around 1890 but later headquartered in Minneapolis, the company was known not only for interior design but also for making fine furniture.

The Glensheen commission was so large that William French worried his small company lacked adequate capital to purchase all of the materials needed for the job. Congdon quickly solved this problem by making a substantial investment in the firm, thereby ensuring that French would have the money he needed. As part of the arrangement, Congdon also became the firm's vice president.

The Congdons were deeply involved in the design process, as well. Chester had an especially strong interest in horticulture and must have closely monitored the landscaping work. Clara, who had written her senior thesis at Syracuse University on

Glensheen's balanced front facade, which features a curved central gable, is a beautiful example of the Jacobethan Revival style. The brick walls are trimmed with white granite from Vermont.

A lion's head bursts out in menacing fashion from one of the wall sconces in the main hall.

Gothic architecture, and who had later taught art, concentrated her attention on planning the mansion's richly decorated interior.

Construction began in 1905 and required four years to complete, largely because little, if any, exterior work could be done during Duluth's long winters. Workers began by building an entry road into the estate and digging trenches for utilities, all of which, including the electric and telephone lines, were placed underground. Building materials—everything from bricks and steel beams to plantings—were delivered via the Duluth and Iron Range Railroad to a siding on East Thirty-Sixth Street about four blocks from the estate. Horse-drawn wagons took over from there.

Work on the mansion itself started in June 1905 when the foundations were laid, after which the walls began to take shape. The mansion was built to last. Its walls are of poured concrete faced with brick, and its floors and roof are supported by steel beams in-filled with hollow tiles designed to prevent the spread of fire. Very few, if any, houses in Minnesota today, even extremely large and expensive ones, are built of such heavyweight materials.

Over the next three years, construction of the mansion, outbuildings, and grounds proceeded simultaneously. The mansion itself was under roof by December 1906, and boilers were installed a month later, allowing interior work to continue year-round. The carriage house, a multiuse structure consisting of servants' living quarters as well as a barn and stables, was completed in 1907, as was a 60,000-gallon concrete reservoir on Tischer Creek above London Road. Water piped in from the reservoir was used for gardens and a fountain on the estate's grounds.

Landscaping the grounds was an enormous task, for which Leavitt was well qualified. Trained as a civil engineer, he established his own firm in 1897 and went on to design everything from estate grounds and racetracks to highways and college campuses. As his work at Glensheen was wrapping up, Leavitt took on one of the most notable commissions of his career—the design of Forbes Field, which served as the Pittsburgh Pirates' baseball park from 1909 to 1970. At Glensheen, Leavitt supervised the planting of more than thirty varieties of trees, along with thousands of shrubs and flowering plants. He also designed all of the estate's gardens, roadways, and paths, as well as a bowling green and a tennis court.

Glensheen remained under construction through 1908. The last big job, begun in July of that year, was to complete the mansion's richly detailed interior. Five decorators from French and Company were assigned full time to the task. Except for a few minor touches, the work was finished by November 24, 1908, when the Congdons and their two younger children moved into the mansion.

Glensheen cost $854,000 (something like $20 million today), and what the Congdons got for their money was a truly extraordinary property,

A large carriage house and barn that also included living quarters for servants are among several outbuildings scattered around the estate, which originally encompassed twenty-two acres.

not just because of its architecture but also because of its superb grounds and matchless natural setting. The grounds, which were maintained in the manner of an English estate, required a full-time gardener, who lived in his own cottage not far from the mansion. George Wyness, son of a Scottish master gardener, was hired to work at Glensheen in 1911 and stayed on for decades. One of his sons, Robert, who was raised on the estate, later succeeded him, living in the gardener's cottage through the 1970s. The mansion itself was originally staffed by six servants—a butler, a coachman-chauffeur, a houseman, a cook, and downstairs and upstairs maids.

The 27,000-square-foot, thirty-nine room mansion that forms the heart of the estate is a finely crafted version of the late Tudor style often called Jacobethan Revival, which takes it name from King James I of England. The style combines Gothic and Renaissance elements, and it was very popular for big American houses in the early twentieth century. Chester and Clara had traveled in England, and it's possible they dictated the style, although Johnston probably would have proposed something along its lines in any case. The estate's name was apparently derived from the ancestral home of Chester's family in the English village of Sheen, although some accounts suggest the "sheen" of sunlight in the deep "glen" of Tischer Creek may have been the inspiration.

The mansion is among Minnesota's finest examples of the Jacobethan Revival style. It displays many of the style's hallmarks: parapeted gables, including a curved Flemish gable above the arched front entry; light stone trim in the form of white Vermont granite that plays off against reddish-brown brick walls;

The mansion's vestibule, which includes stained-glass doors and sidelights surrounded by honey-toned oak woodwork, is exceptionally welcoming.

Clarence Johnston, Minnesota's Architect

By the time Clarence Johnston designed the Congdon mansion, he was a varied and productive practitioner well known for his design proficiency. Like most other architects of his time, Johnston moved from style to style as tastes changed, beginning in the 1880s with Queen Anne–style Victorians and moving all the way through the sleek Moderne style of the 1930s. He was not as dazzlingly original as Frank Lloyd Wright, nor did he ever build a national architectural practice like his fellow Minnesotan Cass Gilbert. Instead, he was Minnesota's go-to architect, a model of steadiness and competence, able to deliver consistently high-quality designs to his clients, who ranged from families like the Congdons to church congregations to state agencies. No other Minnesota architect can match his built legacy, which consists of more than four hundred homes, buildings, and structures scattered around the state.

Johnston was born in 1859 in Waseca County in southern Minnesota. His parents hailed from New York but moved to what was then Minnesota Territory in 1856. Johnston's father, Alexander, was a lawyer-turned-journalist who wandered from job to job and drank too much. In the 1860s, the family settled in St. Paul, where Johnston was raised and attended public schools. He must have known early in life what he wanted to do, because at age fifteen he was already working in the office of Abraham Radcliffe, one of St. Paul's pioneer architects. It was there Johnston met Gilbert, and the two men would be friends—and occasional rivals—for many years to come.

In 1878 Johnston and Gilbert left to study architecture at the Massachusetts Institute of Technology. Money was in short supply, however, and Johnston had to leave after a single term. Back in St. Paul, he went to work for another architect but soon secured work with the prestigious New York decorating firm of Herter Brothers, whose client list included the likes of William H. Vanderbilt, owner of the New York Central Railroad, and financier J. Pierpont Morgan. After two years at the Herters' firm, Johnston returned to St. Paul, where he established his own practice in 1882, at the age of just twenty-three.

Johnston later formed a partnership with architect William H. Willcox, but by 1890 he was back on his own. He managed to weather the deep depression that began in 1893 before acquiring new duties as Minnesota's state architect in 1901. The design of state schools, colleges and universities, hospitals, asylums, prisons, and office buildings all fell within his purview. Even as public commissions poured in, Johnston and his large staff of draftspeople continued to produce a wide range of private buildings, including numerous mansions. Glensheen was one of the two largest residences of his career, approached in size only by another estate—Stonebridge—built in 1916 in St. Paul for industrialist Oliver Crosby. Stonebridge, unfortunately, is gone, demolished in 1953.

Two of Johnston's sons eventually joined his practice, which began to decline in the 1920s. It took a further dip when the office of state architect was eliminated in 1931. By then, Johnston was all but retired, and his son, Howard, took charge of running the firm. When Johnston died in December 1936, a newspaper columnist memorialized him as "among the really great architects of the country. But he will be remembered by many rather for his fine rich-flavored personality which took the rough edge off the day's work. . . . There is a sort of mental and spiritual restfulness in just remembering him as he was."

The sprawling Stonebridge estate in St. Paul, designed by Glensheen architect Clarence Johnston, circa 1930.

A fireplace made of Numidian marble from Algeria is the centerpiece of the mansion's spacious living room. The room is also notable for its rich mahogany woodwork and damask wall coverings.

classical balustrades along the roofline, porches, and rear terrace; and carefully balanced front and lakeside facades, although neither is perfectly symmetrical. Overall, the mansion ranks among Johnston's finest designs. As historically "correct" designs often are, however, it's a bit dry, opting for restrained elegance rather than any sort of theatrics.

The interior is another matter. It's a lively gathering of architectural delights, rich in texture and detail, mixing Jacobethan features with Arts and Crafts and Art Nouveau influences—an amalgam by no means rare at the time. Because members of the Congdon family were the only private owners of the mansion, it underwent few alterations to its major rooms and today retains many of its original furnishings and the Congdons' collection of paintings by prominent American and European artists. As a result, Glensheen is the most intact home of its kind in Minnesota, a preserved-in-amber architectural artifact that offers visitors an incomparable look at how one of the state's wealthiest families lived.

Much of what makes Glensheen so appealing is the quality of its design. It's a huge home, yet it feels inviting and livable. The trick lies in the warm materials chosen by Johnston and the interior designers, as well as their use of ornamental detail to scale down what might otherwise have been overweening spaces. This careful detailing creates a surprising sense of intimacy—a quality not always associated with mansions built by the rich and powerful.

Only the finest materials were used throughout the mansion. Light fixtures, andirons, and even curtain rods are made of silver. Lampshades showcase the exquisite work of the Quezal Glass Company, an

The main hall features warm oak paneling, ornate plaster ceilings, and elegant light fixtures with Quezal glass shades. The staircase's intricate strapwork railings were carved by hand.

offshoot of Louis Tiffany's famed design studio. Doors are double paneled, with wood matching that of the rooms on either side. Rugs, wall coverings, and furniture—all meticulously chosen by the Congdons and their designers—are of similarly high quality.

The mansion's welcoming presence begins at its gorgeously paneled double front doors, which open into a vestibule resplendent with stained-glass inner doors and sidelights. Past the vestibule is the front hall, which branches out into a longitudinal hall to form a cross-shaped plan. Finished in honey-toned fumed-oak paneling with pilasters, the entry hall leads straight to the main staircase, which features hand-carved strapwork railings of stunning intricacy and six art-glass landing windows abloom with stylized Tudor roses. A similar design appears in stencilwork atop the stairway's paneled walls. The staircase is typical of the mansion's pleasing scale. It's undeniably grand, yet it doesn't seem over the top, its elaborate ornament carefully integrated into the home's overall design.

The rest of the first floor is equally outstanding. There's a reception room adorned by gold-leaf ceilings and Circassian walnut woodwork, a smoking room and den finished in Japanese-style *jin-di-sugi* cypress and chestnut wood by Minneapolis decorator John Bradstreet, a huge living room with mahogany paneling and beams that centers around a dazzling fireplace made of Numidian marble from Algeria, a library also finished in mahogany where Congdon kept a fine collection of books, a Georgian-style formal dining room, and a large kitchen. Both the dining room and library, which overlook the lake, open out to a two-level terrace that leads down to a walled garden with a central fountain. An open porch on the west side of the mansion, off the living room, provides another fine view, toward a delightful little arched stone footbridge that crosses Tischer Creek near the lake.

The mansion's most irresistibly charming room is another of Bradstreet's creations—an Arts and Crafts–style breakfast- and sunroom that juts out to take in views of the lake. It features walls and floors of green faience tile made by the famed Rockwood Pottery Company of Cincinnati, art-glass windows with naturalistic oak-leaf and acorn designs, and a peaked *jin-di-sugi* ceiling. When the sun pays a visit, the room takes on a gentle glow and is in its own small way the mansion's glory.

At the south end of the stair hall, a flight of steps leads down to the basement. Here was the more casual part of the mansion, including a billiard room, a playroom, and a large recreation room where the Congdons often entertained. Next to the recreation room is the "little museum," where the family preserved many keepsakes. All of these rooms faced an enclosed porch, or "subway," as the Congdons called it, set beneath the home's upper terrace. The dug-in north side of the basement includes furnace, cold storage, laundry, milk, and wood rooms. The wood room was used to store

The mansion's delightful, light-filled breakfast room was designed by Minneapolis decorator John Bradstreet, who used green faience tile made by the Rockwood Pottery Company of Cincinnati.

Duluth Millionaires

At some point, nearly every historical reference to Duluth includes the claim that at the turn of the twentieth century, the city boasted more millionaires per capita than any city in the United States. Whether this claim is true or not, there's no doubt that hardworking Duluth has been the backdrop for many fortunes made and lost. The city has a shipping route to the Atlantic Ocean via the Great Lakes, and its natural resources of fish, fur, lumber, iron ore, grain, and stone have made it ripe for industry throughout the years. Eventually connected by railroad to the West Coast, the centrally located port has always been a crossroads for trade.

The region was first settled by the Anishinaabe (Ojibwe) and Dakota. In the seventeenth century, French trappers and traders descended from Canada to exploit the thick-furred northern fauna—especially beaver—and the Native tribes and Canadians alike profited from this trade. One such Frenchman, Daniel Greysolon Sieur du Luth (after whom the city is named), negotiated a treaty with the Indians in 1679. The nearby fur trading post at Fond du Lac was eventually taken over by John Jacob Astor and his American Fur Company in 1809. Astor became one of America's first millionaires.

Duluth was mapped as a township by George Stuntz, a pioneer from neighboring Superior, Wisconsin. Stuntz made his money in gold, silver, and iron ore. Members of the Lewis Merritt family also jumped on the ore bandwagon and helped develop the Mesabi Iron Range, only to lose their business in 1894 to John D. Rockefeller.

Meanwhile, lumber was booming, and speculators like Roger Munger plucked Lake Superior's north shore of its thick pine forests, making millions of dollars in the process. In the 1860s, Philadelphia businessman Jay Cooke built the Northern Pacific Railroad from Duluth to Seattle's Puget Sound, and the Lake Superior and Mississippi Railroad from St. Paul to Duluth. The Duluth Ship Canal was dug in the 1870s, providing clear and safe access for major shipping concerns. With railroad, grain, and shipping businesses flourishing, jobs were plentiful, and the region drew immigrants from throughout the United States, Scandinavia, Europe, and Canada.

But industrial progress was never a steady climb. Depressions in both 1857 and 1873 saw Duluth's fortunes fall, only to recover again and repeat the pattern. The 1880s saw a great revival, however, which boomed well into the new century. By 1907 Duluth's shipping industry outstripped that of New York City, and as iron ore poured in from the Mesabi and other ranges, New York financier J. P. Morgan announced his intention to build his U.S. Steel plant in Duluth. It was during this great age of growth that Chester Congdon became Duluth's wealthiest man. Prosperity continued through World War I, when a group of investors including Alexander McDougall, Marshall Alworth, Julius Barnes, and Congdon started churning out freighters for the war effort.

Duluth's population hit an all-time high of 112,000 in 1928, and the city weathered the Great Depression intact even as timber, fur, and other resources became depleted. Today, the city still enjoys a healthy shipping trade, but finance, tourism, and medicine are now its chief businesses. There are still plenty of millionaires in Duluth.

A lion—symbol of power and wealth—forms the base of a lamp on the staircase leading up to the third floor.

combustibles for the mansion's fifteen fireplaces. In the milk room, servants prepared dairy products from the estate's cows for family use.

As built, the mansion was equipped for both gas and electric lighting, although within a few years electricity became the sole source of illumination. A central vacuuming system and security and communications systems were also installed. The mansion and its outbuildings originally required up to one hundred tons of coal a year for heating, but no delivery trucks ever soiled the grounds. Instead, coal was dumped into manholes built along London Road and then fed by augers into bins inside the mansion. The furnace room was also equipped with an ingenious system whereby water was sprayed over hot radiators and turned into moist air, which was then sent through the mansion via ducts to provide humidity in winter.

The second floor of the mansion contains nine bedrooms and five baths. The master bedroom, trimmed in walnut, is at the west end of the mansion and includes a fireplace and a balcony that overlooks Tischer Creek and the lake. The five other family and guest bedrooms are decorated in a range of styles and colors. Three smaller bedrooms, on the east side, were for female servants. Six additional bedrooms, including some used by the Congdons' sons, are on the third floor, beneath a large attic.

Among the family bedrooms on the second floor is one called the "grey room," located immediately east of the main staircase. It was here, on June 27, 1977, that eighty-three-year-old Elisabeth Congdon was smothered to death by an intruder, who also killed her night nurse, Velma Pietila. The long investigation that followed eventually led to Elisabeth's adopted daughter, Marjorie Caldwell, and her husband, Roger, being charged with the murders. In separate trials, Roger was found guilty of the crimes, to which he ultimately confessed, but Marjorie was acquitted.

It's certain Chester and Clara Congdon, who always maintained strong family bonds, could never have imagined such a tragic event in their beloved home. Chester, however, would enjoy Glensheen for only eight years. Although he had retired from his law practice in 1904, he continued to travel frequently in the ensuing years to oversee his far-flung business interests, among them copper mining in Arizona and agriculture in Washington's Yakima Valley, where he'd begun buying land in the 1890s. In 1895 he built a canal in the valley to irrigate three thousand acres devoted to fruit orchards, wheat, alfalfa, and hops. Congdon must have liked Yakima because in 1914 he began building his second mansion there. Designed by architects from Minneapolis, the mansion—a towered stone minicastle that Congdon called Westhome—is even bigger than Glensheen. It was completed in 1916, only a few months before Congdon's death, and remains privately owned to this day.

Back in Minnesota, Congdon had taken on a new assignment in

1909, winning election to the Minnesota legislature as a Republican and a staunch opponent of a proposed state tonnage tax on iron ore. He helped defeat the tax and then served a second term in the state house of representatives from 1911 to 1913. Congdon moved into the national political arena in 1916 when he became a member of the Republican National Committee and campaigned for the party's presidential candidate, Charles Evans Hughes. That work, however, was cut short by his death.

In August 1916 Congdon experienced bouts of what he thought was indigestion but may well have been symptoms of heart disease. Even so, he kept up his busy schedule and was feeling better by November 7, when he cast his vote for Hughes, who narrowly lost the election to Woodrow Wilson. That same day, Congdon went to St. Paul on business. He had an apartment at the St. Paul Hotel, and he was staying there when his health began to fail. Doctors were duly summoned, but his condition rapidly deteriorated and he died on November 21, at age sixty-three. His death produced numerous encomiums in the Duluth and Twin Cities newspapers, which hailed him for both his business acumen and his contributions to civic life. Three days after his death, he was buried in Duluth, on what Clara in her journal described as "a cold but lovely and quiet" afternoon.

Congdon's mark on Duluth did not include only Glensheen. In 1908 he donated more than thirty acres of land along Tischer Creek north of London Road to the city, to form what is now Congdon Park. He also donated a thirteen-mile strip of land along Lake Superior just east of the city limits to be used for construction of a highway but otherwise left undeveloped. The road, once a portion of U.S. Highway 61, is today called Congdon Boulevard.

Clara Congdon survived her husband by more than thirty years, living at Glensheen until her death in 1950 at age ninety-six. Elisabeth Congdon, who never married, also remained in the mansion and raised Marjorie and another adopted daughter there. In 1968 Elisabeth decided to will Glensheen to the University of Minnesota Duluth, with the proviso that she could remain in the mansion until her death. Four years later, she permitted the mansion to be used as a location for the filming of a spooky-old-house movie called *You'll Like My Mother*, starring Patty Duke and Richard Thomas. The movie was no masterpiece, but it did turn out to be an eerie foreshadowing of things to come.

After Elisabeth's death, the University of Minnesota Duluth took possession of Glensheen and opened the estate for public tours in 1979. The

The breakfast room's art-glass windows depict oak leaves with acorns.

Westhome, Chester Congdon's mansion in Yakima Washington, about the time it was completed in 1916, just before his death. The mansion was even larger than Glensheen.

The mahogany table and chairs in the Georgian-style dining room were custom made, as were almost all of the mansion's furnishings.

estate was added to the National Register of Historic Places twelve years later. Preparing the mansion for tours required a good deal of work to make it more accessible, and initially only the basement and main floor were open to the public. The second and third floors were added to the tours in the early 1990s. Since acquiring the estate, the university has undertaken numerous maintenance projects, including repairs to the mansion's tile roof, but much other work awaits funding. The cost of operating the estate is substantial—the heating bill alone can run to $40,000 a year. Torrential rains that caused unprecedented flooding throughout Duluth in June 2012 took a heavy toll on Glensheen's grounds, and the repair bill ultimately came to more than $3 million.

Today, Glensheen is the scene of numerous weddings and special events, along with the popular tours. There was a time when the murders of Elisabeth and her nurse were never mentioned by tour guides. That stance has since softened, however, and the tragic events of 1977 are now treated as simply one part of Glensheen's extraordinary story.

Members of the far-flung Congdon family retain a special attachment to the property, and in 2010 more than one hundred descendants gathered in Duluth for a tour of the mansion and grounds. "It was real magic," one of Chester and Clara's great-great-grandsons later told a news reporter. "It was like stepping back in time. Yes, it's a museum, but it's [also a] family spot. And it has a lot of significance and memories for people." Those memories, of an estate like none other in Minnesota, seem destined to last, as does Glensheen itself, which the Congdons built to be a home for the ages. ꙮ

The "blue" bedroom, one of nine on the second floor, has the only four-poster bed in the mansion. The crisp white woodwork is enameled birch.

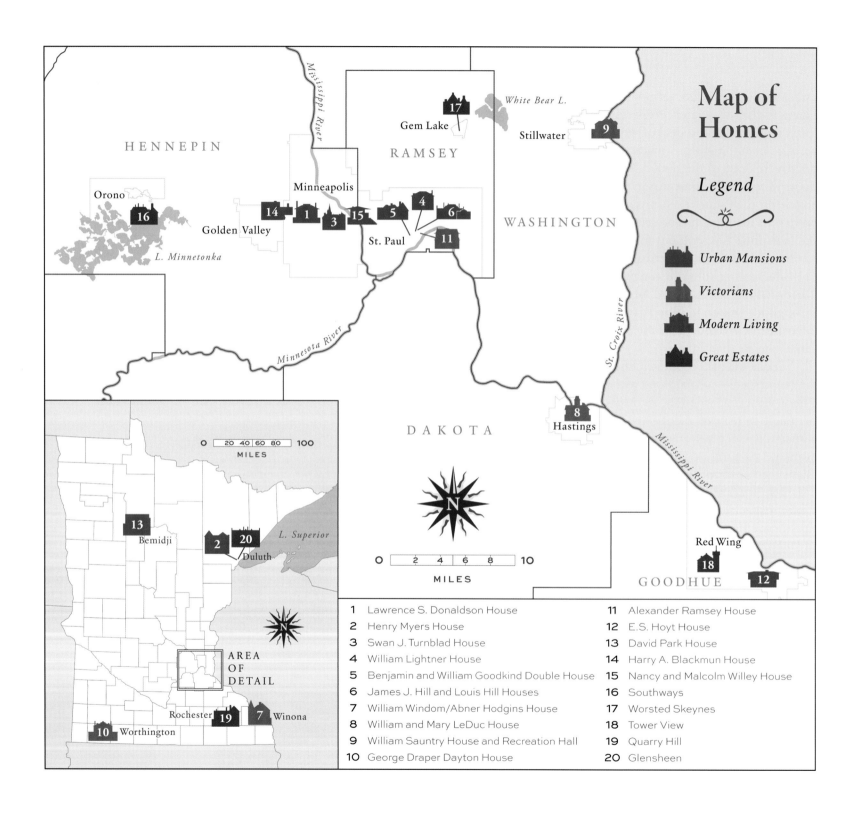

Map of Homes

Legend

- **Urban Mansions**
- **Victorians**
- **Modern Living**
- **Great Estates**

HENNEPIN

RAMSEY

WASHINGTON

DAKOTA

GOODHUE

Orono

Minneapolis

Golden Valley

St. Paul

Gem Lake

Stillwater

Hastings

Red Wing

L. Minnetonka

Mississippi River

Minnesota River

White Bear L.

St. Croix River

Mississippi River

0 2 4 6 8 10
MILES

0 20 40 60 80 100
MILES

Bemidji

Duluth

L. Superior

Rochester

Winona

Worthington

AREA OF DETAIL

N

1	Lawrence S. Donaldson House	11	Alexander Ramsey House
2	Henry Myers House	12	E.S. Hoyt House
3	Swan J. Turnblad House	13	David Park House
4	William Lightner House	14	Harry A. Blackmun House
5	Benjamin and William Goodkind Double House	15	Nancy and Malcolm Willey House
6	James J. Hill and Louis Hill Houses	16	Southways
7	William Windom/Abner Hodgins House	17	Worsted Skeynes
8	William and Mary LeDuc House	18	Tower View
9	William Sauntry House and Recreation Hall	19	Quarry Hill
10	George Draper Dayton House	20	Glensheen

294

Acknowledgments

So many people contributed to the creation of this book that naming them all would take up many pages, and I have room to acknowledge only a few here. My thanks must begin with a salute to the homeowners, both individual and institutional, whose generous cooperation made this book possible. "Cooperation," in fact, is too weak a word to describe the enthusiasm with which the owners approached a project that required no small commitment of their time and energy. It was truly an honor to meet so many wonderful people and see their beautiful homes. A special note of thanks goes to Dennis Lamkin of Duluth, who went out of his way to share his vast knowledge of that city's history and architecture.

I am grateful to Thomas Jeffris and his family foundation—the rock upon which this book is built. I have written a good many books about architecture and history but never one more generously supported than *Minnesota's Own*.

At the Minnesota Historical Society Press, the expert team behind this book, led by director Pamela McClanahan, included design and production manager Daniel Leary, managing editor Shannon Pennefeather, editor Mike Hanson, color specialist Tim Meegan, volunteer Sallie Haugen, and researcher David Katz, who quickly dug up answers to every question, no matter how obscure, I threw his way. I wish to thank MacDonald and Mack Architects, who prepared the book's lovely color drawings, my son, Matt, who created the map of the homes, and the design team at Mighty Media for their excellent work.

I greatly benefited from working on this project with Matt Schmitt, who is not only an outstanding photographer but also a genial traveling companion. It was a pleasure working with him. Finally, I want to thank my wife, Jodie Ahern, who shared every step of this book-writing adventure with me. Jodie helped with everything from writing sidebars and captions to copyediting my rarely pristine prose. I couldn't have managed it all without her.

Larry Millett

It was a remarkable experience to work on this project with so many talented, knowledgeable, and generous individuals. There were so many beautiful homes and intriguing human stories about the people who built them, the people who lived in them, the people who restored them, and now, the people who pulled it all together for this book. My role as the photographer was just one of many in this project, and I have many people to thank for their individual contributions to this collaborative venture.

Thanks go to author Larry Millett for sharing his vast knowledge of and insights into the historic homes and sites found in this book. It was a pleasure working with Larry and his wife and writing partner, Jodie Ahern, throughout our many months and miles of scouting Minnesota for the final twenty-two homes.

I thank editor Mike Hanson for his management skills and for keeping the project rolling forward.

Thanks go to Jim Stanislaw for his location assistance and for sharing his photographic expertise throughout the process.

I thank the homeowners and the organizational staffs of the many beautiful houses we visited while making the difficult choices leading to the final home selection. They graciously opened up their homes to us for what must have been somewhat disruptive visits.

I am grateful to Pamela McClanahan, director of the Minnesota Historical Society Press, and her staff and others who offered so much help, including design and production manager Daniel Leary, managing editor Shannon Pennefeather, volunteer Sallie Haugen, researcher David Katz, and color specialist Tim Meegan.

For their help in guiding our final home selection, thanks go to Royce Yeater of the Jeffris Family Foundation, Craig Johnson, Denis Gardner, and Dennis Lamkin.

I thank Thomas Jeffris for his vision and commitment to historical preservation and his most generous support and funding of this book.

Finally, I thank my wife, Deb Robinson, for her constant support, encouragement, and helpful assistance throughout this project.

Matt Schmitt

Selected Bibliography

Allsen, Ken. *Old College Street: The Historic Heart of Rochester, Minnesota*. Charleston, SC: History Press, 2012.

Anderson, Alexander P. *The Seventh Reader: Short Stories with Some Verse*. Caldwell, ID: Caxton Printers, 1941.

Anderson, John P., Jean M. Chesley, Lydia E. Hedin, and Louise A. Sargent. *Alexander P. Anderson, 1862–1943*. Red Wing, MN: Privately published, 1997.

Andrews, Jack. *Samuel Yellin, Metalworker*. Ocean City, MD: Skip-Jack Press, 2000.

Bemidji State University. *David Park House*. Bemidji, MN: Bemidji State University, n.d.

Blanck, Thomas R., and Charles Locks. "Launching a Career: Residential and Ecclesiastical Work from the St. Paul Office." In *Cass Gilbert, Life and Work: Architecture of the Public Domain*, edited by Barbara S. Christen and Steven Flanders. New York: W. W. Norton, 2001.

Brookins, Jean. "A Historic Mansion: The William G. LeDuc House." *Minnesota History* 37, no. 5 (1961): 189–203.

Caron, Barbara Ann. "The Alexander Ramsey House: Furnishing a Victorian Home." *Minnesota History* 54, no. 5 (1995): 194–209.

———. "The James J. Hill House: Symbol of Status and Security." *Minnesota History* 55, no. 6 (1997): 234–49.

Christen, Barbara S., and Steven Flanders, eds. *Cass Gilbert, Life and Work: Architecture of the Public Domain*. New York: W. W. Norton, 2001.

City of Red Wing Heritage Preservation Committee. *Footsteps through Historic Red Wing*. Red Wing, MN: City of Red Wing Heritage Preservation Committee, 1989.

Clapesattle, Helen. *The Doctors Mayo*. Rochester, MN: Mayo Foundation for Medical Education and Research, 1990.

Conforti, Michael, ed. *Minnesota 1900: Art and Life on the Upper Mississippi, 1890–1915*. Mississauga, ON: Associated University Presses in association with the Minneapolis Institute of Arts, 1994.

Dayton, Bruce B., and Ellen B. Green. *George Draper Dayton: A Man of Parts*. Minneapolis: Privately published, 1997.

Dierckins, Tony, and Maryanne C. Norton. *Lost Duluth: Landmarks, Industries, Buildings, Homes, and the Neighborhoods in Which They Stood*. Duluth, MN: Zenith City Press, 2012.

Doermann, Elisabeth W., and Ellen M. Rosenthal. "Introducing the Hill House." *Minnesota History* 46, no. 8 (1979): 328–36.

Downing, Andrew Jackson. *Victorian Cottage Residences*. 5th ed. New York: John Wiley and Sons, 1873. Reprint, New York: Dover Books, 1981.

Doyle, Marcy. *A Face of Red Wing, MN, from My Perspective*. Red Wing, MN: Privately published, n.d.

Duluth Preservation Alliance. *Historic Duluth's East End Walking Tour*. Duluth, MN: Duluth Preservation Alliance, 2010.

Dunn, David J. "Study of Dr. Henry Stanley Plummer's Life and Contributions to Medicine and the Mayo Clinic." Unpublished paper, 2011.

Dunn, James Taylor. *The St. Croix: Midwest Border River*. St. Paul: Minnesota Historical Society Press, 1979.

Firestone, Mary. *Dayton's Department Store*. Charleston, SC: Arcadia Publishing, 2007.

Forester, Jeff. *The Forest for the Trees: How Humans Shaped the North Woods*. St. Paul: Minnesota Historical Society Press, 2004.

Fourie, Ada. *Their Roots Run Deep*. Duluth: University of Minnesota Duluth, 1985.

Furness, Marion Ramsey. "Childhood Recollections of Old St. Paul," *Minnesota History* 29, no. 2 (1948): 114–29.

Gaut, Greg. *Abner Hodgins House, Local Designation Nomination Form*. Winona, MN: Winona Heritage Preservation Commission, 2013.

Gebhard, David. *Purcell & Elmslie: Prairie Progressive Architects*. Edited by Patricia Gebhard. Salt Lake City, UT: Gibbs Smith, 2006.

Gebhard, David, and Tom Martinson. *A Guide to the Architecture of Minnesota*. Minneapolis: University of Minnesota Press, 1978.

Greenhouse, Linda. *Becoming Justice Blackmun: Harry Blackmun's Supreme Court Journey*. New York: Times Books, Henry Holt and Company, 2005.

Grief, Martin. *Depression Modern: The Thirties in America*. New York: Universe Books, 1975.

Hammel, Bette Jones. *Legendary Homes of Lake Minnetonka*. Photographs by Karen Melvin. St. Paul: Minnesota Historical Society Press, 2010.

Hammerstrom, Lawrence. "The Swedish American Publishing Company Stockholders' Lawsuit Against Swan J. Turnblad." *Swedish-American Historical Quarterly*, January 1984.

Hanson, Krista F. *Minnesota Open House: A Guide to Historic House Museums*. St. Paul: Minnesota Historical Society Press, 2007.

Hendry, Sharon Darby. *Glensheen's Daughter: The Marjorie Congdon Story*. Brule, WI: Cable Publishing, 2009.

Historic Irvine Park Association and Preservation Alliance of Minnesota. *Historic Homes of Saint Paul's Uppertown & Irvine Park*. St. Paul: Historic Irvine Park Association and Preservation Alliance of Minnesota, 2001.

Hoover, Roy O. *A Lake Superior Lawyer: A Biography of Chester Adgate Congdon*. Castro Valley, CA: Kutenai Press, 1997.

Hudson, Lew. *From New Cloth: The Making of Worthington*. Worthington, MN: Calvin-Knuth American Legion Auxiliary, 1976.

Irish, Sharon. *Cass Gilbert, Architect: Modern Traditionalist*. New York: Monacelli Press, 1999.

Johnson, Craig. *James J. Hill House*. St. Paul: Minnesota Historical Society Press, 1993.

Johnson, Frederick L. "Professor Anderson's 'Food Shot from Guns.'" *Minnesota History* 59, no. 1 (2004): 4–16.

———. *The Big Water: Lake Minnetonka and Its Place in Minnesota History*. Minnetonka, MN: Deep Haven Books, 2012.

Kennedy, Roger G. *Historic Homes of Minnesota*. St. Paul: Minnesota Historical Society Press, 1967.

Kimball, Joe. *Secrets of the Congdon Mansion*. White Bear Lake, MN: Jaykay Publishing, 2002.

Koop, Michael. *National Register of Historic Places Registration Form, Glensheen*. Duluth, MN, 1990.

Lane, Michael. *Glensheen: The Construction Years*. Duluth: University of Minnesota Duluth, 1980.

Larson, Agnes M. *The White Pine Industry in Minnesota: A History*. Minneapolis: University of Minnesota Press, 2007.

Larson, Paul Clifford. *Minnesota Architect: The Life and Work of Clarence H. Johnston*. Afton, MN: Afton Historical Society Press, 1996.

———. *A Place at the Lake*. Afton, MN: Afton Historical Society Press, 1998.

———. *A Home of Versatile Talents: The William and Carrie Lightner Residence*. St. Paul: Privately published, 2006.

———. *Louis and Maude Hill Residence*. St. Paul: Privately published, 2007.

Larson, Paul Clifford, and Jeffrey A. Hess. *St. Paul's Architecture: A History*. Minneapolis: University of Minnesota Press in cooperation with the City of St. Paul Heritage Preservation Commission, 2006.

Lathrop, Alan K. *Minnesota Architects: A Biographical Dictionary*. Minneapolis: University of Minnesota Press, 2010.

Lee, Dr. Arthur O. *The University in the Pines*. Bemidji, MN: Bemidji State University, 1994.

Legler, Dixie, and Christian Korab. *At Home on the Prairie: The Houses of Purcell & Elmslie*. San Francisco: Chronicle Books, 2006.

Lewis, Anne Gillespie. *The American Swedish Institute: Turnblad's Castle*. Minneapolis: American Swedish Institute, 1999.

Lindeberg, H. T. *Domestic Architecture of H. T. Lindeberg*. New York: William Helburn, 1940. Reprinted with introduction by Mark Alan Hewitt. New York: Acanthus Press, 1996.

Malone, Michael P. *James J. Hill: Empire Builder of the Northwest*. Norman: University of Oklahoma Press, 1996.

Martin, Albro. *James J. Hill and the Opening of the Northwest*. New York: Oxford University Press, 1976. Reprint, St. Paul: Minnesota Historical Society Press, 1991.

Millett, Larry. *The Curve of the Arch: The Story of Louis Sullivan's Owatonna Bank*. St. Paul: Minnesota Historical Society Press, 1985.

———. *Lost Twin Cities*. St. Paul: Minnesota Historical Society Press, 1992.

———. *Twin Cities Then and Now*. St. Paul: Minnesota Historical Society Press, 1996.

———. *AIA Guide to the Twin Cities*. St. Paul: Minnesota Historical Society Press, 2007.

———. *Once There Were Castles*. Minneapolis: University of Minnesota Press, 2011.

Mulfinger, Dale. *The Architecture of Edwin Lundie*. St. Paul: Minnesota Historical Society Press, 1995.

Okabena Media. *The Dayton House*. Worthington, MN: Okabena Media, 2007.

Pennoyer, Peter, and Anne Walker. *The Architecture of Warren & Wetmore*. New York: W. W. Norton & Company, 2006.

Perrin, Mark, and Ron Beining. *A History of the Lawrence S. Donaldson Residence*. Minneapolis: Privately published, 2011.

Pillsbury, Eleanor Lawler. *Southways: Random Reminiscences*. Privately published, 1985.

Poatgieter, Alice Hermina. *The Alexander Ramsey House*. St. Paul: Minnesota Historical Society Press, 1965.

Prospect Park History Committee. *Under the Witch's Hat: A Prospect Park East River Road History*. Minneapolis: Prospect Park History Committee, 2003.

Prouty, F. Shirley. *Master Carver: Johannes Kirchmayer, 1860–1930*. Portsmouth, NH: Peter E. Randall Publisher, 2007.

Purcell, William. "Parabiography." Northwest Architectural Archives, Minneapolis.

"Residence at Duluth." *Western Architect*, April 1910, 48–54.

Rice, John G. "The Swedes." In *They Chose Minnesota: A Survey of the State's Ethnic Groups*, edited by June Drenning Holmquist. St. Paul: Minnesota Historical Society Press, 1981.

Richter, Bonnie, ed. *The Ellerbe Tradition: Seventy Years of Architecture & Engineering*. Minneapolis: Ellerbe, 1980.

Roberts, Norene. *North Hill (Original Town) Stillwater Residential Area, Stillwater, Washington County, Minnesota*. Stillwater, MN: City of Stillwater Heritage Preservation Commission, 1995.

Rosenblum, Gene H. *Jewish Pioneers of St. Paul, 1849–1874*. Chicago: Arcadia Publishing, 2001.

Sandeen, Ernest. *St. Paul's Historic Summit Avenue*. St. Paul: Living History Museum, 1978. Reprint, Minneapolis: University of Minnesota Press, 2004.

Schrenk, Lisa D. *Building a Century of Progress: The Architecture of Chicago's 1933–34 World's Fair*. Minneapolis: University of Minnesota, 2007.

Scott, James Allen. *Duluth's Legacy: Architecture*. Vol. 1. Duluth, MN: City of Duluth, 1974.

Sik, Sarah. "John Scott Bradstreet: The Minnesota Crafthouse and the Decorative Arts Revival in the American Northwest." *Nineteenth-Century Art Worldwide*, 2013–2014.

Spraker, Jean E. "Samuel Yellin, Metal Worker." *Minnesota History* 50, no. 3 (1986): 118–26.

Storrer, William Allin. *The Frank Lloyd Wright Companion*. Chicago: University of Chicago Press, 1993.

Sturdevant, Lori, with George S. Pillsbury. *The Pillsburys of Minnesota*. Minneapolis: Nodin Press, 2011.

Swanhold, Mark. *Alexander Ramsey and the Politics of Survival*. St. Paul: Minnesota Historical Society Press, 1977.

Upper Mississippi River Interpretive Center. *River Town Winona: Its History and Architecture*. 2nd ed. Winona, MN: Winona County Historical Society, 2006.

Werle, Steve. *An American Gothic: The Life and Times of William Gates LeDuc, 1823–1917*. South St. Paul, MN: Dakota County Historical Society, 2004.

Willius, Fredrick A. *Henry Stanley Plummer: A Diversified Genius*. Springfield, IL: Charles C. Thomas, 1960.

Wingerd, Mary Lethert. *North Country: The Making of Minnesota*. Minneapolis: University of Minnesota Press, 2010.

Yarbrough, Tinsley E. *Harry A. Blackmun: The Outsider Justice*. New York: Oxford University Press, 2008.

Young, Biloine W., with Eileen R. McCormack. *The Dutiful Son: Louis W. Hill*. St. Paul: Ramsey County Historical Society, 2010.

Zelle, Carol. *Final Report: The LeDuc-Simmons House: A Report on Research and Recommendations for Interpretation*. Prepared for the Minnesota Historical Society, 1989.

Illustration Credits

Historical Images

Pages 33, 35, 36, courtesy of the American Swedish Institute.

Pages 253, 256, 257, reprinted by permission of the Anderson Center for Interdisciplinary Studies.

Page 241, from the collections of Anthony Scornavacco and Michael Garrett.

Page 69, courtesy of the Avery Architectural and Fine Arts Library, Columbia University.

Page 118, courtesy of the Brookings County, South Dakota, Historical Society, via the Dakota County Historical Society.

Page 281, provided by Glensheen, the Historic Congdon Estate.

Page 167, courtesy of the Goodhue County Historical Society, Red Wing, Minnesota.

Pages 137, 138, 145, courtesy of Historic Dayton House.

Page 21, courtesy of the Kathryn A. Martin Library, University of Minnesota Duluth, Archives and Special Collections, Northeast Minnesota Historical Center Collections.

Page 49, courtesy of the Library of Congress.

Page 267, by permission of the Mayo Historical Unit, Mayo Clinic, Rochester, Minnesota.

Page 168, courtesy of the Minneapolis Institute of Arts.

Pages 5, 6, 7, 8, 20, 22, 26, 38, 47, 48, 56, 61, 64, 65, 75, 79, 86, 87, 95, 98, 101, 109, 111, 112, 125, 128, 130, 143, 151, 152, 154, 157, 161, 172, 190, 191, 198, 218, 225, 227, 230, 232, 239, 243, 254, 261, 268, 271, 274, 287, from the collections of the Minnesota Historical Society.

Pages 209, 213, from Nancy Willey's photo album, courtesy of Russell Burris, copyright Wright at Home, LLC.

Page 249, courtesy of the Northwest Architectural Archives, University of Minnesota Libraries.

Page 196, courtesy of Ralph Dauphin for Walker Art Center.

Pages 181, 182, from the personal collections of Robin M. Ward, granddaughter of David Park.

Pages 195, 203, from the collections of the Supreme Court of the United States.

Page 123, from the collections of the Washington County Historical Society.

Pages 97, 107, courtesy of the Winona County Historical Society.

Page 211, courtesy of the Wisconsin Historical Society.

Page 292, courtesy of the Yakima Valley Museum.

Page 229, courtesy of the Yellin Metalworkers.

Elevations and Floor Plans

Thanks go to the following for their help in securing blueprints and providing information for the elevation and floor plan illustrations.

Lawrence S. Donaldson House, Northwest Architectural Archives, University of Minnesota Libraries.

Henry Myers House, Johan and Nicole Bakken.

Swan J. Turnblad House, American Swedish Institute.

William Lightner House, John Fallin.

Benjamin and William Goodkind Double House, Northwest Architectural Archives, University of Minnesota Libraries; Daniel Leary and Sallie Haugen.

James J. Hill House, Minnesota Historical Society.

Louis Hill House, Richard and Nancy Nicholson.

William Windom/Abner Hodgins House, Daniel Leary and Sallie Haugen.

William and Mary LeDuc House, Minnesota Historical Society.

William Sauntry House, Thomas and Sandra Lynum.

George Draper Dayton House, Historic Dayton House.

Alexander Ramsey House, Minnesota Historical Society.

E. S. Hoyt House, Northwest Architectural Archives, University of Minnesota Libraries.

David Park House, Bemidji State University Foundation.

Harry A. Blackmun House, Bill Lyons.

Nancy and Malcolm Willey House, Northwest Architectural Archives, University of Minnesota Libraries.

Southways, Northwest Architectural Archives, University of Minnesota Libraries.

Worsted Skeynes, Northwest Architectural Archives, University of Minnesota Libraries.

Tower View, Anderson Center for Interdisciplinary Studies.

Quarry Hill, Plummer House of the Arts.

Glensheen, University of Minnesota Duluth.

Index